FINDING RIGHT RELATIONS

MARIANNE O. NIELSEN AND BARBARA M. HEATHER

FINDING RIGHT RELATIONS

Quakers, Native Americans, and Settler Colonialism

THE UNIVERSITY OF
ARIZONA PRESS
TUCSON

The University of Arizona Press
www.uapress.arizona.edu

We respectfully acknowledge the University of Arizona is on the land and territories of Indigenous peoples. Today, Arizona is home to twenty-two federally recognized tribes, with Tucson being home to the O'odham and the Yaqui. Committed to diversity and inclusion, the University strives to build sustainable relationships with sovereign Native Nations and Indigenous communities through education offerings, partnerships, and community service.

ISBN-13: 978-0-8165-4409-7 (hardcover)
ISBN-13: 978-0-8165-5029-6 (paperback)

Cover design by Derek Thornton / Notch Design
Cover image of a beaded Lenape purse from the National Museum of the American Indian, Smithsonian Institution (24/4153). Photo by NMAI Photo Services.
Typeset by Leigh McDonald in 10.75/14 Arno Pro with Worker

Parts of this text are based on the following previous publications: Marianne O. Nielsen and Barbara Heather, "An Opportunity Lost: Quaker and Lenni Lenape Peacemaking in the 1700s." In "Indigenous Peoples, the Law and Restorative Justice," special issue, *Restorative Directions Journal* 2, no. 2 (2006): 236–73; Marianne O. Nielsen and Barbara Heather, "The Universality of Peacemaking: A Real Possibility?" *International Journal of Restorative Justice* (2008), www.crjcs.org; Barbara Heather and Marianne O. Nielsen, "Quaker Ideology, Colonialism and American Indian Education," *Culture and Religion* 14, no. 3 (2013): 1–16; Barbara Heather and Marianne O. Nielsen, "(Dis) armed Friendship: Impacts of Colonial Ideology on Early Quaker Attitudes toward American Indians," *Culture and Religion* 16, no. 3 (2015): 308–26; and Barbara Heather and Marianne O. Nielsen, "Quakers, North American Indians, and the Paxton Boys, 1763–1764" (paper presented at the Quakers, First Nations, and American Indians from the 1650s to the 21st Century Conference, November 10–12, 2016, Philadelphia, Pa.).

Publication of this book is made possible in part by the proceeds of a permanent endowment created with the assistance of a Challenge Grant from the National Endowment for the Humanities, a federal agency.

Library of Congress Cataloging-in-Publication Data
Names: Nielsen, Marianne O., author. | Heather, Barbara M., 1938– author.
Title: Finding right relations : Quakers, Native Americans, and settler colonialism / Marianne O. Nielsen and Barbara M. Heather.
Other titles: Quakers, Native Americans, and settler colonialism
Description: Tucson, Arizona. : The University of Arizona Press, www.uapress.arizona.edu, 2022. | Includes bibliographical references and index.
Identifiers: LCCN 2021041173 | ISBN 9780816544097 (hardcover)
Subjects: LCSH: Indians of North America—Middle Atlantic States—History—Colonial period, ca. 1600–1775. | Indians, Treatment of—Middle Atlantic States—History—17th century. | Indians, Treatment of—Middle Atlantic States—History—18th century. | Quakers—Middle Atlantic States—History—17th century. | Quakers—Middle Atlantic States—History—18th century.
Classification: LCC E78.M65 N54 2022 | DDC 970.004/97—dc23/eng/20211018
LC record available at https://lccn.loc.gov/2021041173

Printed in the United States of America
♾ This paper meets the requirements of ANSI/NISO Z39.48-1992 (Permanence of Paper).

CONTENTS

ACKNOWLEDGMENTS

W E WOULD like to express our profound gratitude to the librarians and staff of the Quaker Special Collections Library at Haverford College for their invaluable assistance and even prescience in finding research materials for us.

For Barbara, this book would not have become a reality without the help and support of Edmonton Monthly Meeting Friends, and members of a local housing cooperative where she lives. In particular Barbara would like to acknowledge with gratitude the academic and friendly support of Jeff Dudiak of Kings College Edmonton; Linda Kreitzer, who has been a supporter in every possible way, including editing Quaker content in early papers; Canadian Yearly Meeting (CYM) Education Committee for sending her to the Truth and Healing: Right Relationship with Indigenous Peoples conference in Philadelphia in May 2018; and her brother and sister-in-law David and Eileen Humphrey who are her British support team. For going above and beyond, grateful thanks also to the McEwan University librarians; Kristner of Vintage Quaker Books, www.vintagequakerbooks.com; and Audrey of the Friends General Conference Bookstore, audreyg@fgcquaker.org.

Marianne wishes to express her appreciation to her graduate assistants in the Department of Criminology and Criminal Justice at Northern Arizona University who, through their diligent work over the last fifteen years, have given her time to work on this research; their help with literature reviews and brainstorming is also greatly appreciated. As well, Marianne would like to acknowledge Northern Arizona University for its commitment to Native American communities and students and for its support for the writing of this book through the Scholarly and Creative Activities grant program in 2019–2020.

Both Marianne and Barbara would like to express their appreciation and gratitude to the three peer reviewers whose suggestions (and, we'll admit, occasionally borrowed words) made this a much stronger book.

FINDING RIGHT RELATIONS

INTRODUCTION

QUAKER SETTLER COLONIALISM

Its Disastrous Impacts on American Indians

THE RELIGIOUS Society of Friends (Quakers) was one of the early settler-colonist groups to invade the continent known today as North America. William Penn (1644–1718), who envisioned a government based on Quaker religious principles, set out to develop "a Holy Experiment," or utopian colony, in the area now called Pennsylvania. Quakers had begun immigrating to North America in the mid-1600s in search of religious freedom, prosperity, and safety. Compared to many settler colonists, and for the times, they were more egalitarian and pacifistic in their dealings with the Indigenous inhabitants. Many joined with the Swedish and Finnish settler colonists, creating villages, and living comfortably beside Lenape Peoples (Soderlund 2015). Quakers followed values that today would be called social justice principles and at first, caused relatively few social harms to the Indigenous residents. William Penn, however, who founded Pennsylvania in 1682 from land previously part of the New York colony owned by the Duke of York, wanted to integrate the local Lenape People into his new society on Quaker terms and within English laws as required by his charter. For the Lenape People, this claim to ownership was shocking and changed their lives forever.

Penn's willingness to abide by these imperial conditions on the inclusion of American Indians, was the first sign that Quakers, despite their beliefs, were not immune to, and failed to question, colonial ideas and goals. Neither did they pay attention to the possibility of harms that colonization could cause to Indigenous Peoples and to the settler colonists themselves; thus the seeds of colonialism were sown at the very beginning and were fertilized by the many non-Quakers who soon settled there. With each new wave of non-Quaker settler colonists, Quaker relations with American Indians were further undermined.

During this time, Quakers saw themselves as having very positive relations with the Indigenous Peoples with whom they interacted. Soderlund (2015, 4) comments, "Like English colonists in Jamestown, Plymouth, and Massachusetts Bay, the Friends wove a creation myth of exceptionalism, claiming for themselves a special relationship with the Lenapes based on Quaker principles of justice, peace, religious freedom, and respect for people of different backgrounds." Based on our research, we agree with Soderlund's observation and argue in this book that the Quakers were not as exceptional as they thought, but instead their relationships with the Lenape began as somewhat less colonial than some earlier settler colonists—such as the British and Dutch—but soon became more colonial and were certainly more colonial than the relationships between many other earlier settler colonists and Indian Peoples such as the Swedes and Finns. Despite their social justice ideals, Quakers, like their non-Quaker counterparts, committed violence and other social harms against American Indians, as will be discussed throughout this book.

The Delaware Valley, the center of Penn's colony, had been settled by earlier settler colonists, including Swedes, Finns, Dutch, and English, before the Quakers began to arrive, but these settler colonists were few in number and on the whole respected the sovereignty of the Indigenous inhabitants (Soderlund 2015). The early Quakers added yet more diversity to the regions. Beginning in the late 1600s, newer immigrants, most of whom were not Quakers, arrived in boatloads, some ships carrying as many as three hundred settler colonists at a time. They were among the thousands who heard of Penn's policy of religious tolerance, and flooded Pennsylvania. Many, including those of Scots Irish background, wanted to eliminate and replace the Indigenous Peoples who occupied the lands the settler colonists coveted (Wolfe 2006). Wilbur Jacobs (1969) argues that, in general, these settler colonists regarded themselves as superior to the Indians and were repulsed by all aspects of Indigenous secular and religious practices as well: "Indians were seen as treacherous and unreliable" (Jacobs 1969, 85) and even Indian friendliness was distrusted by the newcomers (Jacobs 1969, 84).

The Quakers, on the other hand, arrived in Pennsylvania with inclinations toward respecting what we would now call the human rights of their Indigenous (and other) neighbors. Penn set out to live with American Indians in friendship and peace. He was concerned with their rights to be treated fairly and justly, human rights they shared with all others. Quakers believe everyone holds the potential to heed the "Light Within" themselves or have "an Inward light of Christ" (Worrall 1980, 5), meaning to have a direct relationship with God. This relationship was also called "The Light," "Inward Light," and "That of God." (We will use the term "Inner Light" throughout.) This meant that Penn saw everyone as spiritually equal, having a right to be treated with respect and to not be harmed, although he seemed to assume that all his "planters" (settler colonists) would be Christian, appointed only Christians to administrative positions, and expected to convert the Lenape, as per his orders from King Charles II (Dunn and Dunn 1982). Penn had a tendency, therefore, to equate acceptable, or perhaps "civilized," humanity with Christianity. Today, we would say that the limited support of human rights by Penn and the Quaker settler colonists was unusual among colonists during the start of this period of intensive colonization, and led the Quakers to the promotion and support of social justice, but their focus on "civilization" was also a symptom of later eighteenth- and nineteenth-century Quaker paternalism and benevolence, causing deep social harms, such as forced boarding school attendance and coerced learning of gender roles that the settler colonists considered appropriate.

The foci of social justice include egalitarianism and the fair distribution of society's advantages (Matwick and Woodgate 2016). Because of their own history, Quakers were well aware that oppression and marginalization through laws, prejudice, economic inequities, and "social dominance" act to prevent social justice and cause social harms (Matwick and Woodgate 2016). According to Matwick and Woodgate (2016, n.p.), "throughout history social justice as a concept is implied rather than explicitly stated." This is certainly the case with the Quakers. Rooted in their spiritual beliefs, social justice is implicit in their Testimonies. Of these, the Peace Testimony is of central interest to this book because of its role in *not* preventing or restraining the social harms, including violence, committed against American Indians by both non-Quakers and Quakers.

In this introduction, we outline who Quakers are as well as the Holy Experiment and its tenets; who American Indians are; the early relations between Quakers and American Indians; early relations between Quakers and non-Quaker settler colonists; what colonialism is in relationship to social justice and social harms; the limitations of our project; and an overview of the book.

By employing modern-day social science concepts such as social justice, social harms, ethnoviolence, structural violence, and organizational structures, we hope to shed new light on the relationship between American Indians and the Quakers who strove with the best of intentions to develop an ideal society where Indigenous Peoples and settler colonists could live in harmony. Because of the inherent contradictions between settler colonialism and their beliefs, they failed terribly and committed grave social harms against the Indigenous Peoples.

WHO ARE QUAKERS?

Quakers are members of the Religious Society of Friends, a group that originated in England with the preaching of George Fox and others who eventually called themselves "The Children of Truth," "The Children of the Light," and other names but are now formally known as the Religious Society of Friends. Quakers are also referred to as "Friends" in this book.

Quakerism was born in the mid-seventeenth century. The ideals of democracy and the philosophy of liberalism, although having deep historical roots, were fertilized during the Enlightenment period in Europe. John Locke's writings (published in 1690) were being written when Penn began his work on a government structure for Pennsylvania in the 1680s, at a time when democracy was anathema to most European rulers. Democracy requires structures allowing all citizens to have a voice in their own governance, and liberalism emphasizes the rights of the individual, but in seventeenth-century Europe it might be fairly said that some monarchs, determined to hold on to their power, were becoming more tyrannical; for example, Charles I of England believed in and acted on the divine right of kings to govern. It took two wars for Cromwell's soldiers to depose Charles I and establish the protectorate that replaced him and for supporters of the monarchy to restore it and put Charles II on the throne in 1661 (Punshon 1984).

Quakerism was built from groups of dissidents attracted by the teaching of George Fox, their beliefs not only part of the democratic and liberal ideals but also part of a religious revolution in which worshippers were turning against the power of the established Christian church and claiming their individual right to communion with God. In Britain the Church of England was the only officially permitted church, and its hierarchy of ministers or priests dominated society and government (Punshon 1984). Many Quakers suffered as a result of Church antagonism, which they aroused not just for their egalitarian beliefs but also for their tendency to stand up during a church sermon (rather than afterward as was typical) and argue forcefully with the priest. Quakers learned quickly that in order to survive it was best to find ways of not antagonizing the church hierarchy. Quakers became past masters of something now called "speaking truth to power," but also of working around the power of tyrannical governments. The Peace Testimony was born out of the foment of these times.

There are two interpretations of the origin of the word "Quaker." One suggests it originated in reference to their practice of silent worship during which they waited for "leadings of the spirit." When they fervently voiced a "leading," it often manifested itself in physical shaking (Dorland 1968, 1). The second states that it began when Quakers on trial would admonish judges to "tremble before God" as the judges delivered prison sentences for dissident religious beliefs (Punshon 1984, 51). In both cases it became a term of disrespect used by non-Quakers to jeer at Friends' fervor. It has since been reappropriated by Friends as a term of pride and popular usage.

Early Friends, such as George Fox, steered a hazardous path between conflicting royal and commonwealth factions in England as they attempted to gain the support of both sides to end persecution and avoid the fighting. He was an acknowledged founding member of the Quakers, who preached against the need for priests or church but rather for a direct relationship with God (Hamm 2003, 18, 14–22).

Early Quakers suffered discrimination and severe persecution, ranging from imprisonment to death, in England and some of the new American colonies. Quakers, including William Penn, spent years of their lives incarcerated, sometimes dying in filthy and dank prisons, for offences against the Church of England, whose ministers were fighting to retain the power they had from the Crown. Quakers offended the established church with their belief in equality as well as their understanding that having a direct relationship with God negated any need for priests or churches. Hamm (2003, 18) cites many Quaker practices that upset the British government, such as refusing to take oaths. But Sharpless (1898) suggests their Testimonies were likely tinged with the pragmatic desire to survive as a faith. The Testimonies were formalized much later in the history of Quakerism. The original beliefs were simplicity, honesty, equality, and peace, and referred to individually (see also Barbour and Roberts 1973, 41). The Peace Testimony was first stated by Margaret Fell in a letter to Charles II (Quakers in the World n.d.).

Quaker enthusiasm knew no bounds. "Hardly the benign, benevolent, charitable people they are today, Friends in this first, prophetic period of early Quakerism did not care to suffer the mass of mankind to go unconverted" (Worrall 1980, 3). In later years, proselytizing waned and eventually turned into a desire not to proselytize at all. Birkel (2004, 27) writes that, "The robust confidence of the earliest Quakers gave way to greater circumspection and to an unrelieved doubt concerning their own purity of motive." Rather than proselytizing, they expected their faith-based actions to be their witness and were more careful about "mistaking one's creaturely creations for the Leadings of the Light" (Worrall 1980, 75).

THE HOLY EXPERIMENT

In 1681, King Charles II of England granted a charter to William Penn to lands in what is now the USA, to be called Pennsylvania in honor of William Penn's father. The king owed a debt of £16,000 to Admiral Penn, an officer who not only lent money to the king's navy "for the victualing of the Navy [in] 1667" but also served a year without pay in 1668, leaving him in debt himself (Dunn and Dunn 1982, 31).

Although the first Quakers, including George Fox, came to Pennsylvania in 1655 to spread their faith (Jennings 1965, 52–53), Penn's reasons for establishing a colony were somewhat different. They included: his failure to get Charles II to adopt a policy of religious tolerance in England; the failure of Quakers to achieve broader political representation in England; his inability to heal divisions among English Quakers, which included a debate between total denial of war and violent defense as appropriate (Sharpless 1898); but perhaps most importantly, the need for a fresh source of income. While in part this was due to a rather lavish lifestyle as well as loans related to his Quaker activities, the debt also came from expenses incurred during the application for a charter, the tenants on his estates in England defaulting on their rents, and the dishonesty of the manager of his English estates, Philip Ford, who was enriching himself at Penn's expense (Fisher 1919). This "knavish steward" put him so deeply in debt that Penn served time in debtor's prison (Jones 1962, 425; Dunn and Dunn 1982, 21–22). Penn's Quaker beliefs brought all of these reasons together. The Peace Testimony, in particular, underlay the new order of human relationships that Penn set out to create in Pennsylvania (Hamm 2003, 27–29).

Penn's first visit to Pennsylvania was not until 1682 due to time spent clearing up his debts (Jones 1966; Soderlund 1983). Dunn and Dunn (1982) record that Penn's first action, on receiving the charter to his land, was to begin work on a written constitution that improved on the unwritten constitution of England and in doing so, embedded Quaker principles and created a kind of theocratic democracy that permitted religious freedom for all Christians. "I shall have a tender care to the Govern[ment] that it be well laid at first," he wrote to Robert Turner (Dunn and Dunn 1982, 137). Penn's draft constitution attracted many Quakers wishing to escape the persecutions in England, and as word of his tolerance spread, many Christians and members of other persecuted faiths such as the pacifistic Mennonites and Jews, joined the early settlers (Kenny 2009, 25; Adler and Rosenbach 2011).

In other Quaker-dominated provinces, mass settler-colonist invasions created conflicts over governance, so that, for example, in Rhode Island the Quaker government established religious tolerance but modified its pacifist beliefs by providing for a militia and allowing conscientious objection to military service (Pointer 2007). This assisted them in the integration of settler colonists with a wide variety of religious and political beliefs. In the Pennsylvania government, however, Penn also instituted religious tolerance but insisted on total absence of defensive structures and ordered settlers to come unarmed (Pointer 2007; Bronner 1968, 2).

WHO ARE AMERICAN INDIANS?

American Indians are Indigenous groups and individuals "who trace their ancestry in these lands to time immemorial" (Morse 1989, 1), a definition appropriate to early colonial times, or today, according to the U.S. Bureau of Indian Affairs (BIA n.d.),

An American Indian or Alaska Native person is someone who has blood degree from and is recognized as such by a federally recognized tribe or village (as an enrolled tribal member) and/or the United States. Of course, blood quantum (the degree of American Indian or Alaska Native blood from a federally recognized tribe or village that a person possesses) is not the only means by which a person is considered to be an American Indian or Alaska Native. Other factors, such as a person's knowledge of his or her tribe's culture, history, language, religion, familial kinships, and how strongly a person identifies himself or herself as American Indian or Alaska Native, are also important. In fact, there is no single federal or tribal criterion or standard that establishes a person's identity as American Indian or Alaska Native.

"Native American" is a more general term that we use here to include "*all* Native peoples of the United States and its trust territories, i.e., American Indians, Alaska Natives, Native Hawaiians, Chamorros, and American Samoans, as well as persons from Canada First Nations and indigenous communities in Mexico and Central and South America who are U.S. residents" (U.S. BIA n.d.; italics in the original).

In common usage, Native Americans also refers to individuals of mixed Indigenous descent. The overarching term "Indigenous Peoples" is used to describe both American Indians and original inhabitants of other now-colonized lands, such as Canada and Australia. The Lenape were the first American Indian Peoples Penn met when he visited West Jersey to try to (unsuccessfully) establish a Quaker colony there. The Lenape Indians, members of the Algonkian linguistic group, call themselves the Lenape, a word meaning "ordinary," "real," or "original" (Bierhorst 1995, 4; Soderlund 2015, 6) or "common person" (Weslager 1972, 31). After this meeting, Penn shifted his focus to the western shore of the Lenapewihittuck (Delaware) River, also occupied by the Lenape, to land that became Pennsylvania. The English colonists called the Lenape the "Delaware" because their villages were located on a river the English baptized the Delaware River in 1610 when an English explorer renamed it after the first governor of the Virginia colony, Thomas West, third Baron De La Warr (Soderlund 2015; Delaware Historical Society 2019). Out of respect, in this book we use the name Lenape ("Lenni Lenape" is an older term used by some historical texts), since it is the name the people originally and currently call themselves, though it should be noted that serious depopulation by disease led to communities of Lenape and Munsee merging, some of whom adopted the name "Delaware" (Soderlund 2015, 178). Today, the Lenape define themselves as: "the original inhabitants of Delaware, New York, Eastern Pennsylvania, and Southern New York. For over 10,000 years they have been the caretakers of these lands and of The River of Human Beings, more commonly known as the Delaware River" (Lenape Nation 2018).

Though the Lenape were the Peoples with whom Quakers had most of their original dealings in Pennsylvania, the Quakers soon had to interact with members of other Indian Nations fleeing settler-colonist depredations. Over time, as the so-called frontier moved inland due to settler-colonist incursions and violence, and as American Indian individuals joined other Indian groups as a result of depopulation and social disorganization, Quakers came into contact with members of many more American Indian Nations such as the Conestoga, Susquehanna, Shawnees, Nanticokes, Conoys, Munsee, and others (Silver 2008, 105).

Today, Indigenous communities are among the most marginalized, economically, politically, and socially in the United States and elsewhere (Coates 2004), conditions that communities and Indian Nations are actively fighting using innovation, resilience, and the assumption of de facto sovereignty (see Nielsen and Jarratt-Snider 2018). There are still many social harms that affect Indigenous Peoples, including violations of human rights and socioeconomic marginalizations, because of the colonial mechanisms that were and still are used against them. These include various forms of violence; discriminatory and acquisitive laws; economic disadvantage from the loss of lands and resources; cultural and language loss as a consequence of boarding schools and assimilationist government policies; and the weakening, distortion, and loss of social institutions, such as family structure, leadership, education, and social control (Coates 2004; Dunbar-Ortiz 2014). Because of the actions of early settler colonists, these marginalizations were already underway by the time Penn began his colony, despite the Lenape still maintaining a position of strength (Soderlund 2015, 7).

EARLY QUAKER AND AMERICAN INDIAN RELATIONS

Quakers' principles served them well when meeting and negotiating with American Indians in the early years. In his papers, Penn writes that he is resolved to live in peace with the Indians and that, in spite of being granted Pennsylvania by the king (Dunn and Dunn 1982, 127), he would purchase the land from the Lenape. This was common practice among early settler-colonist groups such as the Dutch and Swedes, perhaps because as Jones (1962, 495) writes, "The neglect to do it had led to massacres and the extermination of several colonies in the south." Penn bought a few strips of land at a time. "Penn did not buy all of Pennsylvania at one transaction, or any considerable part of it. He had at first no use for any but a little strip along the Delaware, and this was bought of various tribes at different times by separate treaties. . . . Penn would buy from one creek to another and the unit of measure up the creek was a day's walk, in his time about twenty miles, though vastly extended later" (Jones 1962, 495–96).

Penn wrote to the Pennsylvania Indians in October 1681, stating that he came in peace as a friend and neighbor, and that he desired to deal fairly with them (Dunn and Dunn 1982, 261; Myers 1970). In 1682, Penn arrived in his new colony. The famous and nearly mythological Treaty of Shackamaxon, a document that is missing but that is recorded in Quaker minutes and in Indian oral history (Keyser 1882), likely took place in 1682 on Penn's first visit to Pennsylvania. He promised that he would be with the Lenape "as one Body, one heart, one mind." (Kelsey 1917, 63–64). That same year, the Lenape negotiated a memorandum of agreement with Pennsylvania deputy governor William Markham that provided the framework for the Lenape-Pennsylvania dealings and informed some of Penn's policies (Soderlund 2015, 170).

That covenant held until Penn's sons Thomas and John, along with James Logan, broke it, as described later (Soderlund 2015, 5). Penn argued that if you do not abuse the Indians and do ensure justice for them, "you win them," (Myers 1970, 40; Jennings 1984, 242) which sounds somewhat manipulative, undermining claims to equality, along with his goal of Christianization. As well, Penn wrote to his Pennsylvania commissioners in 1681 that they should "Be tender of offending the Indians . . . lett them know [yet] you are come to sitt downe Lovngly among them" (Myers 1970, 57). In 1682, when William Penn was planning his form of government for Pennsylvania, he wanted "unarmed friendship" with the Lenape whose land (he thought) he was purchasing. The conflicting attitudes between Indians and settler colonists about land and natural resources were the key sticking point. The Lenape believed land and natural resources to be under the control of the spirits and not the property of any individual or group. The settlers saw them as something to be owned outright (Kraft 1974, 49; Pencak and Richter 2004, 9–10, 25–36). Penn, for example, became angry and threatened reprisals when the Lenape returned for their annual usage payments (Dunn and Dunn 1982). The Lenape believed in shared usage, with settler colonists paying for the privilege of that use; they granted the rights to build trading forts and small settlements to the Swedes, for example, but they kept their own right to keep using the land for hunting, fishing, and agriculture, and expected regular gifts from the Swedes (Soderlund 2015, 200). If the land was not used for its stated purpose by the settler colonists, the right was lost (Soderlund 2015, 81). This is the same arrangement they expected to have with the Quakers.

For Penn, the treaties were not only land sales but formed "leagues of friend-ship" where "eternal amity and mutual good-will were promised and the prom-ises sealed with wampum belts" (Jones 1962, 496). Such friendship made sense both economically and spiritually. This human rights-type approach used by most Quakers to ensure respectful relations with the Indians was significantly different from that of other colonies according to Quaker writers:

> In some colonies the Indians were made drunk, and in this state signed away valuable claims. In others, false maps were shown them, or false weights deceived them in selling their furs. The land unpurchased was not always excluded from settlement. They were killed, and no penalty was meted out to the white mur-derer. Their food was taken, in their eyes unjustly, often by irresponsible whites, but the acts were not disowned by the authorities. They were treated as inferior, and their pride was hurt. The land bought of one tribe was not bought of another which possibly had, or thought it had, superior claims. Rumours of Indian inva-sions were excuses for bloody attacks. From all of these things the Pennsylvania Indians were preserved. (Jones 1962, 496)

This is not to say that there were not incidents of theft and fraud between the Quakers, the old settlers, and Indigenous Peoples (Soderlund 2015, 163), but in general, the Lenape saw Penn as a benefactor, a man who was generous, a peace-maker, and someone who believed in harmony among peoples (Gerona 2004; Schutt 2007). Weslager (1972, 163) reported that Indian groups described Penn with phrases such as "he spoke from his lips but also from his heart." Penn seems to have had their respect, friendship, and confidence "because his government gave the Indians 'a new deal,'" (Weslager 1972, 170) at least compared to other colonies. In his Frame of Government, Penn incorporated the just, truthful, and equal treatment of American Indians (Dunn and Dunn 1982, 441).

Good relations existed not only between Indians and the Quaker treaty-makers and other important Quaker leaders but also among Indians and ordi-nary Quaker settler colonists. Jones (1966, 497) writes of shared meals in both Quaker and Indian homes, Indians babysitting Quaker children while their parents went to Meeting, Quakers buying wild meat from the Indians and pay-ing a fair price, and Indians being "good neighbours in times of need." Though the communities of the Lenape and Europeans remained distinct, they shared cultural similarities, and some Lenape intermarried with the Swedes and Finns as well as with Quakers (Soderlund 2015, 69, 181–82). Quaker social justice

practices proved to be effective in establishing for them what Quakers sometimes referred to as a "right relationship" or "right relations" between peoples
from a variety of social backgrounds and cultures.

Penn, the Quakers, and the Indians of his time had a relationship that included
some degree of mutual respect and led to a relatively peaceful coexistence that
lasted for seventy years, although this "Long Peace" has been described as prob-
lematic by some scholars (Merrell 1999; Soderlund 2015). For the Quakers this
was based on the similarities in some of their spiritual beliefs. Keil (2001, 1)
comments that, "Though coming from very different cultures, the two groups
found common ground in their strikingly similar beliefs. As Friends believe in
the presence of God—or Inner Light—within every individual, many American
Indians recognize the presence of the Creator or Great Spirit in all individuals.
Accordingly, the belief in the value and dignity of every human being is important to both Friends and Native Americans." Penn, however, saw "five clearly dis-
tinguishable aspects of the Indians: souls to be shown the Truth, exotic objects
for study, claimants to the soil, subjects of government, and trading partners,"
(Jennings 1965, 56–57). As a result, some, but not all of this relationship might
be interpreted as respectful of Indian human rights.

The Quakers' fundamental belief in the Inner Light led them to a general
"levelling down"—a refusal to accept subordination (Birkel 2004, 108–9). At
the same time, Quakers were not revolutionaries; they accepted the right of
governments to govern. These beliefs led them to treat individuals as spiritual
equals, placing them in a difficult situation when even that level of egalitarianism was confronted with government power as occurred more frequently as
colonization intensified, and government interests conflicted with their ideals.

Quaker beliefs and actions changed over time under the subtle and not so
subtle pressures of colonialism. In the early years of colonization, Quakers supported egalitarian ideas whole-heartedly. They originally saw American Indians as spiritual equals, as mentioned above, with basic human rights such as
freedom, peace, and security, since their spiritual beliefs were similar; but as
Gimber (2000, viii) puts it "[the] 'Children of Light' remained confident that
through the mystical and subtle workings of the spirit of God within, the Native
people would convert," but they were also in agreement with widely held beliefs
that saw American Indians as "primitive," that is, less culturally, socially, technically, and politically developed than themselves and hence inferior because,
for example, they had no written language. It was therefore a duty to civilize—to introduce Indians to a "superior" way of living, and this was linked to

Christianization (Gimber 2000, vi; Swatzler 2000, 21). One consequence of this was that by the mid-1800s Quakers were deeply involved in the boarding school era that removed American Indian children from their families. In response to the terrible massacres of American Indians that were decimating their numbers, Quakers felt the only way to save them was to assimilate them, mainly through education. Quakers seemed unaware of, or justified to themselves, the inherently violent assimilative nature and policies of the schools amounting to cultural genocide and how these social harms contradicted their beliefs. They did, in time, end this involvement.

EARLY QUAKER/SETTLER-COLONIST RELATIONS

At the same time that Penn was drafting his 1681 letter to the Indians, he was also busy promoting Pennsylvania and selling land lots to settlers, initially mostly Quakers, and also charging an annual quitrent on each. Penn needed to make money as quickly as possible. His promotions very soon extended to non-Quakers, and he organized large influxes of colonists prior to his first treaty with the Lenape (Spady 2004, 31). He insisted only that the settler colonists come unarmed and treat the Lenape and other smaller resident Indian groups with respect (Gimber 2000). The new settler colonists did neither.

While this made for quick settlement, it also led to Quakers becoming outnumbered. For as long as there was peace with the Indians this caused relatively minor problems, but most settler colonists did not share the Quaker view of American Indians and were far greedier for land than Penn had envisaged, nor had the Lenape anticipated the large numbers who came wanting the Lenapes' land (Spady 2004, 31).

The American Indians initially perceived the Quakers, idealized in Penn, to be very different from other settler colonists (Weslager 1972, 163) but as violations of treaties and human rights continued, American Indian rebellions against the settler colonists increased. By this time Quakers had split into two groups—those who supported William Penn's sons, who were now the non-Quaker proprietors (the governors of Pennsylvania), and those who supported the "anti-proprietary group" of Anthony Morris, John Evans, William Brown, Israel Pemberton, and other Quakers. This latter group came uninvited to several treaty conferences in an attempt to protect the Indians from the rapacity of the government. An example of this was the infamous Walking Purchase committed by Penn's sons and other proprietors (Dewees 1912, 124). As well, even after the Quakers were out of power in Philadelphia, this group of wealthy, concerned, and pacifist Quakers, tried to stop direct violence against and by the Lenape and other Indian Peoples by forming the "Friendly Association for Regaining and Preserving Peace with the Indians by Pacific Measures" (Sharpless 1898, 181; Jones 1966; Ream 1981), which was informally approved by the Philadelphia Yearly Meeting (PYM). They worked from "their own self-understanding as protectors of Native Americans" (Thompson 2013, 77) and so set up conferences with the hostile nations, which included paying restitution for fraudulent purchases of their lands, persuading government and Indians to the negotiating table, and defended American Indian rights at treaty sessions. They also recorded the history of the Delaware, in the Indian speakers' own words, and kept those documents (to this day they can be found in Haverford College's Special Collections). They also attempted to have tracts of land permanently set aside for Indian settlements, but government officials balked at the idea of permanence (Mekeel 1981; Spady 2004, 38).

Penn's form of government contributed to later tensions in that it set up a Legislative Assembly and Executive Council with separate responsibilities leading to inevitable conflicts, especially when those raised issues related to Quaker beliefs. Rothenberg (1976) argues that Quakers had also become so enamored of their new wealth that they lost sight of Quaker values, including their agreement to renew their treaty with the Lenape every year. This contributed to Indian anger over their treatment by settler colonists and eventually led to the Lenape participation in the French and Indian Wars (Seven Years War) in Pennsylvania (Soderlund 2015, 176).

COLONIALISM AND SOCIAL HARMS

Quakers took a different approach in North America than most other colonists, one related to social justice, but they did not challenge the underlying basis of settler colonialism, which centered on resource acquisition at all costs, including committing structural and cultural violence that led to intense social harms to anyone challenging settler colonialism's goals. The Quakers, like other European invaders, were there to acquire land and resources so they could thrive. Quakers undoubtedly felt a divine leading to immigrate and colonize but also carried with them a sense of the superiority of their truths and by extension, also of themselves (Jones 1966, xiv). The material needs of Quaker settlers also appears to have overwhelmed many, leading to some ostentatious displays of wealth and great inequality of conditions in Pennsylvania (Rothenberg 1976; Moulton 1971), undermining Quaker values.

Colonialism is the expansion of European powers into non-European lands by conquest or other means. According to Osterhammel (1997, 16) colonialism starts as "a relationship of domination between an indigenous . . . majority and a minority of foreign invaders. . . . Rejecting cultural compromises with the colonized population, the colonizers are convinced of their own superiority and their ordained mandate to rule." According to Blaut (1993, 23) colonialism was "an immensely profitable business" aimed at acquiring the resources of Indigenous Peoples for the ruling powers of Europe.

Like other Europeans of the time, Quakers believed implicitly that they were entitled to what they wanted because they were superior due to God's will; "the religious argument was so nearly universally accepted down to the nineteenth century that other arguments were not seen as necessary to many European intellectuals" (Blaut 1993, 60). Later, white European superiority was based on the premise that they were "brighter, better and bolder than non-Europeans because of their heredity" (Blaut 1993, 61). Both of these culturally violent ideologies impacted the treatment of American Indians by Quakers and the settler colonists. Quaker beliefs, however, tempered them so that the actions based on these beliefs were initially more respectful and less likely to cause harm. These beliefs of superiority were rooted in what J. M. Blaut terms "Eurocentric diffusionism," the belief that progress developed and flowed out of Europe, which was the center of the world:

> The era of classical diffusionism was the era of classical colonialism, the era when European expansion was so swift and so profitable that European superiority seemed almost a law of nature. Diffusionism, in its essence, codified this apparent fact into a general theory about European historical, cultural, and psychological superiority, non-European inferiority, and the inevitability and absolute righteousness of the process by which Europe and its traits diffused to non-Europe. (Blaut 1993, 26)

Blaut (1993, 16) explains that according to this colonizers' model of the world, "compensating in part for the diffusion of civilizing ideas from Europe to non-Europe, is a counterdiffusion of material wealth from non-Europe to Europe, consisting of plantation products, minerals, art objects, labor, and so on. Nothing can fully compensate the Europeans for their gift of civilization to the colonies, so the exploitation of colonies and colonial peoples is morally justified."

Law reflected these colonial ideologies of the time and was an early tool of colonialism. For example, terra nullius (or "land that belongs to no one") was a legal fiction that permitted Christians to take any land occupied by non-Christians, without the permission of the inhabitants, since these inhabitants "lived in a state of nature" according to international law (Nielsen and Robyn 2019; Nayar 2015, 153). This was the foundation for the Doctrine of Discovery, a particularly repugnant declaration of superiority by Europeans claiming lands new to them as uninhabited and available for possession unless the inhabitants were Christians. Anaya (1996, 22) describes it as follows: "Under this fiction, discovery was employed to uphold colonial claims to indigenous lands and to bypass any claims to possession by the natives in the 'discovered' lands." Taking Indigenous lands was therefore "justified" because "lands not put to the highest agricultural use (again, as defined by Europeans) were essentially 'vacant' or in a state of 'waste,' subject to European discovery and occupation" (Pommersheim 2009, 94–95). Since Indigenous Peoples had no say in defining "agricultural usage," legal reliance on this definition ensured they lost their land. The Doctrine of Discovery and various papal bulls also overtly encouraged forced conversion to Catholicism and the murder of Indigenous Peoples who refused (Nielsen and Robyn 2019). Law continues today to contribute to the political, economic, and social marginalization of Indigenous Peoples (see, for example, Nielsen and Jarratt-Snider 2020).

Such colonial beliefs were "unquestioned and usually unnoticed" (Blaut 1993, 60) by the settler colonists and were certainly central to the beliefs of the non-Quakers to whom Penn offered land and who believed they "could use the land better than they [Indigenous Peoples] could" (Wolfe 2006, 389). Wolfe (2006, 391) contrasted such settler colonists to the more educated elite such as Penn, writing that these "irregular, greed-crazed invaders . . . had no intention of allowing the formalities of federal law to impede their access to the riches available in, under, and on Indian soil." In Pennsylvania, this describes the incoming Scots Irish settlers (also called Ulster Irish) who were escaping religious intolerance and economic crises, and who shared none of the Quakers' values. Rather they embraced violence, including murder, and other harms against Indians.

Their beliefs also infected the beliefs of Quakers. A concept discussed by Soderlund (2015) is that of mythologizing colonization. She argues that Quakers, like all historical winners, mythologized their colonial activities into a "creation myth." Such creation myths basically represent the winners' history, only from their point of view and in the most positive light possible. But as Dunbar-Ortiz (2014, 2) writes,

> The history of the United States is a history of settler colonialism—the founding of a state based on the ideology of white supremacy, the widespread practice of African slavery, and a policy of genocide and land theft. Those who seek history with an upbeat ending, a history of redemption and reconciliation, may look around and observe that such a conclusion is not visible, not even in utopian dreams of a better society.

American history is not a "consensual national narrative" (Dunbar-Ortiz 2014, 2) although that is how its history is perceived today by the majority of the population, though not its Indigenous Peoples and other people of color. Indigenous Peoples have been the victim of history rewriting and, despite active resistance through their own representations, are still victims of it. In the case of the Quakers, such origin myths become ideological justifications for the great harms done because they were done "with the best of intentions."

Quakers used a framework of Christianization and civilization from the beginning not only because they were obliged to by King Charles II's Charter for Pennsylvania but because of their belief in European diffusionism (Blaut 1993) and the justifications provided by the Doctrine of Discovery, covenants with God, and the Columbus myth (Dunbar-Ortiz 2014, 3). For the Quakers, that framework was bolstered by the mythical retelling of their founding stories, including mythologizing of the Treaty of Shackamaxon (which was likely real, but no physical evidence of it exists today); the claim that Divine Providence was the cause of Lenape hospitality and friendship (Bowden 1850, 400; Angell 2003, 5); and the stories of Quakers exempted from Indian violence during war; however, implicitly, the framework is also based on the assumption of their own superiority, based on their testament to Truth. Quakers seemed unaware of the inherent cultural violence in that. While integration can include the equal sharing and melding of two cultures, assimilation only refers to the absorption of one culture into another, and by the nineteenth century, Quakers were willing to accomplish that by force.

SOCIAL HARMS

Settler colonialism relies on direct, structural, and cultural violence and the threat of violence, as described by Galtung (1990) to achieve political and economic ends. The World Health Organization (WHO) (2002, 4) defines violence as "the intentional use of physical force or power, threatened or actual, against oneself, another person, or against a group or community, that either results in or has a high likelihood of resulting in injury, death, psychological harm, maldevelopment, or deprivation." This definition recognizes that violence may be self-directed, interpersonal, or collective.

Quakers abhorred direct interpersonal violence but like other settler colonists participated in collective violence, that is, "the instrumental use of violence by people who identify themselves as members of a group against another group or set of individuals, in order to achieve political, economic or social objectives" (WHO 2002, 5). Settler colonial and American government policy supported such collective violence. This can be seen not only in the "Indian Wars" but in forcing American Indian children into boarding schools where they were subjected to direct interpersonal violence committed by their supposed guardians. Violence in the schools included all the types found under this category: physical, sexual, psychological, and deprivation or neglect (WHO 2002, 5). Many of these forms of violence were what Passas (2016, 125) calls "*lawful but awful* crimes," that is, crimes that were "acts and practices that the law allows, and governments often encourage or even subsidise, which have adverse social, economic and environmental consequences." Nielsen and Robyn (2019) call these "legal crimes" and describe them as one of the foundational elements of colonialism.

Johan Galtung (1990) proposed a typology of violence that comes at violence from a different though related perspective. It differentiates among direct, structural, and cultural violence. Direct violence is committed by depriving people of their basic human needs, that is, survival, well-being, identity, and freedom—through death, a life of misery, alienation from identity, and repression. Structural violence is committed by social institutions such as religion, the military, economics, and law—through exploitation and permanent misery, limiting people's access to information (segmentation), internalized inferiority (penetration), marginalization, and fragmentation (basically divide and conquer) (Galtung 1990; Dutta 2020). Cultural violence "refers to the prevailing attitudes or beliefs used to legitimize violence of direct or structural nature.

These include the prejudices or stereotypes existing in society, which have been internalized by individuals" (Dutta 2020, n.p.).

Cocks (2012, n.p.) extends Galtung's discussion of structural violence to add "foundational violence," which she argues is a process more appropriate to colonialism in that structural violence is not able "to disclose the violence entailed by the birth of a new order of things, before it has congealed into something structured enough to be either structurally violent *or* structurally peaceful" (italics in the original). Foundational violence occurs when one order is replaced by another either violently, which agrees with Wolfe's (2006) view of the settler colonial objectives, or peacefully (Cocks, 2012), which is likely what the Quakers were anticipating. Cocks describes the treaty-making process between American Indians and settler colonists as exemplifying foundational violence because, eventually, the treaties were used as a form of assault by a stronger power on a weaker one that has to consent. Cultural violence then must account for the original destruction of the existing Indigenous societies and Peoples (Cocks 2012).

Using this modified typology, Quakers appear to have avoided direct violence but contributed to foundational, structural, and cultural violence against Indigenous Peoples.

Violence is only one form of social harm.[1] Social harms caused by colonialism during the period in question encompassed a number of categories, including direct and structural physical violence, as mentioned above, such as assaults, torture, disease, and food deprivation; financial/economic harms, including poverty and fraud; emotional and psychological harms; and cultural violence, which Hillyard and Tombs call "culture safety harms," that includes depriving people of "autonomy, development and growth, and access to cultural, intellectual and informational resources." (Hillyard and Tombs 2004, 19–20). All of these harms were inflicted on American Indians during the early and later colonial eras, and Quakers contributed directly or indirectly to most of them.

Presser (2013, 2) explains, "humans harm other living beings with alarming frequency in a variety of ways and have done so for as far back as historical

---

1. As Tombs (2016, 220) writes, the social harms framework "is very much a work in progress." In this book, we take the social harms framework beyond relationships in current society to look at the harms caused by colonization to Indigenous Peoples of the past and present. We are not the first to do so, but the use of such a framework has been rare. See, for example, Comack (2018), Nielsen and Robyn (2019), and Wyatt (2014). As far we can determine it has not been applied at all to analyze the historic and continuing relations between American Indians and Quakers.

records go. Harms include the sort of crimes typically handled by local police (e.g., murder, rape, assault, and theft) and the white-collar crimes handled by regulatory agencies (e.g., price fixing and insider trading)." For the purposes of this book, it is important to note that crime also includes "organized collective actions such as war, genocide, terrorism, torture, slavery, *colonization, displacement, and human-trafficking*" (Presser, 2013, 2; italics added). Based on Indigenous histories, we would also include the destruction of food stuffs, such as buffalo and other animals, crops, and others means of livelihood. Pemberton (2016, 9–10) summarizes social harms as "specific events or instances where 'human flourishing' is demonstrably compromised" and sees them as "inherent to the capitalist form of organization." And Quakers were certainly early capitalists, since making money underlay many of their intentions (Rothenberg 1976). It should be noted, however, that not all colonial endeavors, particularly in non-European colonized parts of the world, were capitalist, though they were certainly expansionist and damaging (Coates 2004, 268).

Presser (2013, 2–3) writes, "harms differ from suffering or loss which are its effects" and points out that some harms are structural, such as poverty; some harms result because of taking action, such as firing a gun; and others result "from failing to take action, such as neglectful parenting or tolerance of genocide." The participants in harm have different perspectives on the harm depending on their role. "Most notably, victims are apt to call harmful what perpetrators and bystanders do not" (Presser 2013, 4). Intent becomes relatively irrelevant. Corporate or government negligence, for example, does not intend to produce victims, but does so nevertheless (Presser 2013, 7). Harmful cultural violence may be "unintended and unforeseen," or harms may be tolerated, or the perpetrators may perceive themselves as not doing harm, but the consequences are still harm (Presser 2013, 7, 9). As well, harms can occur if moral indifference is used by perpetrators to release them from their responsibility (Pemberton 2004).

Because of their religious beliefs, Quakers did not fully follow the colonial belief system nor take it to its logical extreme, which was the extermination of the Indigenous inhabitants as advocated by some other settler colonists (see Nielsen and Robyn 2019). They recognized American Indians as human beings with the same rights as other human beings, as limited as those rights might have been in those times. Over time, however, as Thomas Penn and others in power left the Quaker faith and members of other settler-colonial groups came into power, economic and political priorities led to Quakers turning away from or distorting their own sense of social justice and worsened the relationship between many Quakers and American Indians. Quakers became more invested in structural violence in the economy and laws of the colony, and cultural violence more strongly permeated their beliefs.

The Quaker colonists believed that they were doing no harm, in fact that they were doing right by their American Indian neighbors. Thompson (2013, 1) argues in her research on Quaker missions that "despite Quakers' own conception of themselves as unique from other colonists and thus able to provide a superior education for Native Americans than that provided by other Protestants, Quakers were engaged in the same colonizing project as other missionaries and colonists." Quakers thought their religious beliefs, based as they were on social justice, made them incapable of doing harm, unlike the other non-Quaker settler colonists, but as Presser (2013, 12) writes "People do harm in part because to do so is all right in the culture" and as Quakers adopted colonial ideologies, harm became part of their relations with American Indians. Quakers did not intend to cause harm to American Indians, but "the harms that cause the most widespread social injury are not caused by intentional acts, but rather, result from the omission to act or societal indifference to suffering" (Pemberton 2016, 8). Presser (2013, 128) writes that "the business of doing good is dangerous territory. . . . One person's good is another's evil."

While the Quakers were trying to establish a functioning government, colony, and life, they unintentionally caused harm to the Indigenous inhabitants of the colony by ignoring the violence and stress that colonization caused. As they later tried to deal with the influx of non-Quaker settler colonists, they found themselves caught between their capitalist needs and their religious beliefs. According to Pemberton (2016, 8), "harms are . . . a direct consequence of prevailing political, economic and policy decisions." The question becomes: "Could the crimes against the American Indians have been prevented by the Quakers?" Perhaps, but instead, they essentially ignored the crimes against the settler colonists committed by French and Indians when at war, as well as crimes committed against their Indian allies by the settler colonists. Later, they ignored the violence committed in residential and boarding schools, at least for a while.

Quakers, most of whom were staunch pacifists, abhorred the use of direct violence against Indigenous Peoples, or any individuals, and this was indeed a contradiction: Quakers were both pacifists and settler colonists. We argue that, despite their best intentions, Quakers contributed to the violence and social harms committed against Indigenous Peoples and communities. First was their inability to politically and personally deal with violence and harms carried out by others; and second, by integrating cultural violence into their beliefs and not recognizing or ignoring the violence and harms inherent in such colonial processes as the assimilation of Indigenous Peoples, particularly children.

LIMITATIONS

Despite our access to the amazing resources at the Haverford Special Collections Library, there are two main limitations of this book: lack of Native voice and the bias of our non-Native resources. Neither author is of Native American descent, and although Nielsen has worked in and for Indigenous communities and organizations for over forty years, she lacks the lived experience that is the basis for such deep understanding. The second limitation is our reliance on non-Native writings. Some early Lenape history and stories related orally were recorded at the time, but the biases of the settler colonist observers and recorders cannot be discounted. We were rather horrified as we continued our research over the years to realize that when we started, we had bought into the mythologizing of the Quaker creation myth (Soderlund 2015). These myths underlay the majority of our historical resources because most Quakers writers believed them. We learned to read our sources with greater sensitivity and worked hard to try to present Quaker/Native American relations from an even-handed perspective, though we may not have always succeeded (see Soderlund 2015, 205 for her discussion of this issue). Such biases are hard to avoid. Please note that we incorporated the writings of Indigenous authors where possible.

THE BOOK

Our first thought in doing this research was that we could use peacemaking as a way to discuss right relations between Native Americans and Quakers. That proved an unsuccessful approach because of a number of historical factors: the king's requirements for Penn's colony, the impact of colonial ideology on the Quakers, and the Quakers' arrogance in their beliefs. It is still an important theme in the book, however. We use it as the jumping-off point to discuss the early relations between Quakers and the Lenape Indians, and then we revisit it again in the final two chapters where we see it as a present and future tool for finding right relations between Quakers and Native Americans. In the chapters in between, we explain some of the points at which their relations deteriorated from what had looked like promising early days.

The confluence of settler colonialism, the Quaker Peace Testimony (and other Testimonies), and Native American survival is clearly complex. This book focuses on some of the key examples that illustrate the forms of violence and other harms that resulted from this intersection. Over their four hundred-plus years of relations with Native Americans, Quakers participated in many colonial processes either naïvely or knowingly depending on their own colonial goals. We argue that colonial aims and ideologies had serious impacts on the Quaker practices and Testimonies that originally influenced Quaker dealings with American Indians. Their beliefs were corrupted so that Quakers eventually contributed to the social harms that affected American Indians, such as marginalization and destruction of American Indian cultures, lifeways, and lives. They turned away from their social justice approach to American Indian relations and attacked the American Indians' human rights, all the while believing they were doing it for the good of American Indians. As John Echohawk (2019, 313), a founder of the Native American Rights Fund, states: "The efforts went too far by attempting to solve problems by changing the *others* who were being harmed, rather than examining how one's own actions might be contributing to the suffering of others and then attempting to change one's own actions in a way that would not cause the same suffering. In retrospect, it is finally becoming clear to outsiders that the problems for Tribes in the past might often be described as harmful outcomes of well-meaning, but poorly advised, policies of outsiders" (italics in the original).

We provide evidence that Quakers' foundational value of nonviolence was insufficiently grounded to be successfully put into practice. Consequently, it led to cultural and structural violence and the Quakers' well-intentioned but extremely harmful assimilative efforts in boarding schools. At worst, direct violence occurred through their abandonment of Indian allies in danger of lethal violence. We argue that the harmful processes of settler colonialism contributed much to ending any potential that Penn's Holy Experiment had for shaping an America that integrated Native Americans and non-Native Americans in an equal, respectful, and just relationship.

This research originated in 2004, when we applied for and received the Gest Fellowship, funding a month-long residency at Haverford College to study their historical documents. We analyzed original Quaker diaries, county records,

Quaker legislation, and historical writings going back to the late 1600s, and newer ones as well. The research eventually led to the four published articles and a conference paper that form the core of this book. We wanted to discover if the Lenape taught the Quakers how to do peacemaking. The answer to our question was "no." We then began to debate the universality of peacemaking, considering its application within two such different cultures four hundred years ago, and among Quakers and Native Americans today.

As we searched through the historical documents looking for peacemaking connections, we came across unanswered questions that intrigued us. Because of our criminological, sociological, and Quaker history interests, we investigated crimes and violence towards the local American Indians, including the Quaker government's role in preventing such violence, or not, and the Quaker role in boarding schools, which were inherently violent institutions.

In brief, the remainder of the book is composed of seven chapters in which we first examine and compare peacemaking by both Quakers and the Lenape in chapter 1, as well as the relationships based on that peacemaking. Over the course of time, Quakers and Lenape in Pennsylvania grew apart. Given the many compatibilities between Quaker and Lenape spiritual beliefs and practices, it is surprising that the first step in the process of positive relationship building that happened before the arrival of William Penn should break down. But there were inherent weaknesses in Penn himself as well as in his planning. Peacemaking was a part of his plans, but the three levels of government that he designed were weakened by his trust in the superiority of the wealthy proprietors as the Executive Council for his province, with a weaker voice for the elected Legislative Assembly, or lower chamber. Chapter 2 discusses Penn's government, beginning to identify some of the weaknesses that undermined the Quaker-Lenape potential. It also points to possible indicators of why Quakers did not learn from the Lenape. Impacted by imperial orders and politics, by settler colonist desires, and by religious fervor, weaknesses in the Pennsylvania government structure became broad cracks when Penn's need for income led to invitations for non-Quaker settler colonists that met with an enthusiastic response. They came in numbers neither Quakers nor Lenape had anticipated, and they came with a different view of Indigenous Peoples and of the rights of settler colonists to the lands. Years later, when two levels of Penn's government, one elected (representing settlers) and the other appointed (representing proprietors), were unable to agree over funding, frustration, including murderous rage, at the government's perceived failures led to war between the Lenape and settler colonists. Chapter 3 offers a harrowing example of what can go wrong when cultures (especially when one of them displays unbridled greed) collide and the government is unable to respond. Quakers failed to fulfill Penn's promise of protection for his Indian friends.

Both religious and political ideals infused the narratives of all concerned. They led to assumptions about *the Other*—the settler colonist, the Lenape Indian, the Quaker. Each one acted on their assumptions, leading in some cases to years of peace and in others to years of conflict. Behind the fighting and the peacemaking is ideology, and this is discussed with examples in chapter 4, followed by another example of ideology and false assumptions in chapter 5, where we write about Quaker involvement in the boarding school system, how it all began and where it began, at least, to end. Quakers began with the ideals of equality and peace but ended with trying to make peace happen by enforcing "superior" ways of living on supposedly inferior Indians.

In chapter 6 we return to peacemaking as a possible social justice-based resolution to overcoming social harms and speculate about its current and future place as a mechanism of social justice and restoration of right relations. The final chapter recaps the themes of the book and relates how the evidence in each chapter supports the claim that settler colonialism destroyed Penn's Holy Experiment. It looks with renewed hope at the present and future of Quaker and Native American relations.

The purpose of this book is to raise public and scholarly awareness of the power of colonialism to corrupt even colonists with a belief system rooted in social justice and diametrically opposed to the belief systems that drive settler colonialism. As M. Walker (2006, 215) writes, "The importance of truth-telling in cases of extended and systemic oppression is of the greatest importance."

For many Indigenous Peoples, the historical impacts of colonial harms such as socioeconomic marginalization and historical trauma are now just facts of everyday life, but few settler colonist descendants understand the relationship between colonialism and the issues that face Indigenous Peoples today. To do so it would be necessary to understand the violence of settler colonial history and its continuing direct and indirect harms. Many settler colonist descendants have only recently begun to realize the privileges they enjoy are because of the exploitation and oppression of Indigenous Peoples. They are mostly indifferent to Indigenous Peoples and the challenges they face in modern settler colonial society and deny the role of their ancestors in these harms (Nielsen and Robyn 2019).

The descendants of the Quaker settler colonists, however, are not as sanguine; many of them realize that they carry an obligation to take part in ending these social harms and in the healing of today's Indigenous communities. In other words, they acknowledge the harms caused by their predecessors and have returned to the principles of social justice in their efforts to ameliorate some of these wrongs. Telling the truth about the violence and harms of the past is the starting point (Echohawk 2019, 312-313).

We hope this book will assist in the truth-telling that is essential to the healing process that is underway for both Indigenous survivors and the descendants of the settler-colonial perpetrators. We also hope it can in some small way contribute to the building of a better and more inclusive society.

1

QUAKER AND LENAPE
PEACEMAKING IN THE 1700S

What Quakers Didn't Hear

WILLIAM PENN and the Quakers, like so many immigrants since then, arrived in the American colonies hoping to find religious freedom and economic opportunities. The land to which they traveled was inhabited by Indigenous Peoples who already had one hundred years of mostly peaceful experiences[1] with the Swedes and Finns, mainly because of their successful trade relations and these early settler colonists' respect for the Lenapes' undisputed sovereignty (Soderlund 2015, 1–2). The Lenape believed in peace and freedom not only for themselves but for others and in that way differed from many Indian groups in the Northeast (Soderlund 2015, 202). As Soderlund (2015, 149) writes,

> William Penn's "holy experiment" did not develop from a blank slate. The new Quaker settlers obtained assistance, advice, and local perspectives from the Lenapes, Swedes, Finns, Dutch and English who already lived along the Lenapewihittuck and created an inclusive, tolerant, decentralized society based

---

1. This is not to say that this period was one of unrelenting peace. The Lenape, for example, had several violent run-ins with the Dutch, when the Dutch violated agreements and ignored Lenape sovereignty, and with the Iroquois, who attacked not only the Lenape but also the Susquehannock, Lenape allies at the time (Soderlund 2015).

on economic goals. The Lenapes and old settlers had created a culture in which the Quaker colonists in West New Jersey and Pennsylvania easily moved.

These "local perspectives" included the Lenape and old settlers teaching Penn and his officials about "the legal, diplomatic, economic, and cultural practices of their society" (Soderlund 2015, 175). After Penn was awarded the colony, the Lenape and the Quakers continued and expanded these relationships, living what some scholars refer to as the "Long Peace." This was possible because of the Lenape's earlier history with settler colonists, the predilections of both Lenape and Quakers to a peaceful way of life and worldview, and the conditions, described by Soderlund, that the Quaker settler colonists found when they arrived (Soderlund 2015, 175; Merrell 1999, 35).

Both the Lenape and the Quakers were known as peacemakers between conflicting groups and practiced the philosophy of what is now called restorative justice within their own communities. Because of restorative justice's focus on equity, respect, fairness, healthy relationships, individual well-being, peacemaking, and achieving justice, it can be seen as a form of social justice (see Zehr 2015).

At the beginning of our research project, we speculated that because of their good relations, Quakers and Lenape may have learned restorative justice practices and concepts from each other and incorporated them into their own systems; however, we found that this was likely not the case. There were no letters, journals, speeches, minutes of Meetings, court records, or other records that we could find that mentioned or even hinted at discussions between Quakers and Lenape about justice practices or of Quakers witnessing and understanding Lenape restorative justice practices. The Quakers may have learned from the local Indian groups about foodstuffs, climate and natural resources, and other such knowledge essential for survival in a strange land but had little curiosity about their culture or history with earlier settler colonists (Soderlund 2015, 4, 143, 180). The Lenape communicated their history through oral narratives that were only occasionally recorded by the settler colonists, meaning there is a lack of Indigenous records from this time (Soderlund 2015, 4, 68), which had an impact on our research.

The restorative justice practice of peacemaking varies widely depending on the needs of the participants. In general, restorative justice practices focus on discovering all the needs of the victims (e.g., physical, emotional, financial), the offender taking responsibility for the wrongs committed, involving the community, and repairing the harm done to all parties (Hass-Wisecup and Saxon 2018,

51–77). Today, these general principles are followed by almost all restorative justice programs, including Quaker peacemaking and American Indian peacemaking, although the specifics of each process are culturally based.

We could only conclude, based on our research, that despite what we now see as similarities in ideology and practice, the two groups did not have enough common ground—linguistically, ideologically, or simply chronologically—to share their values about justice. In 1755 when the French and Indian Wars (the colonial theater of the Seven Years War) broke out, the Lenape and the settler colonists of Pennsylvania found themselves a part of it. At this point, the opportunity to learn more about peacemaking from each other, if it ever existed, was lost.

This chapter is about why, thanks primarily to various aspects of colonialism, this sharing did *not* occur.

LENAPE HISTORY

At the beginning of the Quaker settlement of Pennsylvania, there was a population of about ten thousand to twelve thousand Lenape Indians living in Lenapehoking, their homeland in the valley along the Lenapewihittuck River (later called the Delaware River by the English), although historians disagree on the exact number (e.g., Weslager 1972, 42; Soderlund 2015, 1; Becker 1976, 25). At the time of Quaker George Fox's arrival, the Lenape were still the dominant power in the area and remained so well into the 1680s despite diminished numbers (Soderlund 2015, 1, 6, 149). It should be noted that their numbers decreased again after the Quakers arrived in the 1690s, as these Quakers brought smallpox and other diseases with them (Soderlund 2015, 168). According to Soderlund (2015, 7–8),

> During the seventeenth century, prior to William Penn's arrival, the Lenapes and early European colonists created a society in Lenape country that preferred peaceful resolution of conflict, religious freedom, collaborative use of the land and other natural resources, respect for people of diverse backgrounds, and local government authority, all facilitating the business relationship the residents sought for profitable trade. Though theirs was a polyglot, negotiated society, it was one in which the Lenapes held the upper hand and remained flexible to win allies and accommodate trade.

This relationship model was perpetuated by the Lenape and the Friends who set-tled in Pennsylvania and New Jersey so that, for example, the Quakers accepted the well-developed travel policies and joint usage of land policies already in place among the inhabitants (Soderlund 2015, 11, 175). While the Quaker settler colonists held many of these practices and beliefs in common with the existing residents, their society was more inegalitarian.

In the early years of contact, the Lenape lived in thirty to forty autonomous though collaborative and affiliated communities along the river, where they held land collectively through the matrilineal line, and moved from family-based farmsteads to hunting and fishing grounds, depending on the season (Soder-lund 2015, 7, 177, 190–1; Kraft 1974, 31; Weslager 1972, 42; Becker 1976, 25; 1980, 20; Wallace 1961). There were several hundred members of each community (or band). They were closely affiliated with the Munsee Indians who lived north of them (Soderlund 2015, 7).

The Lenape "constituted one of the most powerful eastern tribes in the early eighteenth century . . . and sometimes vied with the Iroquois for leadership" (Jennings 1984, 215). They were members of wide-ranging communication net-works (Schutt 2007) and as the colonial era became dominant, Lenape land became home to not only the Lenape but many other groups who were refugees from conflicts between Indian and Indian, and Indian and European settler colo-nists elsewhere along the Eastern Seaboard (Jennings 1984, 215). These groups, along with some of the Lenape, left for Ohio and points west and north as the settler colonists continued their land theft and encroachment. Today, there are Lenape or Delaware Indian Nations primarily in Oklahoma and Canada (Bier-horst 1995, 4–5), although several nations flourish in parts of New England (Ell-wood 2018; Lenape Nation 2018).

Each community had its own leader, called a "sachem" by Europeans, and council of "great men" with independent authority over the territory (Weslager 1972, 33; Becker 1976, 25; Wallace 1961, 53–54; Becker 1976; Harrington 1913, 24). Penn described them as such: "Every King hath his Council, and that consists of all Old and Wise men of his Nation, which perhaps is two hundred People: nothing of Moment is undertaken, be it War, Peace, Selling of Land or Traffick, without advising with them; and which is more, with the Young Men too. 'Tis admirable to consider, how Powerful the Kings are, and yet how they move by the Breath of their People" (Myers 1970, 36). In other words, each sachem led mainly through influence and might be better described as a "spokesman" (Gim-ber 2000, 53; Becker 1976; Hunter 1978, 21). The sachem and his councilors were the main decision-makers in the community even though they had very limited authority (Weslager 1972, 33) and probably were respected heads of lineages or elders who had no special privileges compared to others in the community (Becker 1976, 45). Jennings described their system of government as being based on the "consent of the governed" (Jennings 1974, 99; see also Soderlund 2015).

The sachem was responsible for ensuring order in his communities and that justice was properly dispensed: "it was his responsibility to see that the death of a member of the lineage was avenged, or, if one of his own people had been the killer, to arrange for the payment of blood money to buy his kinsman's life." (Wallace 1961, 51); and "[t]he community had no police to enforce the law. The Delaware, indeed, had no law in the statute-book sense. But individual Indians seldom violated the community's code. If they did violate it, they submitted to punishment without a murmur. 'Their honor was their law'" (Wallace 1961, 52, citing a letter from C. Cukler to L. C. Draper, Feb. 20, 1863). According to Gimber (2000, 53) one of the roles of the sachem also included mediating disputes.

As the European invasions continued to disrupt Indian political and economic alliances,[2] other Indian groups displaced by European settlement attacked the Lenape. Weslager (1972, 102) gives an example, writing (mistakenly) that "Delawares were not warlike prior to the coming of Europeans; and neither by disposition, experience, nor in military weaponry were they a match for Minquas [Susquehannock] attacking parties. They were wholly unprepared for battle." Weslager seems unaware of the Lenape practice of "mourning wars" in retaliation for murders when peacemaking didn't work or the conflicts the Lenape had with the Dutch, the Iroquois, the non-Quaker English, and others (Soderlund 2015, 39, 108, 203). As another example, the Lenape asked the Quaker government for military aid in 1692 to attack invading Senecas but were refused help (Brinton 1885, 117). They were also invited to participate in a war against the French by the Onondagas and Senecas [Iroquois] in 1694 but refused (Brinton 1885, 117) for political reasons (Soderlund 2015). In general, the Lenape avoided "expanded war" and preferred peace but would fight "to protect their families, land and political autonomy" if necessary, and were not pacifists, like the Quakers. They believed that they could preserve their own freedom by respecting that of others (Soderlund 2015, 203). The violent turmoil of settlement and consequent social harms eroded their peaceful ways, however.

---

2. Lenape political organization had broken down because of the scattering of the members of their communities, making getting data about it very difficult (Harrington 1913, 211).

Between 1701 and 1757, the Lenape grew more politically united, and developed "leaders" in the European sense, as a consequence of their political needs resulting from colonial contact and by 1740 could more accurately be called a "Nation," as defined today (Becker 1976, 50, 45; 1980, 20; Thurman 1974, 129).

American Indian tribes fed up with English settler colonists' attitudes and behavior toward them joined the French war with the British over colonial lands and "shot down Braddock's army in the summer of 1755 with a right good will" (Sharpless 1898, 179). Some Lenape felt they had no choice but to join with the French in a war against the settler colonists in the dim hope of regaining control of their land (Jennings 1974, 98). Some fought on behalf of the British, and some tried to be peacemakers (Soderlund 2015, 194). Some used their military abilities to help the French to attack Pennsylvania (Sharpless 1898). By 1755 the Lenape were raiding Pennsylvania's western borders. The Pennsylvania government, no longer influenced by the Quaker Peace Testimony, declared war on them shortly thereafter. This ended a unique era of relative peace among Indians and European settler colonists.

THE LENAPE AS PEACEMAKERS

The Lenape were the acknowledged peacemakers among the Indian Nations associated with the Iroquois confederacy and practiced peaceful relations (most of the time) with the settler colonists who had been living in the area for decades (Soderlund 2015). They also used restorative justice techniques internally. Peacefulness was an essential part of their spirituality. For them, everything had a soul, including animals, trees, water, and rocks and that influenced their behavior. Spirituality was integral to their daily life (Wallace 1961, 63–76). For example, among the virtues listed in the annual Big House Ceremony are "the apostrophe against violence and war" (Speck 1931, 21). While they were not an overtly warrior society at the time of contact with the Quakers, this had not always been the case. Their military aptitude and political influence were well-respected by other Indian Nations who referred to them as "grandfather" based on an "ancient covenant" going back to probably the late 1500s (Brinton 1885, 113). This aggressively warlike phase of their history ended when they were asked by the Iroquois to take on a special role of peacemaker among the Five Nations and their allies. There is a controversy about this role because of the phrase used to describe it, that is, the Iroquois "made women of them." To early European historians this denoted that the Lenape had been forced into a submissive, inferior role by their stronger neighbors. Whether or not they were actually subservient to the Iroquois, as the Iroquois maintained, is a matter of some debate. According to Thompson (2013, 78), "The powerful political organization of the Six Nations appealed to the British colonial authorities, who were willing to negotiate with whomever they thought would give them the best deal. This resulted in the Six Nations over-reaching their own authority."

It is also clear that the Europeans had little conception of the role that Lenape women played in their political system (Spady 2004; Hirsch 2004). The original meaning is very different, according to more modern culturally based interpretations as well as some earlier writers. Women were respected leaders in traditional Lenape and Five Nations (Iroquois) society. As Weslager (1972, 62) describes their role, women "were recognized authority within the family and community." The term "woman" applied to the Lenape was "an ancient ceremonial term, *Gantowisas*, which we might render 'Lady', 'Matron', or 'Dame.' . . . It was a title to be proud of" (Wallace 1981, 59). According to Brinton (1885, 109),

> among the Five Nations and Susquehannocks, certain grave matrons of the tribe had the right to sit in the councils, and, among other privileges, had that of pro-posing a cessation of hostilities in the time of war. A proposition from them to drop the war club could be entertained without compromising the reputation of the tribe for bravery. There was an official orator and a messenger, whose appointed duty it was to convey such a pacific message from the matrons, and to negotiate for peace.

In other words, Lenape women had a much more privileged position than colo-nial women, a fact that likely did not sit well with early observers. In their role of "women," the Lenape had the responsibility to be noncombatants and peacemak-ers (Brinton 1885, 109–12). Jennings (1965, 20–21) disagrees that they were non-combatants; they were not allowed to declare war on their own but often helped the Iroquois on raids. This was a position completely different from being a con-quered nation, as Europeans later insisted they were (Brinton 1885, 112).

A Lenape account explains that after a devastating series of wars at the end of the sixteenth century between the Lenape and the Iroquois confederacy, the Lenape lost (Brinton 1885, 116), and they were asked by the Iroquois to become peacemakers, as follows:

It is not well that all nations should war; for that will finally bring about the destruction of the Indians. We have thought of a means to prevent this before it is too late. Let one nation be The Woman. We will place her in the middle, and the war nations shall be the men and dwell around the woman. No one shall harm the Woman; and if one does, we shall speak to him and say, "Why strikest thou the Woman?" then all men shall attack him who has struck the Woman. The Woman shall not go to war, but shall do her best to keep the peace. When the Men around her fight one another, and the strife waxes hot, the Woman shall have power to say: "Ye Men! What do ye that ye thus strike one another? Remember that your wives and children must perish, if ye do not cease. Will ye perish from the face of the earth?" Then the men shall listen to the Woman and obey her. (Brinton 1885, 110–11, citing Moravian pastor George H. Loskiel)

Contemporary recorder, Zeisberger, a Moravian missionary, vouched for the more respectful interpretation as did Heckewelder later, who emphasized that the Mohegans corroborated this account (Brinton 1885, 112).

Jennings suggests that this peacemaker status of the Lenape was "a by-product" of the establishment of the Covenant Chain, a treaty and alliance among the colonies of New York, Massachusetts, Connecticut, Maryland, and Virginia and the Indian Nations under the protection of the colony of New York, including the Lenape (Jennings 1974, 89–90). The Lenape had many allies (Schutt 2007). Their status as a supposed subordinate Peoples ended with the creation of Pennsylvania when the Lenape came under that colony's jurisdiction and used this to assert their independence as much as possible from the Iroquois (Jennings 1974, 91, 93; 1984, 215, 237). Their role as peacemakers didn't end, however, at this point (Jennings 1965, 25).

This means that at the time of Quaker settlement, the Lenape were a peaceful, noncompetitive society that had been experiencing a long period of relative peace before the arrival of the Quakers with similar ideals, and in fact held a neutral political position that made them the "acknowledged peace-makers over a wide area" (Brinton 1885, 112), which would have put their philosophy and that of Quakers more in accord. This could have been why from 1677 to 1755 there were no "Indian wars" in Pennsylvania (Jennings 1965, 21), although there were conflicts outside its borders.

Internally, the Lenape also practiced a form of peacemaking, as suggested by the description of the role of the sachem, although it was different from modern peacemaking used by Indian Nations such as the Diné (Navajo) (see Nielsen and Zion 2005). As Penn observed, "The Justice they have is pecuniary. in case of any wrong or evil fact be it [to] murder it selfe, they attone by feasts & presents of their wampum w[hich] is proportion'd to the quality of the offence, or person injur'd" (Dunn and Dunn 1982, 454). A feast and a gift of wampum proportionate to the offence and to the identity of the injured, restored justice, though a retributive killing by the family for a murder was also an option (Soderlund 2015, 38, 44). Penn noticed that more value was given to women. If a woman was killed, the offender had to pay double the price for a man, because a woman can have children, and men cannot (Myers 1970, 39–40). Thus, Penn knew that the Indians treated each other with respect, held women in high regard, and had a system of justice that was mainly restitutive.

The more familiar term for these practices today is "restorative justice," which is summarized by Van Ness (1996, 23) in three propositions: crime is primarily a conflict between individuals resulting in injuries to victims, communities, and offenders; the aim of the criminal justice process should be to reconcile parties while repairing the injuries caused; and the process should facilitate active participation by victims, offenders, and their communities. The goal of restorative justice is that "the community seeks to restore peace between victims and offenders, and to reintegrate them fully into itself; the goals for victims can expressed as healing and for offenders as rehabilitation" (Van Ness 1996, 28). In general, the establishing of blame for past behavior is less important than problem-solving for the future (Hass-Wisecup and Saxon 2018). Merrell writes (1999, 167) that early recorders commented on the many ways of reconciliation used by American Indians.

Although not many descriptions of restorative justice procedures have survived in the notes of contemporary recorders, clues can be found in descriptions of other ceremonies or events. Van der Donck, a Dutch trader, for example, describes:

> Feasts and big meetings are not regular events among them, but are sometimes held to deliberate peace, war, contracts, alliances and agreements . . . [in all their councils] persons of some authority are free to state their opinions at such length and as amply as they please without anyone interrupting them, no matter how long the speech or whether it goes against the mood of many. But if they fully approve of what is said they voice their acclamation towards the end of the address. (Van der Donck, 1655, translated by Goedhuys 1996, cited in Grumet 2001, 24)

Reconciliations, proposals, and requests, along with major matters such as "treaties, agreements, peace negotiations, . . . alliances, and promises are sealed and given force with gifts or veneration ceremonies [and] . . . are considered as fully sealed quasi intervenienti testimonio" (Van der Donck 1655, translated by Goedhuys 1996, cited in Grumet 2001, 27). Other observers added that speechmaking, often very emotional, was a part of all ceremonies as was the participation of the spiritual realm (Heckewelder 1876, 57–58; Weslager 1972, 58–59, 66). Restitution for wrongdoing was common (Dunn and Dunn 1982, 454; Merrell 1999, 167), although corporal punishments, even death in the form of "mourning wars" in retribution also occurred if that was deemed proportionate to the offense and would lead to peace (Harrington 1913, 217; Soderlund 2015, 44).

One case of restitution for murder offered by the Lenape for a slain settler colonist was recorded, as described by Merrell (1999, 50): "To restore harmony, [one of the Lenape leaders who had traveled to Philadelphia] invoked the time-honored ritual of clearing the road between peoples, wiping tears from colonists' eyes, and removing from their hearts the 'Spirit of Resentment and Revenge against Us'—each action confirmed by a string of wampum or a bundle of skins. Three days later, armed with wampum belts and strings, [another leader], too, covered the wound, buried the hatchet, and cleared the 'foul and Corrupted' air. '[T]he Sun which was darken'd now Shines again as clear as ever,' he proclaimed."

These descriptions suggest that restorative justice practices were likely composed of discussion, negotiation, ceremonies, and gift-giving, all done with great respect; and that social justice was the objective, that is, to restore harmony and peace within the community or between communities so that the communities could continue good relations and work effectively together.

QUAKERS AS PEACEMAKERS

Quakers developed a system of restorative justice of their own, beginning in England with the institutionalization of the new sect by George Fox and Margaret Fell (Birkel 2004, 26). Their organization also incorporated principles of peace and respect in committees set up to resolve disputes. The persecutions of Quakers and their prison experiences led them to view crime and punishment in terms of a redemptive response. To redeem that of God in offenders meant to find ways to call them back into being at one with their community (London Yearly Meeting 1960). This thinking applied to disputes that arose between Friends as well as with others. They sought to resolve issues in ways that would restore harmony to the community. Penn's original laws and justice system were possessed of a degree of informality and flexibility not present in the Duke of York's laws used in other colonies. Loyd (1910, 48) records that Penn had no liking for formality and preferred the "indefinite jurisdiction in civil and criminal causes."

As early as 1684 (London Yearly Meeting 1737), a system of arbitration[3] was advocated in instances of conflict between Friends. According to these extracts, London Yearly Meeting Minutes, in 1692 and 1697, record the recommendation that "esteemed Friends" be asked to be arbitrators, and advocated a process to be followed (London Yearly Meeting 1737, 30–34). Overseers established committees to settle internal disputes set up for that purpose at the different levels of Meeting. In the 1704 *Book of Discipline* from the Philadelphia Yearly Meeting, as in other Yearly Meeting books from this time period, we see the first rough outline of a system that by 1785 was well established (Hayburn 2005, 14–15). *Books of Discipline*[4] from both England and North America described in careful detail how arbitration was to be handled by Friends' Meetings. When Friends heard of any difference between two Friends "in the Meeting to which they belong" they were first to speak to the Friends involved in the dispute and "tenderly advise" them to bring a speedy end to the matter.

---

3. Today arbitration may or may not be defined as a type of partial restorative justice because it relies on an arbitrator making the final judgment, as opposed to an agreement reached by consensus. Arbitration may focus on discussion of underlying issues by all parties, the involvement of both the victim and the offender, and arbitrators represent the local community (Alford 1997). If one uses a continuum of retributive to restorative justice as proposed by Zehr (2015), Quaker forms of arbitration fall somewhat closer to the "retributive" end (i.e., the regular criminal justice system) than most American Indian practices.

4. Philadelphia Yearly Meeting first wrote a *Book of Discipline* in 1704, and it was revised in 1719 and 1747 (Hayburn 2005). *Books of Discipline* originated in the organization set up by founder George Fox as a series of interconnected Meetings whose geographical area of responsibility increased inversely with the frequency of Meeting (Barbour and Roberts 1973). In other words, Preparative Meetings covered a small area and met for worship weekly, Monthly Meetings covered a larger area and met monthly to conduct Meeting for Worship for Business as well as for a weekly Meeting for Worship, and so on through Quarterly and Yearly Meetings. *Books of Discipline* "codified the tenets of Quaker faith and outlined sinful activities" (Hayburn 2005, 1). They became increasingly mandatory and were read aloud at Monthly Meetings (Barbour and Roberts 1973).

If the Friends in conflict did not comply with the advice given, the advising Friends "take to them one or two Friends more" and again were to "exhort those in dispute to end their difference" (London Yearly Meeting 1737). These "esteemed Friends" were arbitrators whose judgment had to be agreed to by the conflicting parties.

Any Friend refusing the judgment of the arbitrators could face loss of membership. First, however, the matter would proceed through Monthly and Quarterly Meetings to Yearly Meeting. At that time the Yearly Meeting would decide how it should end. In other words, every effort was made from the Preparative Meetings (to establish a new Worship group) all the way to the Yearly Meeting to settle the matter peacefully. The final decision might be to end the membership of Friends refusing to agree to the settlement offered and/or recommending they turn to the law: "And when any pson so refusing [to accept the arbitrators' settlement] is testified against by ye Meeting and disowned, ye other pson may have his liberty to seek his remedy against him at law" (London Yearly Meeting 1737, 34). Friends' traditional distrust of the law, based on their experience of persecution under it, led them to try to avoid its use by members in all possible ways. Hayburn (2005, 17), transcribing the handwritten 1719 *Book of Discipline* in its original form, records: "But if any professing Truth shall Arrest Sue or Implead & Law . . . any other person making the same profession before he hath proceedes in the method herin after mentioned or is so permitted by the Meeting Such ought to be dealt with as other Disorderly persons & to give satisfaction to the Meeting by Condemning his or her so doing & in case of refusal after deliberate dealing & waiting with such they are to be disowned by the Meeting where to he or She doth belong" (London Yearly Meeting 1737, 31). In other words, a Friend who turned to lawyers before completing the Friends' process of arbitration risked loss of membership.

Quaker *Books of Discipline*, first written down by Philadelphia Meeting in 1704 (Hayburn 2005), and copied by other Yearly Meetings in North America, specify arbitration as the preferred means of settling disputes. Philadelphia Yearly Meeting, like other Yearly Meetings in North America, borrowed heavily from London Yearly Meeting. Consequently, the arbitration process appears in most early *Books of Discipline* and has the same format. For example, extracts from "Advices and Minutes of London Yearly Meeting" (1737, 30) record one statement from 1684 that read that Friends agreed that, "the choosing of arbitrators is proper in cases of difference about a man's property."[5] That statement is repeated in New York Yearly Meeting's *Books of Discipline* (1785). Arbitration, according to Loyd (1910, 48), was in fact a common practice for the settling of disputes in English courts.

All of Penn's legal ideals would have been influenced by Quaker principles of the Inner Light, leading to an emphasis on the restoration of harmony through negotiation as well as from Quaker experiences of persecution and imprisonment. Barbour and Roberts (1973, 464–65) write that "[A]lthough they rejected the liturgical abstractions, Friends were highly sacramental in expecting the flow of divine grace through human interchange in family, worship and work."

Barnes argues that there were three stages to the making of Pennsylvania criminal codes: "the English or Puritan system," adopted in 1676; the "Quaker code" of 1682; and the reestablishment of the English or Puritan codes in 1718. The Quaker codes dropped the English settler colonists' more barbarous forms of corporal punishment, such as branding, and substituted prison sentences.[6] The new laws also emphasized restorative justice practices such as restitution for property crimes like theft, though often supplemented by imprisonment (Barnes, 1922, 8–9). These practices were also common

---

5. There is a lack of records from this time period because "The founders were more bent on development of the resources and organizing the administration of the great territory that had come under their control, than on preserving the records of their proceedings for the benefit of posterity, while their immediate descendants, living in an uncritical age and possessed with a passion for rhetoric to the exclusion of history, carelessly permitted the records of the preceding generation to be scattered or ruthlessly destroyed" (Loyd 1910, 1).

6. There were other influences as well. As Loyd (1910, 15) describes it, Penn's court system was a melding of English practices and those left over from the previous Dutch colonists: "As to remedial law it was, in the first place, provided that all actions of debt or trespass under the value of five pounds between neighbours should be put to the arbitration of two indifferent persons of the neighborhood to be nominated by the constable, or if either of the parties refused their arbitration, the justices of the peace should choose three other persons who were to meet at the cost of him who dissented from the first method, and their award should be conclusive. The practice of referring complicated cases to arbitration prevailed in the New Netherlands and this provision has been regarded as a survival of the Dutch custom." As Soderlund (2015, 152) describes, "the old settler justices did their best to resolve issues peacefully among the sometimes quarrelsome Delaware colonists," usually relying on apologies and fines. The regional courts, including the Upland Court in which Quakers participated, were replaced in 1682 by Penn's new, more hierarchical county courts but continued some of their practices. For example, their juries were often a mix of old and new settlers to ensure fairness (Soderlund 2015, 154–57).

in the colony's courts that existed before Penn was granted Pennsylvania (Soderlund 2015, 154). This emphasis was echoed in the constitution of several colonies, including West New Jersey (1676), where "reparation rather than vengeance was the thought behind punishment for crimes" (Concessions 1676, viii–ix).

Penn's system of justice therefore reflects the practices of Friends generally and reflected a peacemaking or restitutive approach. Penn was required by King Charles II, as part of his acceptance of the land, to have his laws consistent with the laws of England, with the exception of treason and planned murder, for which judgments had to be submitted to the Privy Council for approval before enactment. Penn's laws did not completely ignore the harsh laws formulated by the Duke of York, which were based on English law and applied in most of the colonies but as well, developed different ways to deal with offenders that were based on reparations (Barnes 1922). For example, a thief, caught the first time, must "make Satisfaction." The second offence had to be repaid double, and if the thief could not pay this amount, the thief went to jail to do hard labor until it was all paid off. The third offence had to be paid in triple, and if the thief could not do so, the thief became a bondsman to the victim forever. Over time, however, Quaker penal codes took on an increasingly severe moral tone, prescribing rules for dress and behavior, including the proscription of marrying out and being especially harsh on sexual offences (such as sex outside marriage), which often carried penalties, including corporal punishment (Barnes 1922, 7, 11).

Pennsylvania's early courts served as a ground for "legislative experiments" (Loyd 1910, 1). Although it is not completely clear how they operated or related to the more commonly used arbitration, one of these experiments was the peacemakers established in Chester by William Penn on June 27, 1683, and later in Sussex County (Colonial Society of Pennsylvania 1910, 25–28; Turner 1909, 97, 102, 116). The "common peacemakers" were "three members of each precinct" whose task it was to settle disputes voluntarily submitted to them for arbitration by community members (Dunn and Dunn 1982, 455; Colonial Society of Pennsylvania 1910, 34, 55–56; Futhey and Cope 1881, 25; Loyd 1910, 48). According to Bronner (1953, 462), the law stated that judgments of the peacemakers "shall be as Conclusive, as a Sentence given by the County Court." The methods used were similar to those in regular arbitration (Colonial Society of Pennsylvania 1910, 57–58, 100, 164–66), which were based on arbitration in England. English arbitration was usually voluntary and was used especially for merchants' accounts (Loyd 1910, 48). Futhey and Cope (1881, 25) described peacemaking as "a kind of standing board of arbitration." Peacemaking turned out to be less popular than ordinary arbitration and was ended in 1692 when it was decided that the practice was not being used (Loyd 1910, 49). Simple arbitration continued and was formalized in 1705 (Loyd 1910, 49). It should be noted that this Quaker arbitration may or may not be a form of restorative justice since it was not the participants who arrived at the final resolution, but the fact that the experimental process was called peacemaking, and that simple arbitration was inherently supportive, tried to resolve underlying issues, relied on consensus, and was not focused on punishment, strongly suggests that the procedures could have been open to input from the participants about resolutions, and therefore, a type of restorative justice.

Quaker values of restorative justice and egalitarianism underlay the whole structure of government in Pennsylvania. At the same time the word "egalitarian" must be treated with caution, since Friends did not move completely outside the discriminatory racist and sexist ideas of their time.

The Quakers did not just practice their restorative justice internally; Quakers' pacifist and egalitarian philosophy led to peacemaking in interactions with American Indians. This means that all relationships from the Quaker point of view, including treaty making and trading, were founded on a belief in the divinity of the individual. This belief extended to the community as well as individual members. Quakers were also committed peacemakers between conflicting external groups. Penn traveled into Lenape country to make treaties, for example (Merrell 1999).

Penn's own practices, as well as his laws and regulations, emphasized social justice, that is, fair and just treatment in relations with the Lenape, a spirit of neighborliness and friendship with them, and a general penal code based on restorative justice that included the Indians. Perhaps it is not surprising that Quakers experienced Indians as friendly—much more so than many of the colonists they met. Further, they found commonalities between the two cultures that were based in their spirituality (Daiutolo 1988). Yet Quaker equality and peacemaking had their limitations. In their relations with Indians, they continued to insist the Lenape accept English laws and tried to convert them. On the other hand, Penn also followed in the footsteps of George Fox, who was convinced that the Inner Light was common to all men, including American Indians (Vipont 1977, 111; Nickalls 1952, 642).

LENAPE AND QUAKER EXCHANGES ON PEACEMAKING: WHY THEY DID NOT HAPPEN

We could find no evidence that the exchange of ideas between Lenape and Quakers about justice practices occurred or, if it did occur, it had no recognizable impact. The mid- to late 1600s were a time of great social disorganization for the Quakers in America, but even more so for the Lenape. There were also language issues and Quaker ideologies of religious and cultural superiority that likely contributed.

SOCIAL DISORGANIZATION

When individuals and communities are in the midst of great crises, as were both the Quakers and the Lenape, who suffered as the result of the social harms inflicted by colonialism, it is not unreasonable that they have little time or inclination to discuss questions of worldview and spirituality with each other. The Quakers were under a great deal of pressure originating from a number of sources, including the political machinations of the other colonies, the older Pennsylvania settlers, and the Indian groups surrounding them; demands from England (for military support for example); and the increasing number of non-Quaker settler colonists who, although they were there by Quaker invitation, did not have the same values of pacifism, egalitarianism, or respect for their Indian neighbors. Moreover, many were squatters—illegal immigrants who had not paid for the land they occupied, often moving onto Indian lands that Penn had not purchased. As well, Quakers had set up representation in Philadelphia to ensure that they continued to hold three-quarters of the seats in the Pennsylvania Assembly long after their population numbers fell to "a small minority" (Sharpless 1898, 214; Hindle 1946, 462; Soderlund 2015). This fact was known and resented by many settler colonists.

Benjamin Franklin, General Edward Braddock, and others sided with the governors in arguing that Pennsylvania was threatened by the Indians and needed to set up a military defense. This accorded with the views of the British king and queen, William and Mary. Pressure was put on the Legislative Assembly, and eventually the device of forcing Assembly members to take an oath of loyalty was used. This had failed once before in 1715, when all the Quakers resigned and crippled government services. They returned and remained in power until 1756, when most of them resigned again rather than take an oath (Sharpless 1898, 222).

The real issue was the Peace Testimony; it led those outside the faith to regard Quakers as treacherous and dangerous because they refused to engage in war with pirates, Indians, or anyone with whom the colony experienced conflict (Sharpless 1898, 242–44; Weddle 2001). Those same pacifist and egalitarian beliefs led later to accusations that Quakers were siding with the Indians because they tried to return peace to Pennsylvania through negotiating with the Lenape (Kelsey 1917, 74–75). Quakers did not necessarily agree on all of their policies either (Sharpless 1898, 260; Punshon 1984).

Supported informally by Philadelphia Yearly Meeting, the activities of the Friendly Association added to accusations of favoritism (Ream 1981; Silver 2008; James 1963, 178), but also led to hostility from other Quakers. The association quickly became conflated with the Pennsylvania government in the minds of settler colonists, who perceived Quakers as prioritizing friendship with Indians over financial and military support for the colony's borders (Bauman 1971).

This tension reached a boiling point in 1756. Sir William Johnson had established negotiations with the Lenape and Shawonese at Onondaga in March 1756 (Daiutolo 1988). However, Governor Morris of Pennsylvania ignored their advice to hold off until negotiations were concluded, and declared war on the Indians. Johnson, who had been told to go ahead with negotiations, responded to Morris's declaration by wondering "What will the Delaware and Shawonese think of Such Opposition and Contradiction in our Conduct?" (Daiutolo 1988, 9). In the meantime, Friends in England as well as in the Philadelphia Yearly Meeting were advising all Friends to abjure politics and urging those in the Legislative Assembly to leave because political work inevitably led them to face violation of their Testimonies (Sharpless 1898). All Quakers left or were removed by the time of the American War of Independence (Treese 1992).

The Lenape were even harder hit by social disorganization. By the time of contact with the Quakers they were suffering from the harms caused by disease, liquor, warfare, and hunger due to the over-hunting of fur-bearing animals for the European trade (Weslager 1972, 42–43, 134; Becker 1976, 28; Soderlund 2015). As Becker (1976, 28) concludes: "By the time William Penn began to exploit his interests along the Delaware River, disease and intertribal warfare had already 'pacified' the indigenous population," though not as much as Quaker historians assumed (see Soderlund 2015).

The Lenape suffered three great disruptions during the period of early contact with European settler colonists (Becker 1976, 27–30). The first disruption was loss of population due to the epidemics of European diseases that started in the early 1600s (Soderlund 2015, 85). Epidemics continued for many years; there was a smallpox epidemic in 1663, for example, that killed many Lenape (Weslager 1972, 134; Soderlund 2015, 107). A large proportion of the Lenape population died, though not likely the 90 percent death rate of other northeast Indian populations. By 1694 only about a quarter of the Lenape population remained as a result of disease and migrations out of the area. War with the Iroquois also exacerbated this depopulation (Soderlund 2015, 17–18, 108, 113, 168).

The second disruption was the fur trade that began in the early 1600s. The fur trade gave Indian communities and individuals access to very desirable goods that not only provided useful tools and status but also allowed them to engage in more efficient hunting, war, and competition (Zimmerman 1974, 60–61). However, this economic system was based in Europe and was not structured to protect the environments of North America, and so exploitation of the environment replaced cooperation with it (Zimmerman 1974, 60). It stripped the Delaware Valley of fur-bearing animals and led to armed conflict with neighboring groups, such as the Susquehannocks, when anyone strayed beyond their territories looking for game (Zimmerman 1974, 61). The focus on fur-trading meant less time spent on traditional food hunting and raising (which was already being made difficult by settlers clearing land of trees and hence animals) and led to increased trade with Europeans for ammunition, foodstuffs, and textiles (Becker 1976, 28, 27; 1980, 23; Zimmerman 1974, 64–65). By 1682, the fur trade was over in the Delaware Valley (Zimmerman 1974, 68). Grumet (2001) and Kraft (1974) add that the use of liquor ("rum") by traders during this time period and later also contributed to social disorganization. With the decline of the neighboring Susquehannocks, many Lenape moved westward in search of richer hunting territories, fewer invaders, and less conflict with settler colonists (Becker 1980, 27; Zimmerman 1974, 68). There remained behind, however, Lenape groups "hiding in plain sight" continuing "their traditional ways of life—farming on agricultural tracts, hunting in Pennsylvania and the Pine Barrens, and fishing along the river—and [who] preserved the inclusive, decentralized society that they had shared with the old settlers prior to 1681" (Soderlund 2015, 177, also 195).

A third disruption was caused by the political changes that occurred as colonies were formed by the Swedes, the Finns, the Dutch, and then the British in 1664 (Zimmerman 1974, 67), thereby abrogating the treaties and political understandings that had previously existed between Lenape and earlier Europeans (Weslager 1972, 134–5). The Lenape had been dealing with the Dutch and Swedes (who included the Finns at this time) (Soderlund 2015, 220, note 16) over almost one hundred years and were already accustomed to their goods. They shared many trade and communication networks, self-defense alliances, and families, having intermarried (Soderlund 2015). They were also affected by disputes among Penn and the English governors and French trading companies for the fur trade (Jennings 1984). Penn's "creation" of Pennsylvania in 1682 only added to the complicated political situation (Jennings 1984).

A part of the disruption was the waves of new settler colonists placing a tremendous pressure on the demand for land. For example, twenty-four shiploads of new settler colonists with a phenomenal birth rate arrived almost immediately (Spady 2004, 37; Becker 1976, 29, 32). Quakers and other settlers were already spreading inland by 1685, as shown by the establishment of new Quaker Meetings on land abandoned by the Lenape (Becker 1976, 39). Some of these were legitimate settler colonists in that they moved to land for which Penn had paid the Indians; others were squatters (Auth 1989, 27). The Quaker government and the Lenape and other Indians soon found these invaders to be "unmanageable" (Jennings 1965, 140).

Penn was aware of the stress on the American Indians who remained, and insisted that they retain all usage rights (as per his arrangements with the Lenape) to land they sold to settlers as well as setting aside "manors" for them, basically land with a caretaker or simply empty land where they could live, but pressure from non-Quaker settler colonists and Quakers post-Penn made life difficult for Indians on this land, and many of them eventually left or were forced off (Becker 1976, 29–34; Kraft 1974, 1). The Scots Irish settler colonists (Weslager 1972, 174–75), many of them squatters, wanted the Indians off the land that the Indians had worked over centuries to clear (Becker 1980, 22).

Even though the colony of Pennsylvania ostensibly protected the Indians, "throughout two decades land-hungry colonists had encroached upon the reservation lands of the Delawares . . . and Logan [the secretary of the territory and long-term member of Executive Council] had cheated the [Indians] out of much of their promised compensation" (Jennings 1974, 95). This occurred in 1737 when the Lenape were defrauded out of over a million acres of land through the infamous and shameful Walking Purchase (Gimber 2000, 227–34; Soderlund 2015, 184–85). Penn's sons had already begun to sell this land without the

Lenape's permission (Soderlund 2015, 184). It was Penn's son Thomas (an Anglican after his marriage in 1751), whose actions were complicitly approved by his brother, John, who, abetted by James Logan, negotiated with the Iroquois, the head of the Confederacy that claimed authority over the Lenape, to validate the Walking Purchase (Jones 1966, 502; Treese 1992). Thomas knew that his father used the Indian custom of measuring land by how far a man could walk in a specified number of days. William Penn had bought most of southern Pennsylvania in this manner, but Thomas wanted to drive out the Lenape and claim more of southern Pennsylvania for himself. Thomas produced a doubtful, incomplete 1686 deed that gave William Penn the right to a certain valuable piece of land for "As far as a man could walk in a day and a half" (Sharpless 1898, 174; Soderlund 2015, 184–85). Thomas had a path cleared, hired two trained athletes to run rather than walk it, and had them followed with provisions and baggage. The runners also slanted one corner to take in more land. After repeatedly calling for the young athletes to walk, not run, the Indians gave up in disgust (Harper 2004, 167–68). As a result, the Penns obtained the Lenapes' last large piece of excellent agricultural and hunting land (Soderlund 2015, 185).

The Walking Purchase was compounded by fraudulence in the land surveys and the placement of roads on Indian land (Becker 1976, 37) and by Thomas Penn's dealing with the Iroquois (Jennings 1984, 215). The settlers were greedy for land and had very little fear of colonial law (Jacobs, 1969, 99). According to Jennings (1984, 215), "the remnant bands remaining in the Delaware and Susquehanna valleys were adeptly out-maneuvered by Iroquois intrigues with Pennsylvanians who wanted all the rest of the Delaware lands. It was a rankly malodorous business for which colonials and Iroquois must share the blame even though their motives were different." Today, this would be defined as a kind of state-corporate crime (see Nielsen and Robyn 2019).

Even so, the original intentions of the Penn-era Quakers were good, though steeped in colonial ideology. They wanted to trade with the Indians, wanted the Indians as consumers of their goods, wanted to divest the Indians of their lands in a peaceful and fair manner, and wanted to incorporate them into their colony; however, the Indians did not want to change, though they wanted to trade (which was their original purpose for welcoming the settler colonists) (Soderlund 2015). Some Indians tried to live separately, but many others chose to leave (Jennings 1965, 111). The Lenape that remained felt distinctly unwelcome in their old lands (Jennings 1974, 96–7). The maneuvering among the colonies and the encroachments of the settler colonists continued. As a result of this stress on their populations, the Lenape had begun leaving the area in the early 1600s (Grumet 2001), and the diaspora was well under way in the 1660s, according to Dutch records. By 1684, two years after Quaker settlement began in earnest, relatively few remained in the area, compared to before (Becker 1976, 29).

The 1720s saw a continuing decline in Indian numbers from disease and migration, which alarmed the Pennsylvanians who still needed them as commercial hunters and consumers of goods in their economy (Jennings 1974, 95); however, "[a]mong the Pennsylvania provincials, traders and merchants evaded Penn's controls over commerce with the Indians and acquisition of Indian lands." The dishonest traders in Pennsylvania (and elsewhere) left an enduring negative impression of the European settler colonists' honesty and good intentions. According to Hanna discussing the "frontier" traders (1911, 2) "the many opportunities for illegal gain in their dealings, stimulated and developed their cupidity to such a point that many of the Traders did not scruple to cheat the Indians in the most outrageous manner." There were also many murders of Lenape individuals that culminated in a massacre by Scots Irish immigrants at the Conestoga settlement in 1763 (Becker 1976, 52; Brubaker 2010, 8; Harper 2004, 195).

At the time that Penn and the Quakers made contact with the Lenape, the Lenape had already suffered from direct, structural, and cultural violence resulting in social harms, including depopulation, land and resource theft, ethnoviolence, and out-migration. None of these were conditions that encouraged the prolonged, respectful, and meaningful sharing of information about worldviews, values, or justice practices.

LANGUAGE AND CULTURAL ISSUES

Language issues probably also contributed to the lack of sharing of ideas between the Lenape and the Quakers. Pencak and Richter (2004) conclude that misunderstandings occurred even when there were genuine attempts by the settler colonists and the Indians to understand and appreciate each other. David Brainerd believed the Lenape knew English "considerably well" because they had lived among or near the settlers (Brainerd 1745, cited in Grumet 2001, 32), and by the mid-1600s, the Indians had begun to understand the European concept of land ownership (Weslager 1972, 148)—but communication requires the understanding of two parties. It is likely the Europeans understood less than Indigenous Peoples. Penn, for example, had a fairly superficial understanding of Lenape culture. He understood something of their system of government and justice, observing, for example, that the sachems listened to their community members before making any decisions. Further, he noted their system of decision-making was not unlike Quaker practices, and had a restitutive nature in resolutions of conflict and offenses against the community (Myers 1970, 39).

According to Brinton (1885, 75),

> After the English occupation very little attention was given to the [Lenape] tongue beyond what was indispensable to trading. William Penn, indeed, professed to have acquired a mastery of it. He writes: 'I have made it my business to understand it, that I might not want an interpreter on any occasion.' But it is evident, from the specimens he gives, that all he studied was the trader's jargon, which scorned etymology, syntax and prosody, and was about as near pure Lenape as pigeon English is to the periods of Macaulay.

It was a pidginized form of Lenape that had been developed, and this rudimentary trade jargon was used between early European traders and Lenape in the early 1600s. Its usage likely led to many misunderstandings (Goddard 1974, 105; Spady 2004, 19). It continued to be used in Pennsylvania, even though some old settlers who had long-standing trade relations with the Lenape including intermarriage, had a better understanding of the Unami language (the Lenape language), as did at least a few Quakers (Soderlund 2015, 29, 167, 178). Spady (2004, 21) points out that "The jargon worked well for simple trade, but it was poorly suited for more complicated ideas such as sovereignty, property, and the gender dynamics of social authority."

A small group of early Swedish and Dutch traders was an invaluable resource to the Quakers in providing interpretation services, but even so, misunderstandings were rife (Spady 2004, 19; Soderlund 2015). Interpreters sometimes refused to work for Quaker missionaries because they did not like Quaker views, and since the early Quaker missionaries were reluctant to study Indian languages, proselytizing was very difficult (Angell 2003, 7). Earlier and contemporary Swedish and Dutch missionaries had little success with learning the language, with the notable exception of the Reverend David Zeisberger, a Moravian missionary who devoted his life to a study of the language (Brinton 1885, 74–77).

Negotiators who understood the Indian languages (because languages were multiplying as new Indian groups settled in the area) and were trusted by all parties were few. It is likely that there were none who understood or could do the appropriate Indian ceremonies needed for a complete understanding of the culture (Merrell 1999, 104). Without these valuable mediators and translators, conducting business or even simply discussing ideas on an equal basis was very difficult. The Lenape, on the other hand, understood and fully supported the Quakers' need for trade and their stand on pacifism, although they were not above using threats of violence to accomplish their political and trade goals (Soderlund 2015, 168, 179); even so, the Lenape were "known for obfuscation" so that, according to colonist Conrad Weiser, they would verbally "resort to indirection" to avoid unpleasantness, quarrels, and conflicts (Merrell 1999, 184).

Groups that came into political power after the Quakers were not hampered by a feeling of equality with the Indians and made no effort to learn about Indian languages and culture. Instead, they based their perceptions of Indians and their resulting behaviors towards Indians on stereotypes, which made peaceful relations difficult (Pencak and Richter 2004).

In other words, the two groups may have tried to share abstract ideas, but issues in the understanding of each other's languages, and the culture that shaped them, made such exchanges difficult. There is a good chance that their cultural similarities were overwhelmed by a colonial ideology and goals that Penn and the Quakers never questioned and that their successors prioritized.

QUAKER IDEOLOGIES OF SUPERIORITY

One underlying reason for Friends' responses to the Lenape was religious fervor. They believed they had found "The Truth" in their emphasis on a direct relationship with God. Any other religion might be on that road to discovery but needed to hear about the Quaker Truth and live by it. Further, they believed that God's presence in their lives was real, immediate, and would lead to a new era of peace and harmony. While they worked to establish this new state, they also believed it had already arrived, that is, "the Day of the Lord had come," as Fox proclaimed (Punshon 1984, 36).

The early Quakers, with William Penn as their iconic representative, espoused a philosophy of egalitarianism (to varying degrees) between men and women, upper and lower classes, and American Indians and Europeans (for example, Moore 1981, 30, 200); however, the right to vote in Pennsylvania was restricted to those who "profess faith in Jesus Christ" (Punshon 1984, 99). Even so, although they deemed American Indians in need of religious enlightenment, they proclaimed them equals under Pennsylvania law though they were not treated that way (White 2003, 15). This attitude did not extend to Indian justice, laws, or religion. On the first point, Keyser (1882, 1, note 1) cites Bancroft in describing the Treaty of Shackmaxon (1682) with these words, "its sublime purpose was the recognition of the equal rights of humanity"; yet, the Quakers simply did not recognize Lenape as having laws and justice (Spady 2004, 27) and assumed that Pennsylvanian law should form the standard for all inhabitants whether they agreed or not (Smolenski 2004).

Penn established practices that were intended to protect the Lenape from unfair trading or abuse by settlers. Although the attempt ultimately failed to withstand settler colonist corruption and greed, Penn set up an arrangement whereby any conflict or offences incurred between Indian and white individuals would be tried by a jury of six Indians and six Whites so that "We have agreed, that in all Differences between us, Six of each side shall end the matter" (Myers 1970, 40). This showed Penn's good intentions, but there is no evidence that the juries actually included Indians (Jennings 1984, 244; Kelsey 1917, 55; Soderlund 2015, 142). As another example, Indian testimony was received as evidence in court, and there were continued efforts to settle land disputes between Indians and settlers in courts (Kelsey 1917, 55; Bowden 1850, 317). Finally, all trading was to be regulated by the government, including the prohibition of sales of liquor to the Indians (Dunn and Dunn 1982).

The Quakers did recognize and to some extent understand Lenape religion and described it in respectful though still disapproving terms. Penn, for example, states "The poor People are under a dark Night in things relateing to Religion, to be sure, the tradition of it (yet they believe in God and Immortality without the help of Metaphysicks; for they say) There is a great King that made them, who dwells in a glorious Country to the Southward of them (and that the Souls of the) who ar good shall go thither, where they shall live again" [we left out some punctuation that would have made this quotation unreadable](Dunn and Dunn 1982, 451). Quakers, however, were not discriminating against Indians specifically; they were convinced that *all* non-Quakers would benefit from being converted to Quakerism, the Indians being no exception (Jones 1966). Penn's ideas are reflected in his document, the Quaker-based "Frame of Government" finalized in 1682, which allowed freedom of religion to all, *as long as* they were Christians (Dunn and Dunn 1982, 143; Beckman 1976, 16). On the whole, his efforts as well as those of other Quakers, such as George Fox, to convert Indian individuals were unsuccessful (Soderlund 2015, 1); as Gimber (2000, 168–69) describes,

Although some of the Native inhabitants of the Delaware Valley interacted with the Quakers on a regular basis, the lack of evidence in the Friends' meeting minutes of any Indians actually joining the meetings indicates that apparently very few or none were interested in wholly adopting the Europeans' faith. Friends were appreciative and respectful guests for their Lenape hosts but poor proselytizers for their religion in that they provided no compelling reasons for the Lenape to convert to their particular Christian beliefs. For the most part, it seems that while the two peoples' interaction was friendly, peaceful, mutually profitable and warm, by their own choice they led distinct and separate lives which came into contact with varying degrees of frequency.

Gimber also notes that while some Indians attended Quaker Meetings there is no early evidence any joined the Society of Friends, although there are records of some Lenape converting in the mid-1740s (Soderlund 2015, 181).

Some of Penn's successors, who were not as confirmed in the faith as Penn, were more inclined to treat the Indians with disrespect and self-interest, not to mention avarice and dishonesty (Jennings, 1984, 254–57, 320–24). The Walking Purchase of 1737, mentioned previously, is the best-known example. These proprietors' behavior was informed by the prevailing colonial attitudes towards Indians in the British colonies that saw the Indians as treacherous, barbaric, and inferior to Europeans, thus justifying their maltreatment. Conflicting voices were "smothered" (Jacobs 1969, 99, 89–90). Over time, Pennsylvanians became indifferent to the needs of the Indians, transforming them conceptually from human beings into inhuman, mythical creatures, so that the Indians were obliged to get their needs fulfilled by other colonial groups that did not ignore them (Jennings 1965, 462) such as the French. This denial, or ignoring, is foundational to both cultural violence and social harms theory.

The early Quakers had a greater degree of respect for the Lenape than the later settlers who had little to none, but neither group had any interest in learning abstract ideas from them. To the Quakers peacemaking was part of their faith, and while they may have recognized spiritual connections with the Lenape, they thought their own religion superior and did not recognize Lenape law or justice as legitimate or even as existing, in the European sense of written law. As Penn's personal influence lessened in the colony, the settler colonists dehumanized Indians, much like they did in the other colonies.

Even though "Indian veneration for William Penn's recognition of their humanity became one of the powerful intangibles in preserving the Long Peace in Pennsylvania" (Jennings 1965, 462), Quakers were creatures of their times. As White (2003, 12–14) points out, they were part of the colonial discourse of domination and power imbalances because they were more focused on the goodness of their Quakerism and how well they treated the Indians and slaves (including Indian slaves), as opposed to what these groups wanted (see Soderlund 2015, 197–98). Nevertheless, their relations were more peaceful than those in other colonies where there were frequent eruptions of conflict between Indians and settler colonists in the seventeenth and early eighteenth centuries. Even so, land disputes and conflicts among individuals kept Pennsylvania from being the idyllic place of "intergroup harmony" that Penn hoped for (Soderlund 2015, 173).

DISCUSSION AND CONCLUSION

Together, William Penn's Quakers and the Lenape Indians negotiated a significant period of relative peace in settler colonist/Indian relations in colonial America. While there is some disagreement among scholars, it is safe to say that this period lasted at least seventy years (Sharpless 1898, 154). Organized conflict between them did not break out until April 1756, when (non-Quaker) Lieutenant Governor Robert Morris and the Provincial Council declared war on the Lenape, calling them "cruel Murderers, and Ravagers, sparing neither Age nor Sex" and "Enemies, Rebels and Traitors" (White 2003, 127–28).

Both groups practiced restorative justice, both internally and externally, and this no doubt contributed to their skill in managing the interface between their two cultures. The Lenape were the recognized peacemakers in the region and used restorative justice practices to maintain harmony within their own communities. The Quakers were also recognized as peacemakers by their Indian neighbors and used peacemaking and restitutive justice in their own communities.

Even after this period of peace ended, both groups respected each other, within their limitations. Even though Quakers may not have been a large part of the outlying populations in Pennsylvania (Uhler 1951, 36), they still worked as traders, and their envoys met regularly with American Indian groups without harm, when other traders and settler colonists did not have such fortunate fates. The Indians recognized that the intentions of most Pennsylvanian Quakers were peaceful and treated them accordingly.

This relationship could have provided an opportunity for learning more about commonalities and solutions to important social justice issues, one of which could have been justice practices. Penn was very concerned with establishing a model penal code that was based in restorative justice, yet he was oblivious to the opportunity he faced. Penn interpreted Lenape spirituality as having a belief in the Inner Light, as did the Quakers, but saw it as undeveloped. Because he regarded his Holy Experiment as superior to everything that had gone before—European or American Indian—his perception of Lenape justice practices, like his perception of Lenape spirituality, recognized their similarities but failed to legitimize them. He saw these similarities as enabling their conversion and enabling them to become full, equal members of his colony but only under his European-based law. Penn was no exception to the colonial ideology that his ways were superior and that he knew what was best for the Lenape and other Indian Peoples. His paternalism and his failure to learn the true Lenape language and culture blinded him to the possibility of learning from them.

Consequently, there were many lost opportunities, as John Woolman writes, "to spend some time with the Indians to see if I might receive and understand their life and the spirit they live in, if haply I might receive some instructions from them, or they may be in any degree helped forward by my following the leadings of Truth amongst them" (Moulton 1971, 127). Rather, Woolman recalls a day when he did "greatly bewail the spreading of a wrong spirit" (129). Despite the fact that Quakers (including Woolman) experienced Indian hospitality as "an exceptionally endearing trait," they were not immune to a generalized fear of Indigenous Peoples (Angell 2003, 5). Angell also records Fox's words of thanks at the end of his travels that "God had preserved him and his companions from such dangers as 'the fury of wild beasts and men'" (Angell 2003, 5), this in the face of many examples of Indian generosity to Fox and other Quaker travelers (Nickalls 1952; Soderlund 2015, 1). By the time Woolman was writing, in the mid- to late 1700s, settler colonists and Indians were at war.

Further, Quaker acceptance of the right of government to govern continually came into conflict with their Peace Testimony, setting up contradictions and dissonances in their responses (Applegarth 1892). When the Pennsylvania government was expected to fund military ventures by the British government, for example, they were in the same bind as that later created by the Revolutionary War. Caught between two extremes, the right of government and antiviolence, they prevaricated and evaded, trying to delude themselves by providing funds "for the King's use" (Applegarth 1892, 41). Similarly, their failure to take control of squatters and confront the contradictions of securing their borders by negotiating with the Lenape, led many Quakers to simply walk away from representing their constituents in the Legislative Assembly and from the social harms they were causing but that they refused to recognize. In the next chapter we discuss the strengths and weaknesses of Penn's Frame of Government that contributed to this action.

The Lenape were in no shape to initiate abstract discussions about peace-making. They were suffering from the social harms arising from colonial processes, including disease, conflict, economic losses, cultural erosion, and political maneuverings. Certainly, in the early days of Quaker settlement, the Lenape were likely mystified about their new neighbors—their language and culture was unlike any to which they had been previously exposed. They quickly learned that Penn and his Quakers supported American Indian human rights and social justice to the extent possible for the times, and that they had peaceful (though economic) intentions and were less likely to cheat them and engage in violence. At first, the two groups developed trade, legal, political, and social arrangements that allowed them to live peacefully together despite conflicts between settler colonists and Indian groups in neighboring regions. As the Quakers were quickly overrun by non-Quaker settler colonists with little respect or regard for their Indian neighbors and a powerful desire for land, some Quakers became influenced by the paternalistic and stereotypical attitudes the new settlers used to justify their exploitation of the Indians and early attitudes that were mainly characterized by respect and equality dwindled. The dehumanization of the Lenape that followed was in direct contrast to the attitude of most Quakers but indicative of the settler-colonial ideology of the majority of non-Quaker colonists.

Colonial ideologies that are based on the supposed inherent superiority of the colonizers allow settler colonists to justify social harms such as disenfranchising Indigenous Peoples, taking their land, stealing their resources, killing them, enslaving them, taking their children, and pushing them to the edges of the new society in all ways. The Quakers were unusual in American history in that they did not fully buy into these colonial ideologies at first, following instead practices rooted in what is called today social justice; however, so strong was the ideology that accompanies colonialism that after the governance of William Penn and some members of his family, many of the proprietors eventually succumbed, with Penn's second son, Thomas, the first to do so.

The Lenape continued to practice their ideology of peacemaking with the Quakers until they were simply too fed up with the efforts to change their lifestyle and values and were overwhelmed by sheer numbers. Many chose to move west and northward to avoid conflict, and some of those who remained behind eventually joined with the French in fighting the (non-Quaker) settler colonists.

At that point, the opportunity to develop a model colony that could have provided a different roadmap for colonization in America was irrevocably lost. This roadmap based in social justice and supporting American Indian rights had the potential to prevent more social harms and include restorative justice practices that were familiar to both groups. Peacemaking both internally and externally were strong traditions that the groups could have shared and could have served as models of peaceful relations whether with their Indian neighbors or with other colonies. History, however, shows how extremely complex the demographic, economic, cultural, and political relations were at the time, and in hindsight it was naïve (but optimistic) to think that the ideas of peacemaking could have been shared between the two groups.

2

QUAKER GOVERNANCE

Peace, Politeness, or Politics?

It is, of course, vain to expect peace when enemies have been exasperated and over-reached to the point of fighting. You cannot apply Quaker policy in the midst of grossly imperfect and abnormal conditions. . . . The best one can do is to show that with every approximation to the principles of Penn wars have diminished in frequency and consequence.

—ISAAC SHARPLESS, *A QUAKER EXPERIMENT IN GOVERNMENT*, VOL. 1, 1898

WILLIAM PENN saw Pennsylvania as a democratic government in so far as it was based on Quaker "Truth" and processes; however, Penn was working within a context that was far from democratic. While his faith led him to pursue processes based in social justice, it was difficult though not impossible for him to build into his government structure concerns about what we would call human rights today. As a result, the Pennsylvania government under his leadership, and later non-Quaker leadership, committed or omitted important actions that might have prevented and ameliorated direct structural violence leading to great social harms against the Indigenous inhabitants.

As Penn wrote various drafts of his government structure, which he called a "Frame of Government" for Pennsylvania, he consulted widely among "weighty" (well-respected) Friends as well as with non-Quaker lawyers, experts in government, and members of the king's Privy (private) Council (Dunn and Dunn 1982, 211). However, before he could present his ideas to the Privy Council, Penn had to write and negotiate a charter.

In seventeenth-century England, after the restoration of the monarchy, a committee, the Lords of Trade and Plantations, usually known as the "Lords of Trade," was responsible for informing the king on matters specifically related to the new colonies. They and the Privy Council members were a powerful elite. Penn knew he had to get accepted by them before he could reach the king.

Penn was himself born into high status. He was well educated, expected to become a member of that same elite, and well known to the people in power, but when he converted to Quakerism he lost much of that support; however, Dunn and Dunn (1982, 22) comment that his charter, and later his Frame of Government, were probably successful due to his connections. These editors of Penn's documents also comment that the king was likely glad to get rid of a troublemaker by dispatching him to the colonies.

The charter was eventually negotiated and necessarily became a significant factor in the Frame of Government. In writing this document, Penn had to negotiate between his democratic and peaceful Quaker ideals, the Quaker and non-Quaker settler colonists he was encouraging to come to Pennsylvania, and the requirements of his aristocratic superiors. The non-Quakers expressed a colonial culture and attitudes that were opposed to those of the Quakers.

It should be noted that Quaker beliefs also influenced the Quaker-dominated governments of New Jersey and Rhode Island (Jones 1966) so that Penn was not alone in his struggles. Dunn and Dunn (1982, 81) argue that "Founding a successful proprietary colony in late seventeenth century America was hard work. A Proprietor had to be an aggressive, pragmatic businessman who could publicize his colony widely; offer land, trading rights, and powers of government to a broad variety of settlers on attractive terms; and compete effectively with other Proprietors who had the same basic objective—make their colonies pay." As new settlers flooded into Pennsylvania, Penn found himself challenged to maintain a balance between his need to make money, the needs of the settlers, his intention to set up his Holy Experiment, and an authoritarian monarchical British culture with its undertow of colonial values and practices. As well, Penn, as with many, if not most Quakers, had not completely overcome his colonial upbringing so that the needs of the Indigenous inhabitants as seen from an Indigenous perspective, did not figure highly.

In this chapter we look at the difficulties, especially those that could be classified as creating social harms, caused by the charter and embedded in the Frame of Government, as well as some of the impacts on, and responses of, people involved in or under its administration. This included the proprietors group of the first Quaker settler colonists who owned large areas of land and became a dominant elite, city and rural land-owning settler colonists (some of whom also had "manors" they rented out), and American Indians, mainly Lenape. We begin with the charter, which placed limits on Penn's ideals, followed by a discussion of the Quaker Testimonies and the Charter of Privileges, as Penn confusingly called his final 1701 Frame of Government. Finally, we look at the responses of various individuals and groups to his charter, responses that continued until the Pennsylvania government declared war on the Lenape in 1756, ending the Holy Experiment. By that time most Quakers in the Legislative Assembly (see below) had quit, leaving the government with a somewhat hollowed-out reputation as Quaker, having a minority of Quaker members (Treese 1992).

A RIGHT ROYAL CHARTER

Grants of land in English America had to be approved by the Crown and were awarded based on a royal charter that laid out the Crown's expectations of the prospective recipient(s). The roots of Quaker contributions to social harms against Indigenous Peoples can partly be found in this charter, as well as in the Frame of Government, which had to conform to the charter (Dunn and Dunn 1982). Each version of the Frame of Government was submitted to the Lords of Trade and the Privy Council, some of whom distrusted Penn and were focused on restricting his Frame of Government as much as they could (Dunn and Dunn 1982). These additional limitations caused Penn and his heirs much trouble, especially when they conflicted with Quaker principles. For example, because Penn's laws had to be consistent with English law and practice, they were expected to include the death penalty for many offences, which violated the most basic of Quaker beliefs: if the Light was in every human being they could not be harmed or killed but rather appeals should be made to that of God in them (Brinton 2002, 22).

Penn wished to make fair treaties and live in peace with the Indians, living with them "as brothers," albeit under the administration of his government. The king required him to send annual fees, initially in the form of two beaver pelts each January, to Windsor Castle (residence of King Charles II) and one fifth of any gold or silver ore that might be found within the province. A greater impact came from the command that his government would send money for English or colonial military use when demanded.

An ongoing requirement was that all laws made by Penn's government must be submitted to Privy Council within five years of their making, which clearly added to the surveillance over his governing structures and processes. Penn was also required to appoint an attorney, or agent, based in London, who reported to King Charles II. This agent was to call the king's attention to any misdemeanors (Dunn and Dunn 1982).

Penn's land was the largest of the land grants by English sovereigns. Penn was given the right to wage war if anyone attacked him including "savages themselves as of other enemies" (Soderlund 1983, 47) and to sell parcels of his land where he could erect manors. These were often large country houses, owned by wealthy proprietors, on whose land there might be several small farms and dwellings that were overseen by the steward or manager of the entire property. These homes and farms might be occupant owned or rented. The use of land to create a manor was usually legally defined.

According to his charter, Penn "had two distinct rights: he owned all the land, subject to the performance of his feudal due to the crown . . . and he had full power to govern so long as his laws were consented to by the colony's free-men" (Jennings 1984, 241). His "feudal due to the Crown" was used by later Quaker-controlled Pennsylvania assemblies to avoid seeming to spend money for a militia; instead they designated the money just for "the King's use," but Penn's second right meant that he could institute his Quaker ideals in the form of laws. This also, however, created a dilemma in that Quakers had learned to distrust laws and regarded them as generative of conflict (Scott 1982). They also ran into religious conflicts when the monarchy changed. Penn's relationships with Catholic Charles II, and later James II, became a temporary challenge when his Pennsylvania Charter was suspended from 1692–1694 by (Protestant) monarchs William and Mary because of accusations of treason (see Soderlund 2015, 161).

The final revised form of the charter, March 1681, states "our trusty and well-beloved subject, William Penn Esquire, son and heir of Sir William Penn, deceased (out of a commendable desire to enlarge our English empire, and pro-mote such useful commodities as may be of benefit to us and our dominions, as also to reduce the savage natives, by gentle and just manners, to the love of civil society and Christian religion), has humbly besought leave of us to transport an ample colony unto a certain country hereinafter described" (Dunn and Dunn 1982, 41). Penn was now free to complete and submit his design, or "Frame," for the Pennsylvania government, which required imposing structural violence on the Indigenous inhabitants.

QUAKER ORGANIZATION: TESTIMONIES AND GOVERNANCE

Penn's Frame of Government, as stated earlier, was rooted in Quaker values, but it also was influenced by Quakers' own governance (Sharpless 1898, 1–3). Early in their formation, Quakers realized that they needed some recognizable structures if they were to survive (Birkel 2004, 26). Birkel writes that while Friends believed in continuous revelation, they also believed certain principles would prevail (Birkel 2004, 104). These are their "Testimonies." Quakers recognized these Testimonies as holding core truths but also that those truths would change over time. One of the basic beliefs going back to George Fox is that Truth is not absolute but is a continuous revelation; that is, Truth will change as the individuals on their spiritual journeys understand more. During the times covered in our research, there were four Testimonies to Truth to which Quakers were expected to adhere: Peace, Integrity, Simplicity, and Equality. They remain today, with the addition of Sustainability and Community, but their content, or meaning, has been developed fairly extensively.

Peace: The Peace Testimony began as a refutation of war to end disputes. It was an astute and necessary move in the politically troubled times when Quakerism began. Despite this practical reality, or maybe because of it, Fox was firm in his pacifist beliefs. He refused to fight for either Cromwell or the armies of King Charles II. He told Oliver Cromwell that he would not take up arms: "I told the [Commonwealth Commissioners] I lived in the virtue of that life and power that took away the occasion of all wars, and I knew from whence all wars did rise.... I told them I was come in to that covenant of peace which was before wars and strifes were (1651)" (Canadian Yearly Meeting 2011, 114). He repeated his stand to King Charles II when he said, "We utterly deny all outward wars and strife and fightings with outward weapons, for any end or under any pretense whatsoever" (London Yearly Meeting 1960, n.p.).

These are early recorded statements of what became the historic Peace Testimony, the first statement having been made by Margaret Fell in her plea to King Charles II to release Fox from prison. The statement is based on the Quaker understanding that if all humans have the Inner Light, they are equal before God, must not be harmed, and should live in peace and harmony with all things. Fell, who joined Friends after hearing Fox preach, followed Fox's teaching that the Inner Light was common to all men. Fox believed that North American Indians knew this as well (Vipont 1977, 111; Nickalls 1952, 642).

By the time William Penn set up his Frame of Government for Pennsylvania, the Peace Testimony included a refusal to incorporate any measures that could support war, such as armed defense for the province. When war was declared against the Indians by the Pennsylvania government, most Quaker members of the Legislative Assembly quit because they would not support war even in defense; however, some stayed and there were a small group who argued in favor of a defensive war. They were part of a group among Friends who believed that while war was generally against their Testimony, a military action might be used in self-defense (Kenny 2009, 154). A group known as Free Quakers emerged again just prior to the Revolutionary War. They were sympathetic to the revolutionary cause, but this left them "in a cleft stick, for the Peace Testimony could easily be seen either as a refusal to accept the burden of a struggle for liberty or else a treacherous loyalist posture" (Punshon 1984, 118), although they were neither.

Of all the Quaker Testimonies, the Peace Testimony created the most difficulties for a Quaker-dominated government, increasingly so as more of the arriving settler colonists were not Quakers nor pacifists. Fear of the Indians, compounded by all kinds of erroneous and exaggerated claims made against them, led to demands for a military defense of the province which the Quakers refused to provide (Gimber 2000). This was worsened in the 1750s when the Lenape were threatening war, and the Legislative Assembly and Executive Council could not agree on the raising and provision of funds for defense. The failure to provide military defense was a product of the Quaker Peace Testimony but was also embedded in Pennsylvania government policy and structure. This was not the only time that the Peace Testimony created conflicts for Quakers caught between their beliefs and the practical realities of government. The conflict was between the Assembly, under pressure from its constituents, having legislative but not financial powers, and the Council, accountable to a governor who objected to property taxes, having control of finances but not having legislative powers (Sharpless 1898, 212–17, 220–23). For the governing bodies it was not so much the Peace Testimony itself but how it was interpreted.

For their Indian "friends" it meant they were not supported or protected by Quakers in the ways they had expected. The exigencies of working within a colonial context could undermine the benefits of Quaker assistance, as when neither the Pennsylvania government nor the British Army delivered on treaty promises, contributing to Pontiac's Rebellion in 1763 (Silver 2008, 35). This illustrates the considerable difficulties under which a pacifist government of the time would have had to work.

Integrity meant absolute honesty. Honesty was for them a matter of practiced principle, and they went to jail for refusing to take an oath for example in court, since having to take an oath suggested one was not normally truthful. Integrity also led them to refuse to bargain over prices for their goods, leading to an increase in customers who preferred a set price. Quaker businesses often arose because as dissenters they were denied entrance to professions such as medicine or law, but their integrity made them successful businessmen (Sykes 1958, 163). Integrity also meant that Penn in particular was concerned about dishonest traders defrauding the Indians. He set up the Free Society of Traders in England charged with overseeing trade in Philadelphia. It does not appear to have worked, "going defunct" by the mid-1680s (Soderlund 1983, 147–48). Penn's own Assembly rejected the Society's charter (Soderlund 1983, 192).

Equality at first referred to spiritual integrity. All of life was considered sacred. Friends lived each day and each action "in the Light." The principle of Equality was far more than respect for others, therefore. Friends must also speak to that of God in others, to release it and draw it out, if it was not already expressed. This could not be done if the Friend involved was not themselves practicing those values. These Quaker attitudes informed the governing of Pennsylvania in the early years so that Penn incorporated religious tolerance into his Frame of Government, although he retained positions of authority for Christians only (Soderlund 1983, 132).

George Fox argued that God did not discriminate in who he called to ministry. They did not need a degree, nor did they have to be male, because everyone held inside them the ability to hear God's voice. Quakers did have difficulty in opening up their Meetings to Black Americans, however. Black Americans were offered separate pews in the Meeting houses; for example, at the historical Meeting house on Arch Street, Pennsylvania, there is an ornate division between the squares of seats in the main body of the Meeting from the lines of seats in the Black section (personal observation and see Bacon 1986). Interestingly there is also a raised line of seating for elders, overseers, and those recognized for their ministry at the front of the general seating area, facing congregants, giving an impression of greater authority to those in the raised section.

Jones (1966, 367) notes that in New Jersey (as in Pennsylvania and Rhode Island) Quakers dealt fairly with the local Indians, i.e., they treated them as equals. If they did not have enough trade goods in land negotiations, for example, they did not occupy land until it was paid for (but note the misunderstanding over what they were paying *for*—not land itself but the use of it). Penn, however, seems never to have been able to enforce his requirements of settlers that they treat Indigenous Peoples fairly. In fact, the narrative of Friends' relations with their Indigenous neighbors makes clear that they were not treated as completely equal—they were expected to become Christians and live under Pennsylvania law, neither of which respected their cultural beliefs and practices.

The Testimony to Equality might be said to be a testament more in theory than in practice. As outlined above, Penn believed in equality, but in response to outside pressures, and partly due to his concern that Quakers control Pennsylvania governing bodies, the Testimony to Equality did not translate into complete equality in practice. Many Quakers kept slaves and benefitted from the labor of their enslaved Africans (Moulton 1971, 97). Quakers frequently showed themselves to be better at expressing their beliefs than in actualizing those ideals, often revealing an underlying but unrecognized colonialism.

By the eighteenth century there was extreme inequality in Pennsylvania, and writers such as John Woolman recognized that material greed could lead to injustice (Moulton 1971, 238). If an individual prospered in their business at the expense of their employees, for example, or kept slaves, their actions would cause an unfair distribution of wealth and undermine the quality of society generally. This was antithetical to justice and, therefore, to peace. The Testimony to Equality also relates to the relationship between Equality, Justice, and Peace.

Simplicity: Simplicity was essential to a spiritually focused life since it expressed equality by having none of the trappings of wealth (Hamm 2003, 101–8). By the early eighteenth century the Quaker Reformation had turned this testimony into a rigid set of requirements for plain clothing and home furnishings. John Woolman argued that Simplicity "is good for the practitioner, but it affects the wider environment as well." (Birkel 2004, 112). For example, he protested slavery vociferously and refused to wear dyed clothing because slaves produced the dyes.

Simple forms of dress made Quakers more visible both to other settler colonists and to the Indians (Silver 2008). For instance, Graber (2014, 42) uses a cartoon of the later eighteenth century that depicts an unfavorable image of assumed Native American dependence on Quaker benevolence, drawing on the distinctive Quaker dress to identify them. Simplicity was also expressed in restraint. For example, Simmons, trying to run a school in Seneca chief

Cornplanter's village, railed against the revelry, such as at harvest time, describing it as "frolics" (Swatzler 2000, 41).

Other Testimonies to Truth were developed and refined over time, for example, "Simplicity" began as simple "obedience" to the Inner Light but became a testament to plain living and gradually extended to include wider applications such as avoidance of the verbiage that could obfuscate truth, i.e., plain speaking (Dudiak 2015).

While elders cared for the spiritual life of the Meeting, overseers were responsible for care and oversight of Friends' lives. Jones (1966, 151) comments that, "The work of oversight was not confined to moral and spiritual matters. It touched the whole of life." But overseers failed to bring about the general practice of Quaker Testimonies, and in fact, the natural or inevitable development of a Quaker lifestyle throughout Pennsylvania that they expected, never happened. It was the more convenient truths of colonialism that prevailed.

One example of the direct impact a Testimony could have on government follows: while Simplicity underlies all Quaker organization, there are times when that Simplicity combined with Equality in decision-making can create a cumbersome affair. From their first organization, Quakers were organized from the ground up. Important decisions must work their way through each "level" of the Weekly, Monthly, and Quarterly Meetings to reach agreement at the Yearly Meeting, but do not always begin at the Monthly Meetings for Worship for Business. They may begin at any level, but every decision affecting all Friends must be worked out within each Meeting. Consequently, such decisions tend to have near-absolute agreement but can take a long time, sometimes years, to reach that agreement. Consequently, when Indian leaders requested some form of schooling from Quaker visitors in 1773, Quakers replied they would do so "Whenever we can find any rightly qualified and willing to undertake the service." The Indian leaders did not receive a reply for twenty years (Ream 1981, 205).

THE FOUNDATION, OR FRAME OF GOVERNMENT

Penn's Frame of Government, which had to pay attention to the requirements of the 1681 charter, went through several editions between 1681 and 1701 to meet the demands made of it, including by those who would live under its policies and laws. That final version was written in response to the anger of his Pennsylvania settler colonists, furious over the predominance of the proprietary group in the previous designs for government structure and vociferously demanding a government that gave them greater equality of representation. Penn finally agreed and wrote his 1701 Frame of Government in which legislative power was given to the Legislative Assembly, but control of finances remained with the Executive Council. The final 1701 Frame of Government was titled the "Charter of Privileges" because in it, Penn had changed the Frame to reflect more of the wishes of his settler colonists, increasing the power of the elected Assembly, and lessening the power of the appointed Council (Sharpless 1898; Punshon 1984). The Indigenous inhabitants had little to no say in it.

Reflecting contemporary liberal ideas of a separation of powers, Penn created a government with three layers or structures: most power went to the proprietor, or governor (the term used by most scholarly sources), always a Penn family member, and a deputy or lieutenant governor who stood in for the governor when, as happened more often than not, he was absent from the province. The lieutenant governor was not necessarily a Quaker. Second was the upper house, the Executive Council or "Council," also known as the "Proprietors Council." (Generally, we use the terms "Council" or "Executive Council" in this book.) This was made up of men appointed by the governor or his lieutenant. The Penn family members, and the larger landowners were members of, and dominated the Executive Council. Their responsibility was to inform and advise the governor in the protection of *his* interests. The Council had the right to veto funding requests from the Legislative Assembly thus creating a division of power meant to prevent the development of an autocratic government. But the governor's word was final (Sharpless 1898). The dominance of the Penn family interests in the government structures undermined democratic intentions to the extent that some writers have called it feudal.

Third, was the Legislative Assembly or "Assembly," also known as the "Elected Assembly," elected by property-holding colonists. (Generally, we use the terms "Assembly" or "Legislative Assembly" in this book.) The province was divided into counties, each of which had four elected representatives, chosen yearly "upon the First Day of October forever; and shall sit on the fourteenth day of the same month, at Philadelphia. . . . Which Assembly shall have power to chuse [sic] a Speaker and other their Officers" (Penn 1701, article II).

The Assembly was the body that responded to citizen concerns and requests. It elected its own officers and judged "the Qualifications and Elections of their own Members" (Penn 1701, II). It could impeach criminals and prepare bills and pass those on to the Council for assent and funding, but as mentioned previously, did not have control over finances. Although the original numbers of representatives were considered unwieldy, and reduced, the Assembly remained an elected representative body of property-owning settlers, dominated by Quakers, due to the structuring of representation in Philadelphia and rural areas. This ensured such control until 1755, engendering much resentment by settlers.

QUAKER VALUES AND POLITICAL REALITIES

The structure of the Charter of Privileges was permeated with Quaker values, but the people who read and edited its many sections, as well as those who eventually lived under them, many of whom were not Quakers, responded to and interpreted them in widely differing ways. Privy Council members such as Lord North (brother to the king) considered all but the last version of Penn's structures for his government too liberal (Dunn and Dunn 1982, 62) and tried to have them rejected. The first version of the Frame, consisting of twenty-four "Constitutions," each of which defined and described some right or law, was considered far too liberal, and might well have fared better in the twentieth century. Examples include religious liberty, impartial execution of justice, annual elections of representatives to ensure consent to laws, a limit to the number of representatives in government, and that officials in villages or towns should be elected or chosen by the people of that community (Frame of Government of Pennsylvania May 5, 1682). William Penn—if only in this aspect of his work—was a man ahead of his time.

For the people of Pennsylvania, the government structures set out in the Frames were not liberal enough, and eventually their rebellion led to the final 1701 Charter of Privileges version that awarded more power to the lower, elected Assembly (Sharpless 1898; Bauman 1971). Clearly Penn was not able to please all his constituents, but in the last version he "bowed considerably to popular will" (Treese 1992, 7); however, the proprietors—the wealthy landowners—continued to dominate the Executive Council, and the Executive Council could refuse legislation proposed by the Assembly.

Penn incorporated his faith's principles of Integrity, Peace, Equality, and Simplicity into government, particularly the Peace Testimony and the Testimony to Equality, and applied them to all residents of Pennsylvania, including settler colonists and American Indians, such as the Lenape and other

Indians, who continued to live within Pennsylvania's boundaries (Sharpless 1898; Punshon 1984, 98). Social justice permeated his thinking, for example, when defining criminal behavior and response, so that laws included Quaker values. These laws protected Indian lands and trade and established that half the jury in a criminal case involving an Indian would be Indian. When appropriate, the victim would be compensated as part of the sentence. Penn's own jail experience led him to establish his prisons more as "workhouses" where prisoners could learn a trade or work on a project, perhaps related to reconciliation with victim(s) or community (Sharpless 1898; Punshon 1984, 99). Nevertheless, there were two executions for murder in the Quaker colony prior to 1718 (Soderlund 2015, 159).

The Episcopalians (the Church of England outside of Britain) were one particular group who voiced their issues with the Peace Testimony. They opposed Quaker values and argued that the Quaker stand against oaths as well as their Peace Testimony were impractical and should be the cause for their speedy removal from office (Sharpless 1906). This religious component of elections remained until the Revolution, although by that time the Quakers had lost political power, and the Presbyterians were taking over government (Sharpless 1906). But the vote was still not denied on religious grounds as it was in some provinces.

PENNSYLVANIA AFTER WILLIAM PENN

Penn's first wife, Gulielma, died in 1694. In 1696, Penn married Hannah Callowhill (Treese 1992). After Penn suffered a stroke that left him unable to govern, Hannah took over running the province. She continued after Penn died in 1718, until her own death in 1726 (Billypen 2020). It seems that the heyday of Indian/settler colonist relations in Pennsylvania was during the short period of Penn's residence from 1682 to 1712 and until his widow's governorship ended with her death. According to Jones (1966, 485), the period from 1701 to 1746 was a peaceful and prosperous time for Pennsylvania. He wrote, "For thirty years following 1710 we have a state, satisfied, at peace, enjoying popular liberty and security for its continuance. It was prosperous too, beyond precedent" (Jones 1966, 485). This may have been largely due to Hannah's skills as governor, which were recognized by Ronald Reagan in 1984 with the award of Honorary Citizen of the United States. She is one of the few individuals and the first woman to be given this status (Women History 2008).

Lawyers wrangled over Penn's will and which family members should inherit the province for some thirteen years, leaving the province without a governor for three years after Hannah's death. Eventually Penn's will was accepted as it stood; the province went to the sons of his second wife Hannah with a financial settlement to the remaining family of Gulielma. During this time many settler colonists arriving in the province were confronted with some confusion as to how they bought land or paid quitrents. For many this was a good reason to do neither, find some land, and wait until, as Treese (1992, 9) puts it, "the system caught up with them."

Penn's first son by Hannah, John, became governor until his death. During that time younger brother Thomas acted as an onsite administrator (lieutenant governor). When John, who was the more popular, died in 1746, Thomas became governor, taking over John's shares and responsibilities, and appointing a deputy governor to administer the province in his absence. Thomas was an efficient governor, but mainly in his own interest, and quickly became known as "cold, aloof and greedy" (Treese 1992, 12).

By 1755 the province was on the edge of war. Those Friends who had betrayed their Truth, and the many settlers who never subscribed to them, had between them caused intense harm to Indigenous Peoples, betraying the hospitality of the First Peoples, denigrating, cheating, denying their humanity, and, in some cases, murdering to obtain the lands they wanted. The Lenape had had enough.

THE PEACE TESTIMONY GOES TO WAR

The French and Indian War came to Pennsylvania in the form of attacks on settler colonist villages by the Lenape, Shawnee, and members of other French-allied American Indian tribes such as the Hurons, Ojibwas, Abenakis, Algonquins, and Iroquois (Nies 1996, 189; Kenny 2009, 69–75). The structures of Penn's government proved inadequate to provide effective responses, and the Quakers became divided over military defense. For some years, the annual meetings with Lenape had become formulaic and then were dropped altogether. A number of treaty-signings took place (see Kenny 2009) and Thomas Penn had negotiated with the Iroquois to the disadvantage of the Lenape. To make matters worse, Thomas Penn and other proprietors were using forgery to gain more unpurchased lands. In particular, the Lenape were angry about the Walking Purchase (Bauman 1971; Ream 1981; Kenny 2009) and about the settler colonists and squatters who were pushing across the Allegheny Mountains onto more unpurchased Indian lands. In frustration, many Lenape joined the French armies and unleashed vicious attacks on the western borders of the province. Their goal was to get all their lands back and be rid of the settler colonists.

Those settler colonists had been demanding defensive actions from their government for some time. For the settler colonists, there were four anger-inducing grievances:

1. DEFENSELESS SQUATTER SETTLER COLONISTS: The villages attacked by the Lenape and allies were largely defenseless. The Pennsylvania government did not provide defense in the form of weapons or training for a militia. Thousands of refugee settler colonists streamed into towns and villages closer to Pennsylvania, creating a great deal of pressure for lodging and care. Messengers and letters were sent begging for help to harvest their crops before the next round of attacks but to no avail (Kenny 2009).

2. COUNCIL REFUSING FUNDING FOR ASSEMBLY LEGISLATION: Early in the process of settlement, William Penn had lost control of the inundation of settler colonists, and perhaps administrative controls, although in place, were weakened by his necessary absences. He had only two visits of less than two years each in Pennsylvania (Jones 1966).

Many squatters (i.e., illegal settler colonists) were Scots Irish Presbyterians with a wholly different view of Indigenous Peoples from those of the Quakers. The Scots Irish, along with other settler colonists, perceived Indians as a thriftless, feckless, and dangerous group who should be driven from their lands because they were not properly utilizing them (Gimber 2000). The squatters were themselves an aggressive, if not criminal group. They pushed Lenape and other Indian peoples from their lands on the western borders of Pennsylvania, set up villages, and then demanded defense services from a government they were defrauding of funds. They were also not beyond using murder to get the Indians out of their way.

Penn and his administration were not only overwhelmed by the increasing numbers of settler colonists with such attitudes (Angell 2003; Gimber 2000) but also had inadequate administrative structures to address the situation, including insufficient income from land sales and quitrents to meet the government's obligations. This was in part due to the numbers of settler colonists who never paid for their land or never paid the quitrents meant to recoup the costs of buying land from the Lenape.

The lack of money for a militia and weapons became an immediate issue when the French and Indian War entered Pennsylvania borders (Treese 1992; Kenny 2009). The government itself was unable to respond, paralyzed by its own structure and division of responsibilities. To pay for a militia the Assembly would have to tax property. This had been done before, but Thomas Penn had forced an exemption for the Penn estates. He continued to refuse taxation. It was a deadlock that lasted for months, until Thomas Penn pledged a donation of £5,000 to pay for a militia. This was followed by an agreement that property taxes would be charged, but the Penn family estates would be exempt for three more years. That caused much anger among Pennsylvanians, but they needed defense (Treese 1992, 20–22).

3. PACIFIST QUAKERS IN GOVERNMENT DEMAND PEACE TALKS: The pacifist Quakers, members of the Assembly, demanded that the government seek peace with the Lenape by offering reparations for stolen lands. When this request was refused, and when the Pennsylvania government declared war, many more Quaker members of the Assembly quit their seats, leading to the formation of the Friendly Association. This group was hated by colonial negotiators, Assembly and Council members alike, and became a specific target of the Paxton Boys.

4. UNEQUAL REPRESENTATION: As stated earlier, Assembly members were elected by property holding settler colonists. The founding Quakers awarded votes for Assembly representatives to each county, but the allocations were not based on equal representation. The city of Philadelphia had the highest number. Hindle (1946, 462) writes that "Representation was apportioned in such a way that the three eastern counties elected twice the number of representatives allotted to the five western counties." Consequently, those counties had a much weaker voice. Repeated requests from the western counties for more representatives were ignored (Sharpless 1898). Representation was deliberately kept unequal by the Quaker-dominated Assembly, which had no intention of allowing itself to be overcome by the Presbyterian Scots Irish flooding into the western counties (Kenny 2009). This division of government led to infuriation and outrage as much due to the composition of the bodies as to the division of responsibilities, not well understood by many settlers (Kenny 2009).

After the resignations caused by the war, a "Quaker Party"[1] remained in government, but Quaker members were a minority in both houses of government and were associated more with the Executive Council than with the Legislative Assembly. It had a greater number of non-Quaker members and included Anglicans and Presbyterians, both of whom opposed Quakers and their pacifist principles with increasing vehemence (Bauman 1971, 8, 21–22). The Assembly had gained power over the intervening years since 1701 but still could not exercise that power over the Proprietary Party dominating the Council. Among those who remained in the Quaker Party were those who believed that the Peace Testimony did not apply to defense. Partly due to the Quaker Party, popular opinion regarded the government as still Quaker, and Quakers continued to be held responsible for government actions in which they had less voice (Bauman 1971).

While Quakers never dominated by numbers again, their beliefs and practices had a profound effect on Pennsylvania (Sharpless 1898; Punshon 1984; Ream 1981). However, peace in the eighteenth century was a peace gained by power *over* rather than the Quakers' desire for a peace *with*, i.e., with equal partners, not a conquered enemy (Daituolo 1988). This peace *with* was ended by the time of the Paxton massacres in 1763 (Kenny 2009), and the Penn family oligarchy ended with the Revolutionary War (Treese 2002).

The form of Quaker government and the religious beliefs of Quakers proved unable to respond to a colony peopled by a vast array of settler colonists, most of whom were not pacifists. Penn's form of government included a practice we would now call gerrymandering, used to ensure a Quaker majority. In turn that led to settler colonist discontent when they realized they did not have an equal

---

1. The Quaker Party began as what might be described as a "caucus" of Quaker politicians, including the Pendleton brothers (especially Israel and James) that formed to end the internecine conflicts that had erupted while Penn was in England. This group lost many votes in elections to the Assembly because of its stand on pacifism. It quickly gained non-Quaker members and continued after Quakers gradually left the government in 1755–1756, at which time it was headed by Benjamin Franklin, a non-Quaker. At that time members of the party expressed relief that they were no longer hampered by conformity to Quaker principles (Bauman 1971). James (1963, 164) writes that "In fact, the perpetuation of a 'Quaker Party' run by Franklin and the *politiques* flouting Friends' principles and making a name for itself largely by the ingenuity with which it thwarted the moves of the lieutenant governors, was especially repugnant to the [Quaker] moral reformers" (italics in the original). The Quaker Party lasted until the Revolutionary War and resulting changes to Pennsylvania's government, but its connections to Quakerism had become very tenuous by then (James 1963).

say in government. Penn also never really had adequate structures in place to ensure that new settler colonists paid for their land and treated the American Indians with respect. The structures of government and administration in Pennsylvania were therefore the first important factor in the failure of Penn's Holy Experiment, causing major harms to the Lenape and other Indian Peoples affected by Quaker governance.

A second weakness was caused by Penn's need for money, the cause behind his recruitment of non-Quakers and non-pacifists and loss of control over these settler colonists flooding into his province. In failing to control settler colonists and in the settlement process, he caused untold harm to the Lenape. Finally, a third weakness was the restrictions placed on him by his charter with the king and his own understanding that governing a province necessitated hierarchy, which limited his ability to set up a deeply democratic government. Rather, he maintained three levels of government, led by a Penn family member as governor and with an Executive Council of members chosen by the governor. Only the Legislative Assembly was elected and to some extent (they were all property owners) reflected the will of the people. This was an oligarchy of sorts that undermined any real democracy enshrined in the Frame of Government, which was mainly based on social class or wealth and whose members were assigned contradictory responsibilities. These weaknesses led to the end of the dreams of a Quaker utopia and contributed to the social harms arising from it.

Pemberton (2016, 65) argues that a social democratic government is likely to produce the least social harms. He suggests that the more capitalist a government is, the more likely it is to promote social harms. His analysis of five modern-day government types (neoliberal, liberal, corporatist, meso-corporatist, and social democratic) contrasts them on a number of characteristics, such as welfare, criminal justice, and social solidarity, to determine which types produce the fewest social harms. His analysis finds the neoliberal, such as occurs in the USA today, to be the most likely to produce a wide range of social harms and the social democratic to produce the least.

Based on Pemberton's typology it could be suggested that Penn attempted to develop a rough form of social democracy, considering the colonial nature of government, economics, politics, and cultural ideologies of the times. Like a social democracy, his government promoted a "universal" rights-based system, considering the ideologies of the time concerning women, slaves, and others. His criminal justice policies could be described as "addressing the social context of offending through social policies" and likely having a low imprisonment rate

(Pemberton 2016, 62). It is in the characteristic of social solidarity that Penn's form of government most closely fits the social democratic model. Social solidarity in a social democracy means a "high degree of social citizenship that affords a high degree of protection against harmful aspects." There was also a "low level of inequality and a strong commitment to inclusion" as well as a "high degree of collective responsibility and concern for the 'other'" (Pemberton 2016, 63) in the Frame of Government that Penn finalized in 1701.

However, Pennsylvania authorities very quickly moved away from such social solidarity with American Indians to a more liberal approach to government so that "low levels of trust and social cohesion [gave] rise to high levels of anomie and anti-social tendencies at all levels of society" and "high levels of socio-economic inequality [served] to exclude and marginalize subgroups of the population [and a] weak collective responsibility for others" (Pemberton 2016, 63). By 1755 the elected Legislative Assembly was fighting with the Executive Council over raising funds for a militia. The Assembly was no longer pacifist, and the Council had moved more openly to protect the interests of proprietors.

In the next chapter we examine one egregious example of settler colonist reactions and consequent social harms to which William Penn's Frame of Government and weak administration contributed as did the shift in focus to colonial priorities by those at both levels of government, abetted by Governor Thomas Penn's leadership.

3

THE FAILURE OF THE PENNSYLVANIA GOVERNMENT

The Conestoga Massacres

HISTORICALLY, THE pacifist beliefs of Quakers led to tensions with other groups in society including social harms to innocent groups, such as American Indians, who became collateral damage.[1] In the previous chapter, the challenges the Quaker-influenced Pennsylvania government faced by its adherence to the Peace Testimony were discussed. One of the most infamous tragedies resulting from Pennsylvania government dysfunction was the massacre of peaceful Conestoga Indians by the Paxton Boys, a group of Scots Irish frontiersmen who despised what they saw as a Quaker-led government, although most of the Quakers in the Assembly were by that time long gone. In this chapter we illustrate the issues faced by the Pennsylvania government by describing the massacres of the Conestogas and the context for their occurrence. First, we look at the attitude of the settler colonists and the militia unit known as the Paxton Rangers, which soon became known as the Paxton Boys.

---

1. There is a deal of overlap between the opening sections of this chapter, and Nielsen and Robyn (2019) in the description of the Paxton Boys and the Conestoga Massacres since both works use the massacres as a jumping off point to their arguments and use the same resources.

SETTLER-COLONIST ATTITUDES AND THE PAXTON BOYS

Penn's colonial venture put him in debt. Since not enough Quakers bought land, he sold some of it to those who shared Quaker pacifism, such as the Mennonites, but most of it he sold to other Europeans who did not share the Quakers' pacifist beliefs and were hostile to the idea of good relations with the local Indian Peoples. It was not long before many European settler colonists, including often nonpaying squatters mainly the Scots Irish from Ulster, flooded the colony (Kenny 2009, 4). These non-Quaker settlers wanted the Indians to get out of the way and allow them to, in their opinion, use the land "properly." The claim was rooted in religious beliefs, as expressed in the Doctrine of Discovery, about the responsibility of "man" to till the land and make it productive. There was also much fear about settler colonist/Indian violence occurring on the edges of the colony. This violence resulted from increased settler colonist incursions over the Proclamation line into land guaranteed to the Indians by the British Royal Proclamation of 1763 (Bronner 1968, 13); Lenape rage over the theft of their lands; Lenape and other Indian groups joining with the French in the French and Indian War; Executive Council members and the governor (Thomas Penn) defrauding the Lenape out of millions of acres of their lands; and the Pennsylvania government's failure to set up any kind of defense for the outlying edges of the province. The settler colonists' ideologies held that theft of land from the Indians was justified. Settler colonists dehumanized Indians to the point where extreme violence became an "acceptable" option for accomplishing the settler colonists' goals of replacing them. Further, the period of peace and prosperity for most of Pennsylvania between William Penn's departure in 1701 and the death of Hannah Callowhill Penn in 1726 (Billypen 2020) might well have offered a sense of settler colonist security that culminated with the flagrant abuse of American Indian trust in Quakers because of the land thefts by Thomas Penn, James Logan, and others.

The Paxton Boys were Presbyterian, clan-based Scots Irish from Ulster, who had spent generations fighting the English for their ancestral homes (Marsh 2014, 98–99). The English shipped them to Northern Ireland to help control the mainly Catholic population. Marsh notes that the use of the Scots Irish "as frontline colonial shock troops" laid the grounds for centuries of race-based hatred. Some of those Scots Irish emigrated to Pennsylvania drawn by its religious tolerance and access to fertile land. But these settlers "lived in a world of violence, lawlessness, and contempt for distant authorities" (Marsh 2014, 99). James Logan, as commissioner of property, directed immigrants to the province's advantage, sending Scots Irish straight to the contested borders of the Susquehanna River. He turned a blind eye to the fact that they were squatters, many of whom had taken advantage of the Penn estate being tied up in the courts after Penn's death. Indians were reluctant to sell land to Penn's wife and her sons, and settler colonists were reluctant to purchase it under the uncertain legal circumstances, so the squatters simply took it (Kenny 2009, 24). Logan used them as a buffer between the colony's more settled population in the east and the increasingly unhappy Lenape and other Indian Peoples displaced to the west (Marsh 2014, 100).

During the French and Indian War, these settler colonists banded together in loose defensive units (Fisher 1919). Toward the end of the war, and during Pontiac's Rebellion, the Legislative Assembly, finally able to release funds for defense, organized and armed these small units, or Rangers, one of which included men from the village of Paxton. Some community leaders were selected by the British generals in the area under attack and given arms and training to form militia for defense (Camenzind 2004). The Paxton Rangers were authorized to protect their own district (Brubaker 2010). They had little faith in the British Army, expecting it to go down to defeat to the Indians, and much faith in their band of rangers, which they believed would be Philadelphia's salvation. As well, Scots Irish Presbyterian ministers were preaching sermons about the wicked heresy of Quaker doctrines they said could only lead to evil (Fisher 1919). As a result, the Paxton Boys wanted rid of all Indians, suspicious even of the Christianized, peaceful ones not taking part in the Indian wars. If the Pennsylvania government, which they still perceived as Quaker, did not take action against them, then the Paxton Boys would do it for them. Their authority was the Bible itself: "and when the Lord thy God shall deliver them before thee, thou shalt smite them and utterly destroy them; thou shalt make no covenant with them, nor show mercy unto them" (Fisher 1919, 45). It was the fault of the peacemaking Quakers, they said, who had made treaties with the Indians thereby encouraging their murderous ways.

After several unsuccessful attempts to kill any Indians that they came across, the Paxton Rangers focused on the Conestogas (Brubaker 2010; Kenny 2009), primarily because of the rich land on which they lived and because of what they seemed to represent—the Quaker government's indifference to settler colonist lives and coddling of the enemy.

THE CONESTOGA MASSACRES

On December 14, 1763, a group of about fifty Scots Irish settler colonists from Paxton, Lancaster County, murdered six Conestoga men, women, and children. A twenty-member Conestoga community had been living for about seventy years on a four hundred-acre "manor" belonging to William Penn that had once been part of the Conestoga's traditional lands. Mennonite and Quaker farmers surrounded the Christian Conestogas and saw them as loyal neighbors. The Conestogas believed they were safe and protected by the government despite the tensions caused by the French and Indian War (Brubaker 2010). Governor John Penn echoed this belief that they were safe when he refused to fund their removal despite growing tensions (Treese 1992). Brubaker (2010, 21) described the first massacre of the Conestogas:

> The Rangers went about their business in a rush. They dismounted and fired their flintlocks at the Indian huts. They rushed inside and tomahawked the survivors. They scalped everyone. Then they looted the huts, lashed the booty to their saddles and set the buildings on fire.

Brubaker notes that after leaving the massacre site, the killers told a Quaker neighbor of the Conestogas that, "no government should protect Indians" (Brubaker 2010, 23).

Thirteen days later the Paxton Boys, joined by more settler colonists, killed the remaining fourteen members of the Conestoga community, including seven children. The Lancaster town authorities had moved them into the Lancaster workhouse for protection. The Paxton Boys,

> broke open the workhouse door and pursued the fleeing Indians into the snow-filled yard. They hacked to death Will Sock and his wife and murdered two of the little girls over their dead bodies. They discharged a musket blast in another victim's mouth, splashing his brains on the yard wall. With tomahawks, they cut the hands and feet from several Indians. With knives, they scalped them all. . . . The bloodied killers emerged from the workhouse and walked back up King Street hill to the Swan. They mounted their horses and brazenly rode around the courthouse, shouting and discharging their weapons. Then they spurred their horses north on Queen Street toward home. (Brubaker 2010, 39)

The Lancaster authorities had been warned of a possible second attack, and in fact some had walked the streets but had seen no sign of trouble. Most of them decided to attend a late Christmas church service that afternoon, leaving two men—the sheriff and the jailor—to guard the workhouse. These two did nothing to stop the massacre; in fear for their own safety, they stood aside to let the militia enter the workhouse. The perpetrators were never identified or arrested for the crime, even though there were numerous witnesses (Brubaker 2010; Dunbar 1957; Engels 2005). Several writers suggest that there was sympathy by many settler colonists, and at least compliance by authorities, that allowed the massacre. Clearly there was support for the Paxton Boys, for their complaints if not their actions (Fisher 1919).

This violence today would be called ethnoviolence or hate crime, which is the most extreme form of ethnoviolence (Perry 2009, 403). As with other forms of ethnoviolence, the murders were a message not only to the Indians of Pennsylvania to abandon their lands for the settler colonists to take, but to the Pennsylvania government that the Scots Irish would not tolerate the government's protection of the Indians and that they were angry about their own lack of political power.

THE PAXTON THREAT TO PHILADELPHIA

John Penn, grandson of William, arrived in Philadelphia in early 1763 to take over as deputy or lieutenant governor (Treese 1992) under Thomas Penn who remained in England. On hearing about the massacres after they happened in December, his initial reaction was anger at the flouting of his authority, and he issued proclamations demanding the killers be identified, offering a reward for their arrest (Bauman 1971; Brubaker 2010; Kenny 2009). He also ordered county officials in Lancaster and Cumberland Counties to seek out and reveal the offenders (Brubaker 2010). The two men most likely to know the identities of the offenders were two Presbyterian ministers, John Armstrong, who commanded a different militia group called the Cumberland Boys that often fought together with the Paxton Rangers in joint efforts, and John Elder, who commanded the Paxtons. Both stated that they had no knowledge of the offenders, and yet, Kenny (2009, 143) states, Elder "must have known most of them." Penn relieved Elder of his command of the Paxton Rangers, although his reasons for doing so are unclear.

While John Penn was not happy about the killing of the Conestogas, his greatest concern was the response of his Iroquois allies to the murders (Kenny 2009). Penn went to great pains to show that he did not accept the murders as at all justified, hoping to avoid any acts of revenge from the Six Nations. As well, he responded quickly to the threat the Paxton Boys made to attack Philadelphia and kill another group of 140 Moravian Lenape Indians who had been moved to Philadelphia for their protection (Brubaker 2010). Penn tried to have them moved to the New York colony, but Governor Golden turned them back, calling the Indians "obnoxious" and accusing them of having done "mischief" (Kenny 2009, 148). They were returned to Pennsylvania where they stayed until 1765 in protective custody, though only 83 of the original 140 survived. The rest died from disease due to the bad living conditions and bleak cold weather during their confinement. It is not surprising that the survivors left for Ohio as soon as they were able (Brubaker 2010, 57). The implication is that their care was negligent at the least.

The threat to enter Philadelphia and kill the Indians sheltered there was one with strong political overtones. Dunbar (1957, 49–50) suggests that "the march of the Paxton Boys paved the way for internal revolution" in Pennsylvania. Pennsylvania was unique among the colonies in its form of government, its initial refusal to support war, and its supportive relations with the Lenape and other Indian groups (Camenzind 2004). Philadelphia was the center of political and military power in the province. For the Paxton Boys to invade the city was to "throw defiance directly in government's face" (Silver 2008, 175). Not only did their march defy the government, it also challenged the Holy Experiment. In general, the Paxton Boys' threat included killing anyone who stood in their way or otherwise protected the Indians, and there were rumors that they were specifically targeting the members of the Friendly Association, who had aroused much settler colonist anger over their attempts at making amends with the Indians.

Accounts of the Paxton Boys' "imminent intentions" greatly alarmed the city as well as the colonial government (Brubaker 2010, 45). Both were worried about what the Paxtons might do to the resident Indian population, but they were also worried about what the Paxtons might do to the Quakers and "the entire government structure the Rangers held responsible for not doing enough to protect pioneer families" (Brubaker 2010, 42). Many were concerned for the safety of the Friendly Association members, especially Isaac Pemberton, who left the city. In addition to a large military force brought in to defend the city

(Kenny, 2009), a group of non-pacifist Quakers joined the voluntary militia that was defending the barracks where the Moravian Indians were sequestered. Although Sharpless (1898) records that the Religious Society of Friends had accepted nonmilitary resistance as their practice, over the years Quakers had reached a compromise to keep good relations with the British Crown, which did not approve of pacifism, especially where British interests needed protection (Sharpless 1898). Some Quakers believed that violence might be used for self-defense, as they had before during the French and Indian War. According to Bronner (1968, 11), "some Quakers began to differentiate between defensive and offensive wars," but they were still a significant minority of the Society. A Quaker Meeting house was appropriated to shelter armed men from the rain—a spectacle that added to the sight of pacifist Quakers bearing arms, undermining their reputation for integrity considerably (Kenny 2009, 154–55).

The Paxton Boys did not succeed in a third massacre, and in fact did not enter Philadelphia en masse, but did succeed in being offered negotiations rather than being charged under a new riot act of February 3, 1764, stating "'turbulent and evil minded persons' who refused to disperse would be subject to the death penalty" (Brubaker 2010, 46). Instead, John Penn appointed Benjamin Franklin leader of a delegation that went to Germantown to meet with the Paxtons. It was agreed that the grievances of the rioters would be written and presented to the delegation. Most of the Paxton Boys set out for home, leaving two, Matthew Smith and James Gibson, to present their "Declaration" and "Remonstrance" (Kenny 2009, 163, 165).

On February 4, on behalf of the inhabitants of the "Frontier counties" the documents were delivered to Governor Penn; they defended the Paxton Boys' actions and asked for "redress of their grievances" (Dunbar 1957, 47). In the declaration they professed themselves loyal subjects of George III of England and pleaded "necessity" as the cause of the massacres. They declared the Conestogas to be friends of enemy Indians, murderers, and "more capable of doing us Mischief" (cited in Dunbar 1957, 101). They complained about the "excessive Regard manifested to Indians" and that the people of the frontier counties had been "grossly abused, unrighteously burdened, and made Dupe and Slaves to Indians" because the white residents of the counties had the "disagreeable Burden of supporting, in the very Heart of the Province, at so great an Expense, between One and Two Hundred Savages" ("Declaration" cited in Dunbar 1957, 104). They also lumped together the Conestogas with Indians allied with the French during the war, complained the Indians were enslaving white people, and complained about the lack of assistance the government gave the settlers who suffered during the war ("Declaration" cited in Dunbar 1957, 103). They had taken the law into their own hands, were making unfounded accusations against a group of peaceful Lenape, and rebelling against a legally instituted government, but astonishingly, this was overlooked, and the culprits never brought to justice.

In the "Remonstrance," their political agenda became clearer, for example, where they stated that they had rights to the same "Privileges and Immunities with his Majesty's other subjects, who reside in the interior counties of *Philadelphia, Chester* and *Bucks*, and therefore ought not be excluded from an equal Share with them in the very important Privilege of Legislation" ("Remonstrance" quoted in Dunbar 1957, 105, italics in the original). They continued to conflate the Indians sheltered in Philadelphia with the French-allied Indians, accusing them of violence and carrying on a correspondence with enemies of the settlers. As well, they accused the Quakers of giving gifts to the Indians during the war, aiding them with information, and helping them in treaty making ("Remonstrance" in Dunbar 1957, 109).

The only one of the grievances that was responded to by the government was to reinstate payment for scalps. The Paxton Boys did not get greater representation in the Assembly; however, in the next election, more Presbyterians and fewer Quakers were sent to the Assembly, and Council members were now more in sympathy with the Presbyterians' views than those of Quakers (Kenny 2009).

John Penn again issued proclamations demanding the leaders of the killers be turned in but with no better results than before. Penn rejected a request that the Executive Council and Legislative Assembly meet to consider the "Remonstrance," arguing it was a matter for the Assembly to address. He maintained that the powers between the executive and the legislative bodies should be kept separate, and the Paxton Boys' demands had tried to blend them together. His view was that the Paxtons had already broken the law, now they were trying to undermine the Constitution of Pennsylvania (Kenny 2009, 168–69). The Assembly then sent a message to Smith and Gibson that their "Remonstrance" would be addressed in due course, but the Assembly had more pressing matters on hand. They also stated that some parts of the "Remonstrance" would be taken into consideration as they related to the work of the legislature. Satisfied with that, the two men went home, their revolt ending with little gained.

THE CONTRIBUTION OF THE PENNSYLVANIA GOVERNMENT TO THE MASSACRES

The Paxton Boys were angry the Pennsylvania legislature continued to honor treaties with loyal Christian Indians and had not removed them from their land (Dunbar 1957; Kenny 2009, 33). The government continued to honor a commitment to social justice, although more in the principle than in the practice, given government members were complicit in the theft of Indian lands. The Paxton Boys blamed the Legislative Assembly and Executive Council for delays in providing defense. What also lay behind the Paxton massacres was the anger of other settler colonists who openly or covertly agreed with the Paxton Boys' claims (Bauman 1971, 108–9).

During the French and Indian War and Pontiac's Rebellion, settler colonists were experiencing multiple deaths and destruction of their villages and crops by Indians along the western border. They were angry and terrified, fleeing eastward for safety. They were angry about the government's failure to protect or even to arm them and furious that the Indians appeared to get better treatment than they did. They were also frustrated by their lack of representation in the Legislative Assembly that they blamed for seemingly ignoring their pleas for a militia (Dunbar 1957; Brubaker 2010; Bauman 1971). Quakers in the Assembly were similarly stymied by the unresolvable conflict between their Peace Testimony and the desire of other Assembly members to respond with militia on the frontier. At the same time, Quaker members were under pressure from Philadelphia Yearly Meeting and their own Monthly Meetings to honor their pacifist beliefs (Mekeel 1981, 42).

Settler colonists in outlying areas did not distinguish between Quakers and the government (Bauman 1971). They regarded the Quakers as responsible for their lack of support and defenses, even though they knew delays were being caused primarily by conflicts over funding between Legislative Assembly and Executive Council. While Indian raids were killing settler colonists on the edges of the colony, and Indians were pushing further east toward the settlements, the government, as far as the settler colonists could see, was wasting time quarreling (Kenny 2009, 77–79).

In sum, the Paxton Boys were motivated by greed for land, hatred of Indians, and by political conflict within the Pennsylvania government, perceived as Quaker, and which they saw as impeding their need for immediate defense. Their demands for representation were not unreasonable if one overlooks the illegality of their settlements. And even then, they were useful to the Pennsylvania government because they provided a buffer for Philadelphia. They did have less political representation, they did not have any support for defensive measures until near the end of the French and Indian War, and a group of Quakers was caring for the Indians. They were also subject to the authority of Presbyterian preachers, who regarded Quakers as inherently evil and as Indian allies (Kenny 2009, 28; Fisher 1919, 45–6), fueling their rage. All of this can be seen as undermined by their squatter status—they had not paid for their land, and most of it had not been legally purchased, some obtained simply through murdering Indigenous inhabitants; however, the government was so involved in conflicts between Legislative Assembly and Executive Council, as well as in confronting their pacifist conscience and political reality, that they failed to take any substantive measures to calm the conflict, either through force or through negotiation—all of which fueled both Indian and settler colonist anger.

In short, government inaction and denial led to a great increase in violence and hence in grievous harms against not only the Indians but also "legitimate" settler colonists and squatters (Sharpless 1906). Most importantly, the harms caused by the government's failures to the Conestoga were incalculable. The harms caused to themselves led most Quakers deeper into a colonial mindset.

DISCUSSION AND CONCLUSION

The massacres by the Paxton Boys were politically motivated hate crimes. We would now call their actions domestic terrorism because their actions were "criminal acts, including against civilians, committed with the intent to cause death or serious bodily injury, or taking of hostages, with the purpose to provoke a state of terror in the general public or in a group of persons or particular persons, intimidate a population or compel a government or an international organization to do or to abstain from doing any act" (United Nations 2004, n.p.). The political nature of their offenses is apparent when Dunbar (1957) writes that the long-term effect of the Paxton Boys' massacres was both to arouse the sympathies of Pennsylvania easterners who also disliked their government, giving rise to the possibility of the two groups joining forces, and to put the government on warning that continued control by an oligarchy of wealthy Pennsylvanians was unacceptable, as was their inaction. This inaction included first a failure to adequately care for the Conestoga who were also requesting clothing and food at the time of their murders. Greater care should also have included defensive measures, given settler colonist anger and hatred of Indigenous Peoples in general (Merrell 1999, 250); second, an inability to reconcile their Testimonies to Peace and Equality with a social and political context that relied on a belief in European superiority and rights to justify the use of force; and third, a failure to respond to the escalation of this inherent conflict, especially as expressed when the Friendly Association's later concern for the welfare of Indigenous Peoples deepened antagonisms on both sides. Each of these failures contributed to the destruction of Quaker-American Indian relations and undermined respect for Quakers in Pennsylvania generally.

The Conestogas were the victims of politically motivated domestic terrorism that resulted in lethal harms to them (Bankhurst 2009). Even in colonial times, in Pennsylvania at least, crimes such as the murder of the Conestogas were illegal; however, it suited the colonial feeling against Indigenous Peoples, and the settlers and their leaders were not too concerned about it, perhaps even tacitly consenting to it. This is what Presser (2013, 7) calls harms caused by "negligence," in this case by the government. The murder of Indians was "normal" in most colonies (Petrosino 1999). The colonial ideology of the time and contemporary historical incidents encouraged such a lethal view. As Cunneen (1997, 150) points out, there is an "acceptable" level of racism, in this case within colonial societies, that enables such extreme violence.

Sharpless (1906, 204–5) underlines this opposition of ideology and a colonial historical context with his description of the two adversaries:

> [The Scots Irish] were fierce Calvinists in doctrine and equally fierce militants in conduct. The Quaker was to them an object of strong aversion. These disciples of John Knox would not endure the Friends' doctrine of a universal saving light, and the Friends' treatment of the Indians seemed to them weak and utterly unreasonable. . . . To the Quaker mind in the same way the Presbyterians represented all that was objectionable . . . he was continually opposing their plans for maintaining peace with the Indian tribes by resolutely asserting rights which to the Friend seemed untenable, and enforcing these rights by implements of war.

In consequence, both sides were politically and socially wounded.

There is little doubt the Paxton Boys committed ethnoviolence as we call it now and that their intent was political. They issued a warning, not just about the existence of an oligarchy but also about their ability to flex muscle, to scare their victims into leaving the province, and to push the government into action. The government, however, was not exactly the Quaker government they perceived, although it did "play the fiddle while Rome burned"; and yet, the argument over property taxes was caused by Thomas Penn, a former Quaker and member of a Quaker proprietary family, whose greed, in itself abusive of the Lenape, contributed to the violence.

The Paxton Boys' story includes a somewhat complex narrative related to several issues, such as the culture of Scots Irish settlers themselves; their role as a buffer zone along the border; political and cultural differences with Quaker settlers; perceptions of assistance and protection for the Indians but not for settlers; and conflicts between Legislative Assembly and Executive Council over funding militia. As well, government policy decisions led to government negligence as discussed by Presser (2013) and Pemberton (2016). Additionally, the role of the Friendly Association trying to reassert Quaker social justice values by building better relations with the Lenape and other Indians, and intervening in treaty making, added visible evidence to the settler colonists' attempted claim that Indians were treated better than themselves.

These "frontiersmen" saw themselves as left unaided to defend their stolen land against Indian attacks, while government members quarreled, and Indians were given support and assistance (Bronner 1968; Dunbar 1957; Hindle 1946; Kenny 2009). They conveniently overlooked the fact that they were squatters (Kenny 2009). Perhaps this knowledge of their own illegality and their long-standing resistance to a distant authority (Marsh 2014) added depth to their anger. They believed they could do a better job of governing and blamed the Quakers for the mess. As Fisher (1919, 45) writes: "Their increasing numbers and rugged independence were forming them also into an organized political party with decided tendencies, as it afterwards appeared, towards forming a separate state."

The massacres were only peripherally associated with the Quakers who no longer held political power but also had roots in Penn's need for money and loss of control over settlers, as well as in the Quaker faith that led them to a pacifist stance and to treating the Indians equally under Pennsylvania law. Quakers were, however, overwhelmed by the violence and antagonism toward Indians of other colonies both inside and outside the province and were unable to stand against it. Instead, they chose to ignore these harms, thereby indulging in cultural violence. Based on the historical evidence it seems that the Penn family's unwillingness to share governance with its new settler colonists and contribute to the upkeep of the state through taxes were among the instigating events in the massacre of the Conestogas and the threat to Philadelphia.

Violent crimes and other social harms continue today against Indigenous Peoples worldwide, and Quakers today still face the conundrum of how to prevent them and deal with them in a social context in which their views are not widely supported. The tragedy of the Conestogas shows that even if the Quakers still held a majority in government, they could not have prevented the massacres. Quakers may not have the ability to govern a violent society, though they have the potential to offer a positive and ameliorative influence as discussed in the final chapter.

4

THE SUBVERSIVE EFFECTS OF COLONIAL IDEOLOGY

Early Quaker Attitudes toward American Indians

N THIS chapter, we investigate in more detail how a highly principled group such as the Quakers tried to accommodate its beliefs and practices to a wider society that was less principled, including the use of violence against, and land grabs from, American Indians. We examine changes in Quaker attitudes and practices that impacted their relationships with American Indians from incorporating a sense of social justice expressed in Quakers' desire to treat the Lenape as equal citizens of Pennsylvania, to such a profound integration of colonialism that Friends participated in structural violence (Galtung 1990) through coercive practices such as boarding schools and attempts at forced assimilation. In this process Quakers caused serious damage to Indigenous Peoples' cultural and physical well-being but also damaged Friends' own cultural well-being.

Quaker principles caused them trouble with everyone including American Indians who were upset by the lack of Quaker protection for them against rapacious settler colonists (Weslager 1972). What is less clear is the role colonial ideologies played in the distortion of the four basic Quaker principles: Peace, Equality, Integrity, and Simplicity. These are principles that can be difficult to live by, especially in warlike and hierarchical cultures (see, e.g., Guenther 2001; James 1963). As well, Quakers were very new to the challenges they faced. They had no role models such as we have today. The virulent opposition they were facing had previously come from those in authority; now it came against them because *they* were the authority.

Quakers arrived in the American colonies carrying with them their Truth, which they felt a responsibility to teach to all, but their fervent belief in this Truth was imbued with a certain naïveté. They expected Truth to automatically open itself to others and had no plans for what to do if this did not happen. While there are many accounts of the success of Quaker actions, such as treaty making and shared hospitality in early Pennsylvania, other accounts, such as those claiming lack of interest in conversion, and immunity from Indian violence during settler-Indian conflicts, appear to be closer to myths (Punshon 1984, 34; Pointer 2007, 172; Gimber 2000, vii). There is evidence even so, though its provenance is perhaps mythological, suggesting that during the conflicts in Pennsylvania, very few Quakers were killed, although some lost property. Sharpless (1898, 171) cites three deaths that occurred because the Quaker victims had "so far abandoned their ordinary trustful attitude as to carry guns in defense." White (2003, 111) mentions two more.

Over time Quakers moved from a stance of spiritual equality to one of paternalism. In a society that became steadily more hostile, violent, and oppressive toward Native Americans, and with the Quaker need for political and social inclusion in post-Revolution American society, their naïve thinking contributed to the near destruction of American Indian cultures. American Indians slowly became "Others"—outsiders needing integration "for their own good." We briefly look at colonial ideology, summarize the role of Quaker beliefs in Penn's development of Pennsylvania, and then focus on two specific moments in early American history that affected Quaker relations with American Indians—the French and Indian War and the Revolutionary War—and at the influence of the Quaker Reformation that occurred between these two events.

COLONIAL IDEOLOGY

Before Quakers arrived in the New World, American Indians along the eastern coast of the United States were already suffering from the effects of harms brought on by the consequences of typical colonial processes, such as depopulation through disease, starvation, and violence; economic disadvantage resulting from the fur trade and loss of land; laws written to take their land and resources and to control them; paternalism supposedly to protect them but instead justifying land theft and loss of rights; and racist and assimilationist colonial ideologies proclaiming them underserving inferiors, and condemning or ignoring their economic, political, and social institutions, such as laws, leadership, and gender roles (Becker 1976; Weslager 1972; Zimmerman 1974). For an excellent description of colonial processes from American Indian points of view, see Dunbar-Ortiz (2014) and Fixico (2013).

As part of colonization, most European settler colonists and their descendants first used ideologies based on the Doctrine of Discovery (terra nullius), then their supposed religious superiority, and later based on paternalism and Social Darwinism to justify their treatment of American Indians. Social Darwinism was a racist ideology that "offered a comfortable explanation for the primitive condition of the American Indian and his stubborn refusal to accept the benefits of civilization. White Americans could not be blamed for the tragic failure of natural selection over the course of millennia to produce native North Americans who were biologically able to withstand the impact of Western civilization" (Trigger 1985, 16–17). Because of their "obvious superiority," many Europeans believed they had the right to impose their culture, economy, laws, and religion on such "inferior" Peoples.

The Lenape and other American Indian groups were subjected to this diffusionist ideology of European superiority from Penn and his supporters, though in a less virulent and more "benign" version compared to what came later. After William Penn, no Pennsylvania leader showed much interest in the Indians. Merrell (1999, 126) reports, for example, "At a council with Civility [a Conestoga Indian], one scribe made a revealing slip of the pen when he wrote that, besides various leaders, the congress consisted of 'many other People & Indians.'" Few leaders after this time saw a need to travel to meet the Indians on their own lands or terms (Merrell 1999).

Penn's successors, including his son Thomas, no longer a Quaker (Treese 1992), and several appointed lieutenant governors, were more inclined to treat the Indians with disrespect and self-interest, not to mention greed and dishonesty (Jennings 1984, 254–57, 320–24). Their interests in social justice had by now been eclipsed by capitalist goals (Rothenberg 1976). Rothenberg is one of a few writers to draw attention to the capitalist interests of early Quakers. There were many who amassed large profits from their lands in Pennsylvania, including through ownership of both Indian and Black slaves. Fox writes only that their slaves "should be kindly treated and trained up 'in the fear of God'" and be set free after a term of servitude (Vipont 1977, 108). Ptolemy

(2013, 26), writing of Black and Indigenous experiences through the lens of geography, throws light on Quaker attitudes: "Desires for justice and beliefs in the spiritual brotherhood of man did not erase the lure of racial structures that benefitted white objectives at the cost of black and native claims to justice." (See also McDaniel and Julye 2009, 8.) It would appear that a focus on egalitarian relations was overridden by business interests early in Pennsylvania history. Since Quakers were denied entry to the professions (Punshon 1984, 109) their entrepreneurial skills were a matter of survival that transferred well to their new country. By the early eighteenth century, capitalist goals had eclipsed social justice, making ensuing racialized violence only a matter of time (Pencak and Richter 2004).

During and after the French and Indian Wars, as Merrell (1999, 250) describes, "amid all the killing, symptoms of a deeper malaise—blind hatred—became more pervasive, making peace work that much harder." Indians were dehumanized by the Scots Irish and other non-Quaker settlers to the point where violence against even Christianized Indians occurred.

This same racist ideology was reproduced in the educational system for the next nearly four hundred years. Settler children were taught stereotypes of American Indian Peoples as well as learning about them only as "conquered" and "irrelevant." American Indian children were subjected to the same ideas in the boarding school system. Quakers were not immune to these ideologies, and this could most commonly be seen among those who had become materialistic and/or had abandoned their Quaker faith; however, among Quaker educators with good intentions, such ideas were particularly pernicious.

QUAKER BELIEFS

From 1656, Quakers arrived in the colonies of the Carolinas, Maryland, and New Jersey as well as the Delaware Valley and what was to become Pennsylvania. They were seeking a more peaceful and secure life, but some also came as missionaries, intent on spreading Quaker Truth (Jones 1966, 26; Worrall 1980, 6–9). These Quakers' interpretations of "civilizing" differed from those of other Christian faiths. First, they relied mostly on teaching by example, and second, they often preached, using interpreters rather than learning local languages (Gimber 2000, 142, 143). Native American spirituality was in a sense seen as a first step toward salvation through acceptance of Quaker Truth.

Given Penn's Frame of Government, one might expect Pennsylvania to show most clearly the effect of Quaker practices on their relations with American Indians, but although Quakers came to the New World bringing with them egalitarian and peace-loving Truth, they had also caught the pandemic "sickness" of colonizing English culture, including a belief in the superiority of their culture over that of American Indians. Included in Penn's writing is a letter to the Free Society of Traders in which he admiringly describes the Lenape inclusive style of decision-making that had similarities to that used by Friends; but Penn also accused the Lenape of being lazy because their livelihood was easy to obtain—they had plenty of game, fish, and foraged food. Seeing hard work as a virtue in and of itself led him to view getting one's living seemingly without it as immoral. Claims of superiority by settlers were based on religious beliefs but also on more advanced technology. Laziness, treachery, and "backward" socio-economic systems were common colonial accusations used to justify settler colonist superiority (Jacobs 1969, 84). Berkhofer (1979, 25–26) in his book called *The White Man's Indian* sums up sources of these inaccuracies and stereotypes including: "(1) generalizing from one tribe's society and culture to all Indians, (2) conceiving of Indians in terms of their deficiencies according to White ideals rather than in terms of their own various cultures, and (3) using moral evaluation as description of Indians."

Many settler colonist writers, Quaker and non-Quaker alike, compared Indian values favorably with their own (Nickalls 1952, 624; Spady 2004, 31-32). Quaker Josiah Cole wrote, "We found these Indians more sober and Christian like toward us than the Christians so-called" (quoted in Angell 2003, 5), in spite of which, Quakers still assumed their culture was superior. Penn's attitudes toward the Lenape, as expressed in his own writings, were distinctly mixed (Spady 2004, 38-39). Spady (2004, 27) argues, "The new colonists received ample advice about how to deal with the Lenape" but however benevolent sounding, "it was colonial in its implicit assumptions that right order and law were absent among the Native population."

Some Quakers, one of the most respected being John Woolman, expressed in practical terms the Testimony to Equality. In the mid-eighteenth century, Woolman, a Quaker activist against slavery, also wrote about the structural violence committed against American Indians. Looking back at the way in which Penn's settler colonists displaced the Indians, Woolman laments the situation that resulted, comparing Indian displacement with the violence used toward slaves, both being inconsistent with Quaker pacifism and other social justice values (Moulton 1971, 128–29). Woolman was also unique in that he sought to learn from the Indians as well as to share his faith with them (127). Sadly, although Woolman was admired by the more pious Friends, his writing had little impact on the majority of Quakers until after his death (Kershner 2020).

Quaker principles and beliefs led them to support the rights of American Indians to fair settlements in treaty making, but Penn's charter obligations and Quaker acceptance of settler colonist cultural superiority and belief in capitalism also led them to support conversion and "civilization" work. They frequently faced conflicts between colonial values and their religious beliefs (Angell 2003).

Quakers faced specific ideological conflicts that damaged their relations with American Indians, settler colonists, and the colonial government alike. The Penn brothers and other proprietors were dishonest in their relations with Indians over land and trade (Sharpless 1898, 168). The tacit acceptance of their wrongdoings by Pennsylvanian Friends, who saw relationships with the Lenape being undermined, added to the sorrow and anger expressed by the Indians over Quaker failure to live up to the friendship attributed to Penn. Many Lenape, in a letter cited by Harper (2004, 167), "recognized that their people and the residents of Penn's province were fast becoming 'No more Brothers and Friends but much more like Open Enemies.'"

In 1741, perhaps contributing to the sentiments in the letter quoted above, political leader James Logan and others argued that the Quakers should step aside and allow the Pennsylvania government to take defensive military action against Indian Peoples (Mekeel 1981, 35), thus avoiding direct confrontation with the Peace Testimony. Friends arguing for dialogue with the Lenape were overruled. Quaker ideology began to change as their hold on power decreased. Many Friends believed their Peace Testimony was paramount but were divided on how to respond to it. A few felt that the violence of war was necessary to protect Pennsylvanian settlers (Mekeel 1981, 35) and were often disowned for this belief (i.e., expelled from membership). Both parties alienated the Lenape because Friends appeared to have abandoned them.

In the meantime, the Lenape had undergone the same cataclysm as other American Indians decimated by disease, and the sheer numbers of colonial settlers, and were trying to survive both physically and culturally (Gimber 2000, 196–201; Jones 1962, 502). The climax, writes Harper (2004, 167), came with the "bloodbath of the Seven Years' [French and Indian] War."

IMPACTS OF THE FRENCH AND INDIAN WAR
(1754–1763)

Quaker pacifism and support for Indians had disaffected settlers on Pennsylvania's boundaries. According to Kenny (2009), settler colonists considered Quakerism and pacifism as one and the same. This loss of support, but also the actions of some Quakers while still in power in the Legislative Assembly or Executive Council alienated many Indian groups (Harper 2004).

Politically, the type of government set up by William Penn became a problem in itself, since the Assembly initiated legislation, e.g., to set up a militia in defense of the colony, but the Council held the financial reins, was close to the governor's office, and did not want a tax on the lands of the proprietors to raise money for defense. There was a long standoff between the Executive Council and the Legislative Assembly. In Philadelphia, many Friends urged Quaker politicians to resign before provision of funds for defense occurred.

Colonial politics, mercantilism, and, eventually, the outright greed of some Quakers confused Indian groups, as did the poor relations between the governing Pennsylvania proprietors and the Society of Friends (Gimber 2000; Weslager 1972). It bears reminding that Pennsylvania was a proprietary government as opposed to a Crown colony. The proprietor was both landlord and governor, standing between settler colonists and the king. Rothenberg (1976, 118) quotes Wilbur Jacobs: "The growth of population in the colonies was making proprietary government an obvious anachronism, and the few proprieties which survived into the eighteenth century became bywords for corruption and incompetence." After 1701, when Penn departed from the colony for the last time, formal meetings as well as informal contacts faded between Indians and the Quaker government in part because the Lenape were moving away but also because by then very few Quakers in the government shared "the proprietor's affection for and interest in the Native people of the province" (Gimber 2000, 204). For the next fifty years, relations deteriorated (see Marietta 1984) though economically the province prospered. Prosperity was one of the reasons that friendship with the Lenape faded (Pencak and Richter 2004; Rothenberg 1976). The disruption to Quaker-Indian relations was restored somewhat after the end of the French and Indian War in 1763 (Nies 1996, 187) thanks mainly to the work of the Friendly Association.

By this point, Quakers had moved from wanting Indians to accommodate (integrate with settler culture by for example, becoming Christians) to something closer to assimilation (i.e., complete absorption of American Indians into white European culture). Friends, both individually and as a corporate body, continued to press for fair and just treatment of American Indians but convinced themselves that assimilation was desired by the Indians (Ream 1981, 205). They believed that Indians would be wiped out physically if they did not do so. Their attitude was now one of protectionism or paternalism rather than friendship.

QUAKER REFORMATION (CIRCA 1748–1783)

By the 1750s, damaged relationships, loss of government control, and a general movement away from the founding principles of Quakerism led to a sweeping reformation movement[1] throughout the Society in England and North America (Hamm 2003, 31; Swatzler 2000; Marietta 1984; Sykes 1958). Prominent members of the Society urged Friends to return to their original vision and Testimonies. The result was a set of rigid interpretations that impacted the Society of Friends far into the nineteenth century (Hamm 2003, 31; Marietta 1984). This more rigid enaction of Quaker principles shaped the selection and goals of missionaries and teachers to American Indians who had been active in American Indian education for some time. That their goals encompassed the inherent violence of forced assimilation seems to have escaped Quaker notice. Woolman, and Quaker educator Benezet, were among the relatively few voices against assimilation, urging acceptance of American Indian cultures (Moulton 1971, 127–28, 257; Szasz 1988, 41).

James (1963) writes about the development of a stronger focus on charity during the Reformation movement, which evolved from a requirement of individual members to one of institutional support. This developed out of individuals and sometimes Meetings exercising care and discipline among Friends, that is, a duty of both surveillance and mutual aid (James 1963). There were among Friends, especially those living in cities such as Philadelphia, a wealthy elite; Sykes (1958) refers to them as merchant-barons. These were Friends who had prospered since their arrival and who were enjoying the benefits of their wealth.

---

1. The dates for the Quaker Reformation are not distinct. It spread among Friends in both England and America during these approximate dates: 1748–1783. See, for example, Marietta (1984) and James (1963).

Welsh Quakers in Pennsylvania, for example, found their wealth brought issues in the control of their children but at the same time, established their sons on country estates large enough to sustain a family. Sykes (1958, 182) writes that in the absence of an establishment (such as the Anglicans in England), wealthy city Friends filled the "vacuum." They had "established themselves with a sound business, a town house, a country estate, and a seat on the Council or in the Colonial Assembly" (Sykes 1958, 182). Levy (1988) contrasts this success of Quaker families, most of whom stayed out of debt, with rural Anglican families, some of whom were bankrupt.

Sykes (1958) argues that Friends sorted themselves into a hierarchy based on degree of wealth and into an "anti-Levelling tendency" that was far from the democratic anti-status beginnings of Friends. Their new philosophy incorporated such colonial views as those who were less affluent should be "content with their Condition, not envying those Brethren, who have greater abundance, knowing they have received abundance as to the inward Man" (Sykes 1958, 182). The Testimony to Equality was entirely missing in this new interpretation of Quaker beliefs, and paternalism took its place. The reformation, which Sykes describes as an "attempted fresh start" was a reaction to this corruption by success.

With the coming of the Quaker Reformation, Friends were more readily disciplined for violation of Quaker Testimonies. Charity, which Marietta (1984, 187–94) refers to both as philanthropy and "benevolence," once it became institutionalized, was a kind of corporate benevolence. This included a more benevolent internal care of members experiencing distress due to their religious beliefs or other factors as well as outreach or care of community members. Friends were appointed to travel within their Monthly or Quarterly Meeting area, visiting Quaker families to ensure their conformity to Pennsylvania Yearly Meeting's recommendation that they prevent "many growing inconsistencies and customs among us" (Mekeel 1981, 37). This was a form of surveillance that led to numbers of disownments for nonconformity to the religious principles of Friends, especially "marriage delinquency" and "drunkenness" (Mekeel 1981, 37; see also Marietta 1984, 6–7 for a list of offenses); however, the highest percentage of lost memberships was due to adultery (87 percent), and voluntary withdrawal accounted for 35 percent (Marietta 1984, 6–7). The rigidity of the reformation and its surveillance practices shrunk membership in the Religious Society of Friends to a fraction of its former ranks and deepened the contradictions between those beliefs and the colonial ideologies of their time (Marietta 1984). Jacobs (2009) points out that Christian missions by Friends, while practicing patriarchal and racist attempts at reformation of Indigenous cultures, also provided protection for the Indian groups from some of the worst depredations of settler colonists. The Quaker Reformation period distanced Friends from their erstwhile American Indian friends but at the same time recalled their commitment to care and protection.

THE REVOLUTIONARY WAR (1775–1783)

During the Revolutionary War, the Peace Testimony and Quaker loyalty to government placed them once again in an untenable position. Caught between the Peace Testimony for which violations led to disownment, their stance on obedience to government (in this case, the British government), and their support of the republic, they could not agree what to do, and each Friend made their own choice whether to support the war in any way or to remain neutral (James 1962, 371–77; Jones 1966, 559–66; Worrall 1980, 139–140). Their belief in the right of governments to govern but also their sympathy with the American desire for independence upset both the British government fighting to retain its colonies, and the rebels (later the Americans) fighting for independence. This led to the seizure of goods and houses, exile, and death—two Friends were hanged for treason (Jones 1966, 566–67).

Some were not as rigid in their pacifism as others (Kenny 2009) but were still considered to be Quakers by the settler colonists and therefore not to be trusted. Those who refused to fight or support the war in any way, or who tried to remain neutral, were viewed as treasonous by both sides but more strongly so by the Americans (Gimber 2000, 303). The reputation of Quakers in general was seriously undermined (Gimber 2000, 303; Jones 1966, 567; Mekeel 1981, 48–50). On the other hand, many non-Quakers had reason to be grateful for the assistance Friends gave to cities decimated by the war in a deliberate attempt by Friends to improve their image as good citizens (James 1962, 375; Rothenberg, citing Deardorff and Snyderman 1976, 128). Corporate benevolence had become the norm (Mekeel 1981, 50; Kelsey 1917, 15; Worrall 1980, 147). After the Revolutionary War ended, Friends continued the shift from individualized aid work, for which usually a single Friend requested the support of his or her Meeting, to the more corporate approach through which a Yearly Meeting initiated a project (Illick 1971, 285; James 1962, 374; Marietta 1984, 273). Unfortunately, the new approach slowed responses for assistance considerably, although it did include the potential to rehabilitate and reinstate Quakers with the new federal government through their offer of education programs, for example.

At the end of the Revolutionary War, Quakers were also reaching out to their former American Indian friends. In 1795, Philadelphia Yearly Meeting (PYM) began to plan new aid projects with American Indian Nations, for which they had received requests in 1773 (Ream 1981, 206) and again in 1790–91 (Swatzler 2000, 7). For example, several years after a request for assistance by the Seneca, Quaker educators were sent out to live with them and provide schooling for their children (Ream 1981, 206). Such assistance meant a lengthy process of negotiating and collaborating with the federal government and sometimes also Philadelphia Yearly Meeting (Bauman 1971, 209–15; James 1963, 305).

The Philadelphia Yearly Meeting Indian Committee made a point of contacting George Washington, the new president, seeking support for the proposed work, which they eventually received (Gimber 2000, 321; Swatzler 2000, 8; Rothenberg 1976, 128). When Quakers notified the government of the objects and concern of the Indian Committee, their increased closeness to state views of the Indians was made clear by Secretary of State Pickering who assured them their committee was in line with the disposition of the United States toward Indian Nations. President Washington himself had made clear his intention to "civilize" and "Christianize" the Indians east of the Mississippi within fifty years (Gimber 2000, 309; Kelsey 1917, 94–95; Swatzler 2000, 21).

Friends' attitudes toward the Lenape and other American Indians now had a clearer focus on turning the remaining members of the Six Nations (the Iroquois and their allies) into European-style farmers (Rothenberg 1976, 128; Swatzler 2000, 21; Tiro 2006, 363). No attention was paid to Six Nations food production methods and the complex agricultural systems they used, most of which were destroyed by American troops during the Revolutionary War, nor to the role of women as the farmers in their cultures (Barton 1990, 7; Swatzler 2000, 10, 13). Friends ignored that European farming methods might not be appropriate to the climate, soil, or, for that matter, the cultures of those for which it was being advocated.

Quakers believed that the economic situation of, and ills faced by, American Indians after the Revolutionary War called for their assistance to "put them in a way to support themselves" (Gimber 2000, 330) but how that might be accomplished was based on Friends' own beliefs and worldview. For example, Gimber (2000, 330) quotes from the Minutes of the Indian Committee of the Philadelphia Yearly Meeting of 1795:

[Friends would be] ... drawn to unite with the Concern so far as to go among them [American Indians] for the purpose of instructing them in husbandry, and useful trades; and teaching their children necessary learning that they be acquainted with the scriptures of Truth; improve in the principles of Christianity, and become qualified to manage temporal concerns, and it is expected that the Committee will find it expedient to erect Grist and Saw Mills, Smith's Shops and other necessary improvements in some of their villages.

This attitude differs considerably from that of early Friends. They had moved from negotiation and attempts to "civilize," but in a Friendly manner, to a more forceful acculturation. Some Friends such as Joseph Elkington (1859), worked hard at getting Seneca and Oneida to accept severalty, for example, believing Indian land would be safer if privately owned by individual Indians rather than by the tribe as a whole (Elkington 1859; Swatzler 2000) but this, in fact, made it easier for the various land-grabbing entities operating in the Eastern Seaboard to gain control of Indian lands. Other Friends worked toward allocation of permanent reservations—land "to be solemnly secured for them forever" (Milner 1982, 12). Quaker naïveté, added to their colonial thinking, led to harmful results on more than one occasion.

Paternalistic attitudes are humiliating and insulting, unlikely to foster right relations, although, for example, Chief Cornplanter of the Seneca believed that Quakers would be a defense against the deceits of white settler colonists trying to take his land, but those same Quakers were strongly in support of severalty, which weakened Indigenous defenses against settler colonist theft of their land. Quakers believed in teaching by example, but the example they set, if followed, would probably not give the results they expected, since many were not living by their own Testimonies. How these attitudes and beliefs played out in terms of education of Indian children is found in the next chapter.

CONCLUSION

While their Testimonies were not lived up to, or were inappropriately applied, Quakers did put their lives on the line to defend Indian rights. Their regard for Indian welfare went against many popular views of the time (Illick 1971, 283) and cost them a great deal, sometimes threatening their families and homes. Yet, if they had paid attention to what they were seeing, as Rothenberg (1976) points out, they would have seen that, first, there were many cultural similarities. Second, they would have seen that American Indian cultures had enough flexibility to adapt to settler colonialism—accommodation was possible, but the Quakers had other political and economic priorities that prevented them from exchanging information with the American Indians, and they were already beginning to solidify their myths of colonial relations.

There were two sides to Quaker thinking, one being focused on the primacy of their own beliefs and practices, and the other on their intentions in their relations with others. There was a rigidity to their thinking that during the Reformation period especially focused on detail rather than on the implications of their larger overall beliefs and truths. The Testimonies became a list of verbs rather than a list of qualities to internalize and guide behavior. In addition to the focus inward on Friends' outward behavior, they also wanted acceptance by post-Revolutionary American society, again preventing them from being open to a more equal relationship with American Indians. For example, focused on their own view of education as a one-way street in which teachers taught and students learned, Quakers lost countless opportunities to learn from Indigenous Peoples, whose spiritually based agricultural practices would have accorded well with Quaker beliefs. Those beliefs had been slowly corrupted from being based in the principles of social justice to the acceptance of harmful colonial ideology, setting the stage for the commission of great structural violence and its accompanying harms against American Indians by Friends.

5

QUAKER BELIEFS, COLONIALISM, AND AMERICAN INDIAN EDUCATION

Contributing to Cultural Genocide

QUAKER IDEALS not only shaped the Pennsylvania's constitution but also William Penn's attitudes towards the Lenape Indians who inhabited the area. There were, however, inconsistencies between his attitudes and actions, and such inconsistencies became greater during the years of oligarchic governance by his sons and grandson. The colonial foundations of Penn's government are clearly revealed in his desire to Christianize and civilize the Indians. Friends later reiterated Penn's focus on Christianization in their educational objectives.

In this chapter, we examine in depth one of the most infamous examples of colonial influences on Quaker beliefs—the Indian boarding schools. We argue that the initial Quaker beliefs in justice and equality were deeply influenced and ultimately undermined by American colonial ideas as seen in the Quakers' approach to, and rationale for, Native American education in the late eighteenth and nineteenth centuries. Native American children went from being treated as equals with Quaker children in Quaker schools, living with Quaker families and attending school with the children of those families, to being educated in their own communities, to being placed in boarding schools far from their families in order to be more quickly and coercively assimilated into colonial culture. Tiro (1997) partly titled his article on Quaker education work with the Oneida "We wish to do you good." Their intentions may have been good, but schools run by Quakers were steeped in cultural violence due to their assimilative purposes.

Colonial thinking was, and still is, based on a hierarchical perspective in which societies evolved into ever higher orders. Indigenous Peoples were seen as a lower order than Europeans, whose civilization was the "most developed." Bowden (1850, 356) expressed this when describing the impact on Indians of forcible westward removals by the federal government: "Like most others of the uncivilized races, they have been marked victims of the avarice and cunning of the more enlightened sections of mankind, and in the guilt of this conduct, it must be confessed, that the professors of the Christian name are deeply implicated."

Consequently, approaches to education were based on assumptions that once Indians experienced the virtues of European society, they would desire it for themselves. Quakers were largely in agreement with prevailing views, and some were connected to a group of Americans who later founded the Indian Rights Association in the early 1880s, an organization focused on American Indian assimilation (Adams 1995). Their arguments included: Indians must be made to accept individualism through severalty and thereby gain citizenship, American laws would take the place of tribal law, and children would be given an American education. These were the three pillars of "civilization"—of turning Indians into American citizens. When this idea was resisted by administrators in the American government, the reformers turned to the economics of it—educated Indians could participate in the workforce and contribute to the economy (Adams 1995).

QUAKER AND INDIAN INTERACTIONS ABOUT EDUCATION

Quaker attitudes toward education in general changed radically over time. In the early days of Pennsylvania, emphasis was on teaching children to read and write, and education was not supported beyond this elementary level (Sharpless 1898). Gradually education became more important in their thinking, and first secondary and later post-secondary schools were organized. In Philadelphia "in 1689 William Penn instructed Thomas Lloyd to set up a 'Public Grammar School'" (Jones 1966, 527). This became the William Penn Charter School, intended for everyone, including the poor who were admitted free. It is still in existence and was followed by the establishment of Quaker post-secondary education, such as Haverford College in 1833. By the mid- to late 1700s Quakers also viewed establishing and operating schools as an act of benevolence; they educated American Indians (as well as Black slaves and freed slaves) to help them adapt to the American world (Jackson 2009; and see Ptolemy 2013, for a comparison based on geography and contemporary events that include other racialized groups). Anthony Benezet, a well-known Quaker educator, supported education for all. He founded the African Free School in Philadelphia (Jackson 2009) and, between the 1730s and 1760s, was active in advocating equal education for Indians, Black people, women, children, and adults. He was much ahead of his time in promoting the idea of an inclusive education open to all who wanted it (Szasz 1988; Jackson 2009).

Providing American Indian education after the Revolutionary War was part of Quaker corporate benevolence. Rothenberg (1976, 110) suggests that such corporate benevolence was a move to regain status, arguing that "Quaker benevolence does provide . . . a convenient concept by which to understand Quaker behavior, insofar as it became highly instrumental and institutionalized within the Quaker movement." Hamm (2003, 33) goes further, pointing out that it was not the beliefs of the Religious Society of Friends that reestablished their influence, but "they were leaders in certain humanitarian causes," one of which was education to foster the assimilation of American Indians.

Quakers turned to education but now they saw it as a means of integration for American Indian children aimed at protecting them from the genocide that was occurring across the United States. Their approach, however, was paternalistic, condescending, and rooted in their conceptions of Quaker superiority, as discussed in the last chapter. They appear at first to have been more concerned about regaining their standing among ruling American elites, than on their stated aims of educating the Indians to protect them. Their work, especially with the Seneca, was a mixture of benevolence, coercion, and defense of their hosts, and by the mid-eighteenth century they were willing to become part of the boarding school system under Ulysses Grant's Peace Policy. American Indians proved recalcitrant in following European-based education, which was increasingly aimed beyond mere literacy to forcing Indians to give up their culture and lifeways. In turn this led determined Quakers to take a more coercive approach reflecting the assimilative policies and strategies of the American government (Jacobs 2009; Tiro 1997; Swatzler 2000; Rothenberg 1976).

Benevolence regained them some public recognition and access to government circles (Berthrong 1976; Bronner 1981; Marietta 1984; Swatzler 2000). In addition, early U.S. governments were short on funds and glad to encounter a group willing to pay for activities related to social concerns, including American Indian education, and supported them with letters of introduction. The work of Quaker education fell to the Indian Committee, in its early minutes referred to as "The Committee appointed for the Gradual Civilization and Christianization of the Indian Natives," encapsulating Quaker shifts in attitude from a more equal relationship. The Indian Committee reported to Meeting for Sufferings, which in turn found and hired Friends to do the work requested (James 1963). As well, Friends were concerned with settler colonist prejudices against American Indians so that, for example, the Friends' Meeting for Sufferings of Philadelphia in 1819 sent a letter to Congress stating: "With deep concern . . . we have observed a disposition spreading in the United States, to consider the Indians as an incumbrance to the community, and their residence within our borders as an obstruction to the progressive improvements and opulence of the nation" (Bowden 1850, 356).

Regaining status was not their only motivation; they continued to be faithful to their beliefs (and unconscious of the contradictions that were affecting them) and to their support of American Indians, even though such support might jeopardize their relationship with the government. As such, they were very diplomatic when expressing their concerns to governments.

EARLY QUAKER APPROACHES TO EDUCATION FOR INDIANS

Quakers viewed education as universally applicable but assumed that the English emphasis on literacy, numeracy and European history was also universally appropriate. In addition to this, many schools also emphasized practical skills in "industrial" curricula, such as mechanics and farming for boys and domestic skills for girls. Education in American Indian communities became a larger part of Quaker work as Indian leaders began to realize the necessity of education in non-Native ways. For example, Lenape leader Killbuck and his son travelled to Philadelphia in 1771 to request a Quaker teacher, a request that was repeated a year later after receiving no response (Schutt 2007, 142). In 1773, Captain White Eyes asked for Quaker teachers to come to Ohio, also with no success (Gimber 2000, 295). This changed after the Friendly Association was reinvigorated in 1795 when "after much quiet reflection on the Inner Light, Delaware Valley Friends . . . decided that in their effort to live their faith more fully and to honor the vision of Fox and Penn, they would act on the Indians' earlier requests for teachers and missionaries" (Gimber 2000, 310). The slow movement on new ideas and actions in Quaker governance is here aptly illustrated. Between their decision-making processes and the Revolutionary War, it took Friends over twenty years to respond to this request for assistance from Killbuck and Captain White Eyes (Gimber 2000, 295, 310).

At the request of some Indian leaders, Quakers initially held places for Indian students in Quaker schools. For example, when Cornplanter and other Seneca chiefs were in Washington between 1790 and 1791, seeking aid and redress for grievances, Cornplanter requested that three Seneca boys be accepted into a Quaker school in Philadelphia. Three Friends took the boys into their homes and sent them to school along with their own children (Ream 1981; Swatzler 2000). Several other children followed but without notable success in terms either of becoming Americanized or in being able to utilize what they had learned. According to Thompson (2013, 157, 158–69), a few Philadelphia Quakers took Indian boys and girls into their homes to teach them appropriate (Quaker) gender and job roles. She concludes this experience may have affected later Quaker ideas about boarding schools. Mt. Pleasant (2014, 120) records, "the Seneca leader Farmer's Brother noted that one of his grandsons began drinking, gambling, and frequenting brothels while under the care of the Quakers," a rather damaging account of one attempt to send Indian children to Quaker schools. The consequences led Farmer's Brother and orator Red Jacket to be skeptical of missionary offers to educate their children (Mt. Pleasant 2014, 120).

Once peace between the Seneca and the American government was reached in 1794, Quakers began to consider other ways to reach out to Indian children. Individual Friends living in Indian communities could teach the skills they thought were needed for self-sufficiency in the new reality of America, and at the same time they could be a "constant visible example of proper Christian deportment" (Gimber 2000, 331).

Friends' more corporate concern was first relayed in a letter to the "Western Indians" from Philadelphia Yearly Meeting Indian Committee, in 1795. It stated in part:

We were made glad when we heard that . . . many of you have a desire that you may
be instructed in tilling the ground to live after the manner of white people, which
we believe you will find to be more comfortable for you, and your Families, than
to live only by hunting; and we think that it will be good for your young people to
be learnt [sic] to read and write, and that sober honest good men should be sent
among you for teachers. (quoted in Barton 1990, 2)

The Mohiconick or Stockbridge Indians and the Oneida accepted their offer.
For Quakers, this was the first time they had sent Friends to live with the Indians
in their villages, marking a second change in their approach (Gimber 2000, 325).
As well, the addition of practical curriculum to literacy and numeracy was new.
They now offered mechanics, such as construction and operation of gristmills,
manufacture and use of agricultural implements, and European agriculture.
Together with blacksmithing, this offered additions to the local Seneca econ-
omy (Swatzler 2000).

The federal government under Washington focused increasingly on the
assimilation of Indians. The Quakers were eager to participate at their own
expense as teachers, serving their dual purpose of support for, and benevolence towards, the Indians (Keil 2001; Rothenberg 1976; Swatzler 2000). Their
concern was genuine, but despite the recognition of their seventeenth-century
dependence on the goodwill of the Pennsylvania Indians, eighteenth- and
nineteenth-century Friends' more paternalistic attitude towards their Native
American neighbors can be seen in the minutes of Philadelphia Yearly Meeting
1795 (Ream 1981, 205):

Our minds have been measurably drawn into sympathy with these distressed
inhabitants of the wilderness, and on comparing their situation with our own,
and calling to grateful remembrance the kindness of their predecessors to ours
in the early settlement of this country, considering also our professed principles
of peace and goodwill to men, we were induced with much unanimity to believe,
that there are loud calls for our benevolence and charitable exertions to promote
amongst them the principles of the Christian religion, as well as to turn their
attention to school learning, agriculture, and useful mechanic employments especially as there appears in some of the tribes a willingness to unite in the exercise
of endeavours of this kind.

Benevolence is not generally how neighbors having equal regard for one another would act, and the Indians with whom they worked were not unaware of that; however, they needed the Quakers, too. They needed their advocacy and support, and some believed that it was best to become literate in English so that they could read documents, such as those created at treaty signings and land sales. Further, some of the skills that Quakers offered, specifically mechanical skills, looked promising as a way to make a living (Gimber 2000; Swatzler 2000).

This was the case, for example, with the Shawnee of Ohio. After the War of 1812, during the time of the Shawnee warrior Chief Black Hoof, the Society of Friends returned to the Shawnees of Wapaughkonnetta and Hog Creek (Ohio) to set up a gristmill and sawmill and teach the local men how to operate them (Harvey 1855). They also taught agricultural skills to the men so that they could "relieve their women of the intolerable task" of taking care of the crops (Harvey 1855, 140)—a direct contravention of traditional gender roles. Chief Black Hoof had become a strong supporter of education for the Shawnee, advocating for the establishment of a Quaker-run school on Shawnee land to have "their children educated in a knowledge of letters . . . their children evinced an aptness for learning beyond what had been anticipated" (Harvey 1855, 144).

Two extended examples are offered next to exemplify the changed Quaker relationship with American Indians. Quaker reasons for offering education and Indian reasons for accepting it were not the same. As well, Quaker intentions were far from benevolent in their consequences. The two American Indian Nations were the Oneida and the Seneca, both members of the Six Nations Confederacy.

FRIENDS' EXPERIENCES WITH THE ONEIDA

In 1796, the Society of Friends sent a letter to the Six Nations Confederacy (the Five Nations had become the Six Nations Confederacy in 1722) offering free technical and educational assistance. They asked if the Indians desired to learn "useful trades such as Blacksmiths, Mill-wrights, Wheel-wrights and carpenters, that you may build Houses, Mills and do other necessary things, to make your lives more comfortable" (Gimber 2000, 322–23). They also asked if the Confederacy would like to have their children taught to read and write, and urged them to answer candidly, reassuring them there was no hidden intention to demand anything from them in return. They knew that the Indians had little reason to trust them and wished to assure the Indians to whom they wrote they would not request any recompense. Thomas Pickering, Washington's secretary of war, supported the Quaker offer in a separate letter. To their goal of civilization and Christianization, they had now added "school learning," agriculture, and trades (Bowden 1850, 353).

A favorable response came from the New York Oneida who had experienced similar attempts from missionaries in the past, leaving some converted to Christianity, although not united in their acceptance of this teaching. They also were trying to rebuild after the Revolutionary War, during which their villages and lands had been ravaged, and after which pressures were mounting to get them to sell their lands. As if this were not enough, unscrupulous settlers were tricking them into leasing or selling parcels of land. The Quakers became caught up in these tensions (Barton 1990; Swatzler 2000).

Three Friends, later joined by a blacksmith and two women Friends, lived among the Oneida from 1796 to 1799. During their three-year stay, the Quakers manufactured farm implements, repaired a sawmill, and set up a model farm. They ran a day school where they taught classes in literacy and Christianity. The women taught spinning, knitting, sewing, and household management. The blacksmith also gave classes (Ream 1981). While the project was quite successful initially, Friends realized that although some Oneida were enthusiastic, there was a great deal of indifference among others that made Friends' work difficult. Suspicions of Friends' motives, and resistance by traditionalists who did not want European culture taught to their children, contributed to a fraught environment. Some were also convinced that Quakers would demand land in return for their services. By 1799, Friends stated the Oneida had reached a point where they could continue on their own (Barton 1990, 4; Gimber 2000, 359–60). Tensions on the Oneida reservation were increasing, and Philadelphia Friends were interested in working with the Seneca. Friends packed up and returned to Philadelphia but left all their tools and equipment behind, as they had promised to do (Barton 1990; Ream 1981).

FRIENDS' EXPERIENCES WITH THE SENECA

Seneca Chief Cornplanter had requested Quakers educate the children in his village some time previously, and Friends now turned their attention to him. Cornplanter was an astute leader who for some thirty years balanced traditional Indian ways with Western ideas. Swatzler (2000, 13) points out that the Seneca had been agriculturalists for centuries and had grown sufficient food for their subsistence. European-American methods of farming were only needed to produce a surplus for sale. Cornplanter used the pressure from the government and from Quakers for his community members to convert to European-American farm methods as a means to have Quakers come to his village. He believed that Quakers' presence could act as a defense against the failure of the legal system to defend Senecas, and their assistance would be invaluable in any land negotiations that might have to be conducted (Swatzler 2000, 20). Cornplanter is an example of Rothenberg's claim: many American Indian Nations were capable and willing to work with the colonials for the good of both (Rothenberg 1976).

Joel Swayne, Henry Simmons, and Halliday Jackson responded to Cornplanter's request and moved to his village on the Allegany Reservation. They built a school about half a mile from Cornplanter's home and a residence some nine miles away at Genesinguhta on the Allegheny River, in an area approved by the Indians (Barton 1990). Rothenberg (1976) argues this was a more fruitful endeavor than the Quaker presence among the Oneida, due to the greater isolation of the Seneca under Cornplanter. As well, Chief Cornplanter's own experiences led him to see the value of literacy, for at least some of the children, as a defense against fraudulent settler colonists (Swatzler 2000). Swatzler records that the Seneca were facing a crisis. Settler colonists seriously undermined their subsistence economy, and the introduction of alcohol was devastating their community members. Cornplanter, who had held on to a large tract of land in western New York, wanted to find a way to keep as much as possible of the traditional economy while making use of the one being imposed on his community members.

Cornplanter was also playing the diplomat, telling Quakers and government officials what they wanted to hear. Through utilizing Quaker determination that his community members should learn plough agriculture, he established a common ground for diplomacy. Swatzler (2000, 15) records that after acceding to the federal government's obsession with having Indians learn plough agriculture, Cornplanter went on to deliver "a stinging rhetorical question, which made his real point: 'But before we speak to you concerning this, we must know from you whether you mean to leave us and our children any land to till.'" Swatzler (2000) claims that although the Quakers also arrived in Cornplanter's village with their own agendas, they came mainly because he had asked them to, and they remained for over 140 years, again because some leading Seneca continued to want them there.

Of the three Friends who responded to Cornplanter's request, the only one with experience of teaching was Henry Simmons (Swatzler 2000). Simmons's education was probably quite limited (Swatzler 2000, 78). He would have been selected by Philadelphia Yearly Meeting for his religious devotion as much as his teaching skills and experience, and he himself must also have felt a calling to take up the position. Simmons's religious rigidity undermined his chances of success, but he was able to work with Cornplanter who came to appreciate Simmons as an ally against drunkenness in his village. Simmons's exposure to the Seneca religious observances, however, such as the celebration of Strawberry [picking] Time with ceremonies and dancing, shocked his sense of propriety, as he misinterpreted what he called "frolics" and "idolatry" (Swatzler 2000, 41). Simmons expressed in his teaching and his responses to the community's activities, the colonial ideology underlying Friends' growing focus on assimilation (Swatzler 2000, 41, 82–83) and angered many traditionalist Seneca. They resented Simmons's "rants" against their spiritual practices and his attempts to acculturate their children.

Not all Seneca agreed about Friends' presence among them: in fact, some were determined they should leave, and Friends such as Simmons managed to increase that hostility considerably through their determination to force their ideas of Christian behavior, if not complete assimilation. Simmons upset many chiefs and others in the village (Swatzler 2000). A product of the Quaker reform movement, Simmons tried to enforce its practices (such as no dancing and drinking) on the Seneca. He ran a school that had mixed success and failure; children attended when there were no other seasonal activities going on. Children learned by observing and doing in Seneca culture, but Simmons was unable to appreciate their seeming freedom in that light. Swatzler draws a portrait of a fiercely conservative Quaker preaching his truths to Seneca individuals who tolerated his rants out of norms of respect and hospitality. For several reasons, including sporadic attendance at his school, Simmons did not stay long, returning home in the fall of 1799 (Swatzler 2000, 232–33).

The Quaker missionaries who arrived with Simmons bought some seven hundred acres to farm at Tunessasa and at Clear Creek. After Simmons's departure, Jackson and Swayne remained. Their goal was to establish a model farm where they could teach farming, blacksmithing, and millwork and run a school for the children (Swatzler 2000). The farm was more successful than Simmons's attempted teaching. In 1815, Philadelphia Yearly Meeting once again advertised for a teacher at Tunessasa. Joseph Elkinton[1] responded and arrived in Tunessasa in 1816. He began in a rented room at Cold Spring, on the reservation. It was in a private dwelling and was used until a schoolhouse could be built at Tunessasa. Cold Spring was probably a strategic location for Seneca leaders to watch how Elkinton performed because it was close to where many of the Seneca's meetings were held (Nicholas 2006).

Elkinton focused on teaching boys, giving them reading, writing, and math lessons with some lessons being biblically based. Attendance was low at first, and Elkinton had problems due to his lack of understanding of Seneca language and culture and a lack of control over his students (Nicholas 2006). He pressed on with his teaching of self-discipline as well as academic subjects, but distrust broadened when Elkinton was found to have beaten two of the boys, one severely, for bad behavior. This was a violation of Seneca practice. Discipline was the job of the women, not a man. Elkinton had betrayed his role as a father to the boys (Nicholas 2006), although his use of gifts for rewards was approved.

Elkinton had little or no knowledge of Seneca culture. He meddled in reservation affairs, going far beyond his duties as a teacher. Using Elkinton's own diaries, Nicholas (2006) examines the chaos the teacher managed to create on the reservation due to his religious fervor and his ignorance of the village and clan system of the Seneca. Nicholas (2006, 3) writes that Elkinton's work, while benevolent, "almost resulted in the Seneca killing him." Elkinton was threatened with being "tarred and feathered" by angry traditionalist Chief Red Jacket (see above—Red Jacket was determined to prevent acculturation) if he continued to teach at the school the Friends had built (Elkington 1859, 181). Elkinton had heated up an ongoing dispute between those who favored a return to the traditional culture and those who thought it better to learn the ways of the settler colonists and their government in order not to be cheated or sign documents whose contents they could not read (Barton 1990; Swatzler 2000). Nicholas (2006) records a history of such problems with Quaker schools due to Quaker ignorance and insensitivity toward American Indian cultures.

---

1. "Quaker Mission among the Indians of New York State" is a Cornell University scan of the original which is attributed to "Joseph, 1859 Elkington." The account is written by a grandson of Elkinton, founding teacher of the school, and this use is the only occasion of "g" in the spelling. We use the spellings interchangeably depending on the source.

Nonetheless, Elkinton was one of the few Quakers who learned the Seneca language and was given his own Indian name, *We-ne-se-wa*, meaning "fine day" (Barton 1990; Elkinton 1859) by some of the chiefs. When Elkinton realized that his students were not going to attend school when other activities on the reservation required their attendance, he gave them breaks from school during sugar harvesting and haymaking, and in fact worked in the haymaking himself (Barton 1990). This might explain why he had so much support as well as opposition on the reserve.

Despite periods of being closed, the school at Tunessasa survived in various forms until 1938 (Barton 1990, 80), becoming a boarding school in 1852. It was the first on the Seneca lands and always close to them. Over the next few years, various attempts at schooling were made, but the farm remained the more successful enterprise. In 1820, the school was moved into its own building at Tunessasa, on the opposite side of the Allegheny River, off the reservation and about nine miles from Cornplanter's village on land owned by Friends. In the meantime, women Friends had founded a group of Indian women and girls interested in soapmaking, spinning, and weaving. They began in 1805 and were taught on the farm at Tunessasa until eventually a schoolroom for them was built there.

Barton (1990, 10), who worked at the school before it finally closed, writes: "The goal of Friends, both in the field and in Philadelphia, was clearly to teach white man's culture [*sic*] and values to the natives." Barton records Friends "stated repeatedly their belief that this was the only way to ensure survival," stating it was "*a commendable humanitarian concern*" (italics added). Throughout her history of the school, Barton displays the same sanguinity as earlier Friends. The need to drastically change the lives of American Indians is not questioned and almost in passing, Barton notes children not being allowed home for four or more months at a time, sent to a small room for punishment and "switched" for speaking their own language. Such cultural insensitivity is violently abusive and a clear violation of Friends' principles.

A major source of distrust of Friends by Indians was Friends' support of severalty (Elkinton 1859; Swatzler 2000), but for the Seneca, land could not be owned. Friends did not grasp the depth and complexity of Seneca culture, including their stewardship of the land, nor did they see the consequences of the destruction of Six Nations farms during the Revolutionary War that had crippled their economy (Swatzler 2000). Friends also apparently never considered the possibility that Seneca agricultural practices were more suited to the climate and terrain than their own, that they had already been horticulturalists with large and successful farms (Swatzler 2000), and that Seneca farm methods could be modernized without changing to entirely different ones. This disregard of cultural knowledge was a source both of Friends' acceptance of assimilation and of the American Indians' resistance to their offers of education and training. The Quakers did not see the value of the knowledge and skills they were intent on destroying or understand the harmful consequences of doing so (Rothenberg 1976).

This repressive system may not have been necessary for the Seneca to continue along the path of integration into colonial society. Rothenberg (1976, 148) argues that "the Seneca evidence time and again demonstrates flexibility and receptivity to new ideas, techniques, and behavior which would belie the hypothesis that the Senecas were bound within the tight constraints of a previous culture model." Quakers had by now, however, moved away from thinking that Seneca, or other members of the Six Nations, could become full citizens of Pennsylvania without giving up all of their own culture, toward a clear policy of assimilation (Barton 1990, 10; James 1963, 379; Swatzler 2000, 25). When this did not work out, they tended to blame the Indians; for example, Barton (1990, 10) quotes a letter from the farm at Tunessasa in 1811, which states, "Their [Seneca] general progress in mechanical arts is so slow that we sometimes conclude they are not ripe for trade." By the time Ulysses Grant became president, Friends were ready to work hand in hand with the federal government on assimilation.

In the 1850s, Friends in Philadelphia were searching for a more "efficient" system for teaching the Seneca children. They concluded that,

> we apprehend that some method of instructing the children, by which they would be brought more entirely under the control and management of their teachers and caretaker, would facilitate the formation of habits of order, industry and economy on which depend, in so great a degree, the success of individuals in life, and the comfort and happiness of the domestic circle. (Barton 1990, 29)

Not only control but also educational content were affected by this colonial and Eurocentric attitude. While Quakers at Oneida and Tunessasa did teach both boys and girls literacy skills and sent several Indian children on to postsecondary education, most of their efforts were directed towards lower class vocational skills for the boys and girls.

QUAKER INVOLVEMENT IN BOARDING SCHOOLS: ULYSSES GRANT'S "PEACE POLICY"

The success of Quaker efforts to be accepted by governments is seen in the 1871 "Peace Policy" of President Ulysses Grant, who, after he took office in 1869, restructured the Bureau of Indian Affairs and established a program of federal aid to Indian education and missions to be administered by various Christian sects (McKellip 1992; Ream 1981), awarding two of the largest superintendencies to Quakers (Illick 1971, 284).[2] He favored Quakers for their stand on peace and for their integrity. Friends had clearly regained their status in society, but they were also participating in a policy that involved forced assimilation. They believed that in taking up these superintendencies, they offered American Indians the only chance they had to physically survive (Ream 1981, 208) and that their administration would be less brutal than that of previous regimes. Illick (1971) records that Quakers were concerned about working within government but were reassured by the apparent sincerity of Grant and enthusiastic about what they saw as a more positive approach to American Indians. Nonetheless, they recorded the need for watchful care over military officers appointed by the government lest Friends find themselves in a compromised position. Quakers understood they could not carry the Gospel to Indians while those Indians were being subjected to the schemes of unprincipled "Christian" men. For instance, Berthrong (1976) in his discussions of John D. Miles's tenure as Indian Agent to the Cheyenne and Arapaho Indians in Indian Territory, gives many examples of white horse thieves, unscrupulous cattlemen, and bureaucrats abusing their power.

During the eight years of the Grant presidency (1869–77), Quakers controlled the Northern and Central Superintendencies in Kansas, Nebraska, and some parts of what is now Oklahoma (Milner 1982, 3; Ream 1981, 208). Under Ulysses Grant, Quaker and presidential goals were to "speedily advance the condition of the Indians to the status of Christian, educated, self-supporting American citizens, living in comfortable houses on lands held by them in fee simple" (Ream 1981, 209). Milner (1982) makes clear that the degree of Friends' success varied by which tribe they were with, as well as by the superintendent

---

2. When Grant invited Quakers to become Indian Agents, he assigned the two sects (Hicksites and Orthodox) to different superintendencies. Our examples come from the Orthodox Friends.

or teacher, but also that they had developed a bifurcated consciousness incorporating assimilation and justice. They continually fought against the corrupt
structures that riddled the entire administration of American Indian education
and welfare, as it had been when Grant took over, and continued to do so during
his tenure.

Examples can be found in the writings of John Miles, John Seger, Laurie
Tatum, and Thomas Battey working with Seneca, Cherokee, Comanche, Kiowa,
and other tribes located in the Indian Territories. Friends constantly express
frustration in their writing over battles with inefficient and recalcitrant politicians, bureaucrats, and the military, most of whom broke treaties and did little
to protect the Indians from the American cattle and horse thieves or employers
who tried to cheat them of their wages (Battey 1875; Seger 1934; Tatum 1899).
These and other Friends fought for the rights of American Indians and for the
treaties to be honored, even as they pressed on with their own assimilative goals.

When President Hayes took office, changing Indian policy back to a more
authoritarian, militaristic model than Grant's Peace Policy, most Quakers
reconsidered their involvement, and over time, all left their positions (Milner 1982, 95). Hayes and his appointed secretary of the interior, Carl Schurz,
were adamantly opposed to the use of religious orders running and teaching
in the schools, describing them as "sentimental" and replaced them with hierarchical and efficiently run administrative structures. Milner (1982, 188) writes
that, "Between 1877 and 1882, the reform efforts of Carl Schurz and Ezra Hayt
(another appointee of Rutherford Hayes) forced the resignations of all except
one of the Quaker agents."

Between 8 percent and 14 percent of the Indian population had been put into
the hands of Quakers. They were excited by what they saw as an opportunity to
redress a previously corrupt Indian Bureau's actions by bringing in a fair, kindly,
and humane administration (Ream 1981). Friends organized by hiring other
Friends, a kind of patronage that irritated some of the Indians as well as local
settler colonists who wanted access to the jobs. The intent, however, was to end
the corruption that had attended similar positions in the past.

In 1868 Orthodox Friends, at the invitation of President Ulysses Grant, submitted a list of Christian Friends to work with the Indians in western Indian
Territory. Enoch Hoag would be superintendent of this group, with his headquarters in Kansas. Among the nine Indian Agents appointed under his care
were J. D. Miles and Lawrie Tatum. Tatum was sent to work with the Kiowas
and Comanches, whom he called "blanket Indians" and the Wichita, whom

he labelled "partially civilized" (Tatum 1899, 24–25). Miles was sent to work with the Cheyenne and Arapahoe Peoples, north of Tatum's agency. Reyhner and Eder (2004) cite a well-respected non-Quaker teacher and agency worker, John Homer Seger, as saying that the Quakers hired to teach had their hearts in the right place but had too many conditions beyond their control, such as lack of financial support to back the new federal policies and a lack of empathy for the Indian cultures with which they worked. This claim is also supported by Berthrong (1976).

In Kansas, Oklahoma, and Nebraska, Quaker Indian Agents ran boarding and day schools aimed at isolating the Indian children from their language, culture, religion, and families, and used coercive assimilative processes, another stage in the corruption of Quaker beliefs. McKellips (1992, 12) writes "This assimilation was to be accomplished through education and Christianity directed towards behaviors the government regarded as civilized." When Indian parents refused to send their children to school, agents, including Quaker agents, would withhold annuity goods, including food, that were provided for in treaties, until parents consented.

Some Indian students were isolated in schools for years, in consequence of which they found themselves in a no-man's-land of not being able to reintegrate with their community members but not being "white" either, while others returned to their reserves but could find no work, especially related to their education, and among these, many reintegrated, returning to their own cultural ways (Adams 1995; Berthrong 1976; Reyhner and Eder 2004). Further, the near obsession with turning Indians into farmers was at times disastrous because Friends did not assess their chances of successfully raising produce or livestock or persuading Indians to take up farming, much less how the produce might be used. There are examples of hungry Indians rushing into crops, such as melons and potatoes, eating them before they were ready, and becoming ill with the effects (Berthrong 1976; Tatum 1899).

Agent Miles found that the Northern Cheyenne were especially resistant to horticultural farming, whereas Seger had some success in raising cattle with his students (Berthrong 1976; Seger 1934), although Seger writes that "One Quaker in his parting talk to the Indians with whom he had labored for five years said, 'I have been trying to get thee to follow the white man's road and thee has followed it until thee got to the white man's table and there thee have stopped. And I believe some great calamity must befall thee before thee will be willing to go further'" (Seger 1934, 17). Friends experienced a range of reactions to farming depending on the location and the tribe and their own ability to form relationships with the Indians. Sometimes climate was the worst problem, e.g., a drought wiped out crops for the Cheyenne under John Miles (Berthrong 1976). The contextual challenges as well as changing and sometimes conflicting attitudes of Quakers towards American Indians' education can be seen in the following examples.

The complex situation and actions of Quaker Indian agent John D. Miles likely reflect the experiences of Friends generally. His job with the Cheyenne and Arapaho agency in Indian Territory included operating a school and medical facility, distributing annuities or rations related to treaties, and keeping the peace (Bethrong 1976). Initially he worked with the Southern Cheyenne People, perceived as more cooperative, but then Northern Cheyenne People were moved into the territory and proved to be far less willing to cooperate. Miles, however, was determined to make "his" Indians into farmers or cattlemen. His forceful methods provoked complaints to officials under President Hayes in 1879. As with Tatum, who eventually and reluctantly called for military assistance, Miles advocated the retention of a strong military presence in his area (Berthrong 1976, 3). Although he had some successes, the local climate and soil were unsuitable to farming, and while cattle proved to be better suited to the climate and to the culture of the Cheyenne and Arapaho, he had problems with cattle thieves (mostly white people and some from Mexico) as well as bureaucracy, failure of appropriations in Congress, and long delays in the delivery of rations and agricultural supplies, including those purloined by the army. Miles was incensed by the failure of both politicians and bureaucrats to follow the treaties and fought hard to redress their abusive treatment of the Indians (Berthrong 1976). However, Miles was also committed to keeping the children of "his" Indians in school and withheld parents' rations until their children attended. He was both hated for this and loved for his continual fight to get supplies and to create the means to make a living on the reservation. His attempts to find employment for the Indians were finally successful when he created a commercial transportation business, in spite of opposition from white competitors. Cheyenne and Arapaho young males proved to be excellent at this. Berthrong (1976, 67) records they wanted to work; "the number of Indians owning freight wagons soon exceeded the number required to transport goods and supplies."

The main reasons for the popularity of the boarding schools among missionaries and governments were children's erratic attendance in day schools, such as the school at Tunessasa (Barton 1990; Swatzler 2000), and the strength of parental influence on Indian children far outweighing that of day school teachers. Isolating the children from their parents rendered the parents more "docile," as some put it: Agent Miles wrote to Brigadier-General Richard H. Pratt about his new military-style boarding school at Carlisle, Pennsylvania, for American Indian children, congratulating him on the idea because "there are so many points gained in placing Indian children in school. . . . The child being in school the parents are much easier managed; are loyal to the government, to the Agent, and take an interest in the affairs of the Agency, and never dare, or desire, to commit a serious wrong" (Jacobs 2006, 213).

By isolating children from their community as well as their parents, all influences but those of the teachers were removed. Further, enforcement could be more all-encompassing, including rules about speaking English, wearing a uniform, and eating European food (Illick 1971; Reyhner and Eder 2004). Illick quotes Miles talking about the Kickapoo Indians as:

> "enjoying a good degree of the elements of civilization, yet there is much to be accomplished," such as an appreciation of "the difference between what we regard as '*Christian Civilization*' and '*Aboriginal Superstition*.'" Though the children were apt, "what they learn from their books during the day is half lost during the night *lounging in the old wigwam*." (1971, 290; italics in original)

Other Friends such as Lawrie Tatum preferred on-reservation boarding schools, however, or schools close to home such as the one at Tunessasa. Tatum was a Quaker farmer until appointed as Indian agent by his Yearly Meeting in 1869 and took a different approach to his tasks than Miles. Their actions suggest that Tatum placed his Quaker values ahead of colonial priorities, whereas Miles tended to emphasize colonial priorities over Quaker values (Berthrong 1976; Tatum 1899). For example, Tatum opened an on-reservation school and invited parents to observe and make suggestions, resulting in greater participation. When some of the boys showed an interest in the work of a carpenter and a blacksmith near the school, Tatum arranged for them to work with the men after school and on the weekends. Students that stayed with that activity were given a set of tools for themselves (Battey 1875; Tatum 1899).

John Seger, supervisor of the Cheyenne-Arapaho Manual Training and Labor School (Seger 1934), drew on his own experiences to set up a vegetable garden, farm, and livestock operation in which his students worked. As he built up a herd of cattle, he turned its ownership over jointly to the boys and then hired two of them to herd the cattle. Profits from these enterprises were either used to expand them or used for the school. When the boys completed their schooling, they took their share of the cattle with them to build up a herd of their own (Berthrong 1976). Seger's way of converting the Cheyenne and Arapaho to stock-raising tribes was approved in Washington initially, but then as soon as the school herd reached a significant size, the commissioner of Indian Affairs ordered it distributed. Since this gave most families about three cows each, which was insufficient to begin a herd and costly to keep, most of the cattle were killed for food at a time when, due to bureaucratic bungling and funding shortfalls, food was again in short supply (Berthrong 1976). This was the kind of action that created anger among the Indians and outrage among Friends such as Miles. Miles especially exemplified the bifocal vision of Friends, using coercion and violence to pressure parents to send their children to boarding schools and to pressure children into becoming a reasonable facsimile of white American citizens, while also fighting the government, or its bureaucrats, for adequate funding.

The Carlisle Indian Institute offers a clear example of Quaker attitudes. It was the brainchild of a retired army officer who had overseen American Indian prisoners of war and found them very responsive to a work training program. Richard Henry Pratt began his education career under Rutherford Hayes. He observed that the Indians were quick to learn and argued they could be civilized by removing them from their traditional environment and placing them in an American one. He began to focus first on younger male prison inmates, and then on American Indian children, setting up a boarding school in an empty barracks, mirroring army life and discipline. The institute was an industrial education school that incorporated "Outing," or sending students out to work in specific placements such as farms, or as domestics in private homes during the summer months. Despite its military format, the school was financed and supported by local Quakers, some of whom were also hosts for the Outing system. "The association that developed between Carlisle and the Society of Friends, whose members possessed many of the qualities Pratt wanted to instill, assured the success of the outings as the public-spirited Quakers took an active interest in the success of the program" (Trennert 1983, 273).

Another example of this bifocal approach of benevolence and assimilation in Quaker actions is also seen early in Tatum's 1899 book about Quakers and the boarding schools they ran in the Indian Territory. The book is clearly supportive of forcing children into boarding schools, but the introduction by Battey, who probably knew the Kiowa better than any white person of his time, undermines Tatum's sanguinity. In his introduction to Tatum's 1899 book, Battey lists twelve pages of violations of treaties by the U.S. government. Clearly outraged over these, Battey (1899, vii) writes:

> Among civilized nations treaties are regarded of such binding force that each party is held to a strict accountability by the other for any infringement of their provisions; and in the present consideration of international law a violation of a treaty is considered sufficient cause by the civilized world for an appeal to the force of arms.

Battey (1899, xv) further states there is not one recorded instance when the Indians were the first to violate a treaty.

Tatum hired Battey in response to a request from the Kiowa to have a teacher travel with them and teach their children (Battey 1875, 59). Tatum (1899) found funding for this innovative education by soliciting donations from Friends, since the government of the time refused to support him. Battey had taught at the Wichita agency for eight years and knew the Comanche and Kiowa cultures (Battey 1875; Tatum 1899). In travelling with them, however, Battey had to trust that their chief, Kicking Bird, really could protect him, as he taught the children of Indian tribes who had a habit of raiding and scalping and who had no love for white men. Kicking Bird was unusual in his support of European education at the time but also wise in his request for Battey to live with his community, since inevitably Battey came to understand their ways at a deeper level but could also be watched by tribal members. Just as Friends and others noted that having children in boarding schools made their parents more cooperative, so having Battey travel with them added a measure of protection from attack by the army. Battey travelled with them as they migrated seasonally, returning to the agency offices when they needed rations. He became a valued spokesman for them and a go-between who negotiated with various Indian agents and military generals.

At the same time, Battey supported Quakers as superintendents and teachers in boarding schools for Native children, claiming that Grant's Peace Policy would "cast a halo of glory over his character" (Battey 1899, vii). He appeared furious at negligence and betrayal of treaties, resulting in grievous harm to American Indians, including degradation and starvation, and yet at the same time believed the Indians were the ones who must be made to change in order to survive.

It can be seen that while Quakers could, and did, interpret their roles as Indian agents and educators in very different ways, they also had to juggle Quaker ideals with pragmatism and with their acceptance of "civilizing" and Christianizing the Indians. In addition, this acceptance of assimilative policies undermined their position vis-á-vis the Indians with whom they worked. They did not value Indian knowledge and did not appreciate the power of culture, much less its content and vast differences from their own. In fact, they seem not to have been aware of the influence that their own culture, impacted by colonialism, had on their thinking. Even Tatum, respected by the Kiowa and Comanche for his integrity and fairness, eventually turned to the military to control them (Hixon 1981, 21–23). In addition, Quakers were constantly undermined in their best efforts to assist the Indians and stymied by the bureaucracy and politics of the federal government and often also by the military and local businessmen.

Agent Miles called continually for a police or military force to prevent the thefts of Indian ponies but without much success (Berthrong 1976, 20), and Milner (1982, 58–60) discusses Jacob Troth's and his successor Barclay White's attempts to get settlers to pay the Pawnees for wood stolen from Pawnee lands. Not only settler colonists but also the Sioux raided the Pawnees, stole their horses, took away bison meat, killed the hunters, and murdered women and children. In a clear example of Quaker naïveté, Quaker agents first tried to get all parties to the negotiating table, but without success, after which they focused on preventing the Pawnee from fighting back, relying on promised assistance from the federal government that never arrived. In consequence, many Pawnee faced starvation, especially in winter, and died of this and related diseases (Milner 1982, 58–66).

Hixon (1981, 27), in his study of Lawrie Tatum, writes that: "Thomas Battey . . . who probably knew both Tatum and the Indians better than anyone, wrote of Tatum: 'His steady, upright, straightforward dealings, his firmness and decision of character, coupled with great kindness of heart, have procured for him many friends, not only among the Indians but also among the frontiersman of Texas.'" Perhaps, but Hixon (1981) captures another aspect of Quaker work during Tatum's time when he points to a general use of violence to "keep the peace" and questions the causes of Quaker failures in their attempts to protect Indian tribes from the worst excesses of the settler colonists and their governments as well as in preventing those tribes from fighting each other. Friends continued hoping they could encourage American Indian tribes to become part of a more "civilized life" and to adopt Christianity, while both the tribes and

Quakers were in conflict with, and being abused by, the very Christian Eurocentric culture being held up as an example. In some ways, Quakers were facing an impossible situation, but they also undermined their own intentions by acceptance of colonial values and practices.

The accounts above suggest that Quakers were deeply and personally involved in fighting the injustices they encountered but that their attitude had become distinctly colonial and paternalistic. Each decision they made in regard to their relations with American Indian Peoples meant greater acceptance of Indian assimilation and the social harms that encompassed. First, their pacifism included no alternatives for confronting violence; second, their move from individual friendship and assistance for Indians to a corporate benevolence and paternalism, together with a need to reinstate themselves as good citizens after the Revolutionary War, led them to work within federal government mandates; and third, their acceptance of the need to educate Indians into European culture, farming practices, and Christianity led them to support, and then run, boarding schools. During all of these phases, Quakers failed to see outside of their restricted framework. They could not see American Indian cultures as unique, distinct, and valuable or the Indians themselves as resilient in the face of the invasion of settler colonists and able to live beside, and share knowledge with, those settler colonists (Gimber 2000; Rothenberg 1976).

CONSEQUENCES FOR NATIVE AMERICANS

There is no doubt that American Indian Nations and leaders knew the importance of education. Cornplanter welcomed early Quaker teachers, but by the time Elkinton arrived in 1816, there were several schools in the community with Indian teachers (Barton 1990). In the late eighteenth and early nineteenth centuries, the Cherokee, Choctaw, Chickasaw, Muskogee, and Seminole nations set up their own schools. Children were taught how to read and write in their own languages as well as in Greek and Latin; they also studied astronomy, botany, algebra, and music (Trafzer, Keller, and Sisquoc 2006a, 9; see also Mihesuah 1993).

Native American parents much preferred the on-reservation day schools that were the earlier alternatives to off-reservation boarding schools, since they kept the children in the community, though Trafzer, Keller, and Sisquoc (2006a, 12) report that many saw the advantage of boarding schools that provided at least some food, shelter, and healthcare for their children. They were an alternative to starvation on impoverished reservations (Giago 2006, 6).

The consequences of Quaker educational efforts for American Indian individuals and communities were mainly negative, although there were some general benefits in terms of literacy. The boarding schools were the most harmful because of their assimilative goals. While Quakers accepted the goal of assimilation and believed it could be quickly accomplished, they appear to have been less abusive than other groups and willing to change how they approached education, although it took some while for this to happen. The possibility that they were less abusive is supported by the fact that Indian parents, wishing to educate their children, contacted Quaker teachers. Jacobs (2006, 210) describes an encounter between Kicking Bird and Thomas Battey, who was teaching Caddo Indian children on a neighboring reserve. Kicking Bird wrote to request that Battey take their little girl and be a father to her. Battey requested that they bring their daughter to live with him, but Kicking Bird replied that "We cannot leave her; we have lost five children; she is all we have; we cannot leave her here; but we want you to be a father to her, as you are to those children here." Asked if he wanted Battey to go live among the Kiowa, Kicking Bird said "yes."

As Trafzer, Keller, and Sisquoc (2006a, xi) point out, Native American students had extremely diverse experiences of the boarding schools. Some children grew to love the schools and their teachers as they became more assimilated to non–American Indian ways. But they were often met with disgust, anger, and accusations of disloyalty when they returned to the reservations (Trafzer, Keller, and Sisquoc 2006b, 16). More students, however, were very unhappy at the schools, because of the prisonlike structure, the poor food, the disease, the corporal punishment, the sexual abuse, and the prohibition of their Indigenous languages, spirituality, clothes, hairstyles, and any other cultural characteristics. They resisted their captivity with a wide variety of actions ranging from speaking their language in secret to perpetrating pranks to running away to arson (Trafzer, Keller, and Sisquoc 2006a; Nielsen and Robyn 2019). Further, as government pressures on the schools to become self-sufficient increased, and funding decreased, the industrial component of the curriculum tended to take over most of the day, with children used as unpaid slave labor.

In the late nineteenth and twentieth centuries, some schools began incorporating the local Native culture into school life and also added sports and arts. The results were dramatic. The Heard Museum (2000) published a book using photographic documentation of some of these schools, edited by Archuleta,

Child, and Lomawaima. Many of the stories recounted in the book include anguish and anger, but there are also success stories of singers, artists, storytellers, and athletes. Zitkala-Ša (Gertrude Simmons Bonnin) (1976–1938) was a Dakota Sioux who attended a Quaker mission school and White's Indiana Manual Labor Institute. Despite feeling conflicted about these experiences, she used her education to become a violinist and music teacher, created an opera libretto, fought for citizenship for American Indians, and wrote articles, stories, and books that exposed "the profound loss of identity" felt by boarding school students (NPS 2020). Ali-Joseph (2018, 101) describes how boarding school athletics became a path of resistance to assimilation and how many popular American sports today use culturally based strategies developed by American Indian athletes. These are not the typical stories of the time, however; for more horrific examples, see Nielsen and Robyn 2019; Woolford 2015; and the many writings by American Indian survivors.

Quaker educators who returned to the Indian education system in the 1930s were part of this movement to include more Indian cultural materials in the schools. For example, at the Santa Fe Indian School (which later became the Institute of American Indian Arts and Crafts), under Superintendent Chester E. Faris, a Quaker, attempts were made to work with the Pueblo communities from which many of the students originated. Woolford (2015, 105) quotes Faris as saying, "I always made a rule to never to tell an Indian what to do. . . . I waited until he told me what he wanted, and then I helped him get it."

The students' range of perspectives may be accounted for by the significant differences among schools, the groups who operated them, and as Trennert (1983, xi) points out (from a very noncritical perspective), "the definition of assimilation was repeatedly revised between 1890 and 1930." As the federal educational policies changed, the schools were forced to change emphases to meet national trends and ideologies.

The influence of the boarding schools has been intergenerational and all-encompassing because nearly all members of the community "had an aunt, uncle, mother, father, grandmother or grandfather who had been a victim of the boarding school system. Many suffered the extreme problems of collateral damage" (Giago 2006, 5). Duran and Duran (1995), two Native American psychologists, agree with this assessment of the intergenerational impact of the boarding schools. Untold damage was done to the cultures and lives of communities and individuals, particularly in terms of "internalized oppression" (Duran and Duran 1995, 29), a form of intergenerational post-traumatic stress in which "the self-worth of the individual and/or group has sunk to a level of despair tantamount to self-hatred" (29). This self-hatred can also be externalized in the forms of violent crime and domestic violence. Despite the strength and resilience of many American Indian individuals and communities, these repercussions of colonial oppression still destroy Native American families, oppress Native American children, and contribute to self-hatred and despair.

The Seneca and the Oneida, like the Lenape and many other American Indian groups, managed to maintain many aspects of their beliefs and practices throughout the colonial period, despite the best efforts of the Quakers and other groups with assimilative agendas. Good intentions and the practice of benevolence (itself a paternalistic expression) caused devastation. Quakers reproduced racist ideologies and contributed to the near destruction of American Indian cultures, leaving long-term negative consequences.

DISCUSSION AND CONCLUSION

It seems clear that Quakers were gradually drawn into full acceptance of colonial values and their consequent harms in spite of themselves. In search of a way to continue support of American Indians by ingratiating themselves with the colonial and then the American government, and thus gaining authority, they had succeeded more in assimilating themselves into the power structures of colonial society than in assisting the survival of American Indian lives and culture through the boarding schools. All the Testimonies or the Quaker "Truth" became permeated with colonial attitudes. Miles, Tatum, Simmons, Elkinton, and no doubt other Friends used various forms of abuse and physical violence in their attempts to turn American Indians into Americans, from corporal punishment to the withholding of rations from parents. Further, when Quakers did remain true to their pacifism, they created even more harms.

Jacobs (2006, 215) comments that "heavy handed methods" in the boarding schools for American Indians fostered the very conditions they claimed to be designed to end: poverty, hunger, and disease. Further, Jacobs demonstrates that the real motive of the federal government's Indian policies, unlike Quaker goals, was not a naïve assumption that Indians needed to be civilized for their own good but rather that this was justification for colonial control of Indigenous Peoples. This in turn led to the forced removal of children and deliberate breaking of family ties. Tribal and family units were broken, many lives were destroyed, and many Indigenous languages and cultures were lost, or all but lost.

Quakers were very aware of the injustices toward American Indians and the terrible conditions in which they lived, but their solution was to take actions that were destructive of American Indian cultures and identity. They convinced themselves that boarding schools were the only way to save Indian lives, but they lost sight of, or did not recognize, the consequences of losing one's language, identity, and sense of belonging. Further, they were not open to learning much beyond the mundane from the Native Americans or to the benefits of such shared knowledge. Their views were progressive for the time and gained them much enmity from the larger society when they fought for American Indian rights, but they still contributed to a program of forced assimilation that destroyed tribal sovereignty, Native cultures, and generations of knowledge about care and use of the land. This is lost potential knowledge for American settler colonists and remains the lost inheritance of today's Indigenous Peoples. Polly Walker (2006, 29) writes that Friends did come to "recognise that their good intentions during this time actually caused great harm, and learned to use their long connections with American Indians in more constructive ways," but by then the damage was done.

Quaker ideals were clearly shaped and undermined by a colonial mentality. Agent Miles was symbolic of the divide between the Quaker emphasis on justice, which led him to fight for treaty recognition and the keeping of promises made in treaties, but also to maintaining a relentless focus on Westernizing the American Indians living in Indian Territories. The question that remains is: when they recognized what they had done, how did Quakers respond to that new understanding?

6

THE UNIVERSALITY OF PEACEMAKING

Hope for Social Justice?

OTH MODERN-DAY Quakers and many Native American Nations do peacemaking, maintaining the traditions of their predecessors. Indigenous Peoples worldwide practiced variations on restorative justice long before the Society of Friends was founded, very likely from "time immemorial." The peacemaking practices of both groups, however, have been influential in the modern restorative justice movement, along with practices derived from other groups, such as Mennonites and Jews. Mass incarceration and its many dire consequences and costs in terms of human rights to both individuals and societies is becoming a significant social justice issue. Restorative justice, of which peacemaking is just one model, has been acknowledged by scholars and practitioners as an effective and low-cost alternative that promotes social justice as it empowers and heals the victims and community.

In this chapter, we explore the hope and possibility of peacemaking becoming a more universal practice particularly in overcoming unremedied historic injustices or the harms of colonialism (Walker 2006, 205). We look at four "case studies" of peacemaking that we have labeled "Old Lenape,"

"Old Quaker," "Modern Navajo," and "Modern Quaker." First, we provide a brief context for our argument, and then review what peacemaking is, before applying analytical concepts taken from social organizational theory. This is followed by our analysis and answers as to how and why we believe peacemaking has the potential to become a universal social justice practice. Because the source materials are largely the same for the old Lenape and old Quaker discussions here and in chapter 1, we summarize the descriptions found in more detail in that chapter.

CONTEXT

It has been stated that modern-day Navajo Nation peacemaking is *not* a form of restorative justice that can be adopted elsewhere because it contains "meanings with no ready equivalence in non-Indian social life" and "seeks to reestablish a particular way of living in relation to sacred commands" (Goldberg 1997, 1019). We are concerned that statements such as these could unintentionally contribute to deterring the spread of peacemaking specifically, and the restorative justice practices in general, if decision-makers who read them are not familiar with the structures, practices, and values of peacemaking. In 1974, criminologists were shaken by Robert Martinson's meta-analysis of the existing research on the effectiveness of rehabilitation programs (Martinson 1974). His article concluded that "nothing works." He later retracted his conclusion, and other scholars successfully challenged his work (Cullen 2005), but by then, it was too late. His article had appeared at a time when the justice paradigm was shifting, and his work became the justification for the mass closure of treatment programs. It took forty-plus years before rehabilitation programs began to make a comeback (Cullen 2005).

We, the authors, may well be overreacting, but the potential for a movement away from restorative justice and its contributions to social justice is definitely present during "law and order" political times, despite successful initiatives in specific cities, counties, states/provinces, and countries (see, for example, Hass-Wisecup and Saxon 2018; Van Wormer and Walker 2013). With the intention of assisting in averting such a fate for peacemaking, we explored the characteristics of four peacemaking programs in different parts of the USA and Canada, and in different time periods. In response to Goldberg, our argument is that even though the cultural and sacred specifics of Navajo peacemaking, and Quaker peacemaking for that matter, might not be transferable, the principles, processes, and structures are. We build on our findings to support our contention of the universality of peacemaking.

We used historical data on the Lenape Peoples (pre-1750) and early Quakers in colonial America (pre-1750) as well as current data on Navajo Nation and Canadian/American Quaker justice practices. The data on the early Lenape Indians and early Quakers are particularly interesting because these two groups were the first peacemakers recorded in early American records. Based on the characteristics of these four case studies, we argue that significant characteristics of peacemaking can be found in different cultural settings, and therefore could be transferred into yet more cultural settings, and especially into settings in which settler colonial descendants are working with Indigenous Peoples to overcome the harms done by colonialism. In support of this hope of universality, we look to Zion (1983) who states that the Navajo consulted Quaker writings when modifying their traditional practices for modern times.

WHAT IS PEACEMAKING?

Peacemaking is a form of restorative justice, a theory of justice defined by Van Ness and Strong (2006, 43) as an approach that "emphasizes repairing the harm caused or revealed by criminal behavior. It is best accomplished through cooperative processes that include all stakeholders." Restorative justice practices and principles were soon adopted outside of the criminal justice system, although the concepts came into common public usage there first. "Restorative practices" is the term used outside of the criminal justice system to differentiate the two arenas. Restorative practices are commonly found in schools, large and small businesses, and government agencies and NGOs, such as the post office and the United Nations (Van Ness and Strong 2006). Van Ness and Strong (2006, 33, 41) point out that many forms of restorative justice developed independently and long before the concept was used in the literature; as a result, the concept is complex and has been defined many ways. The practices of restorative justice have been adopted in "diverse cultures, economies, political systems, and legal systems" (Van Ness and Strong 2006, 33). According to Van Ness and Strong

(2006, 43–48), the three principles of restorative justice are: (1) to accomplish justice it is necessary to work "to heal victims, offenders and communities injured by crime"; (2) "victims, offenders and communities should have the opportunity for active involvement in the justice process as early and as fully as they wish"; (3) the community, not the government, is responsible for "a just peace." The goal of restorative justice is that "the community seeks to restore peace between victims and offenders, and to reintegrate them fully into itself; the goals for victims can be expressed as healing and for offenders as rehabilitation" (Van Ness 1996, 28). These principles, though expressed differently, inform restorative practices as well.

The concept of peacemaking is found in the cultures of many Indigenous groups, both historical and modern (see, for example, Lednicer 1959; Price and Dunnigan 1995; Making Peace 1997; Stuart 1997; Van Wormer and Walker 2013; NARF n.d.). The modern term has been adapted from its original European usages as found in Quaker and other writings but seems to be most commonly associated by scholars with Indigenous restorative justice practices. Although the concept has existed since time immemorial in the majority of Indigenous cultures, Navajo Nation scholars brought the English term into popular American usage in the early 1980s. Since then, its usage has spread to include other forms of restorative justice, not necessarily Indigenous, such as peacemaking circles in non-Indigenous communities (Hass-Wisecup and Saxon 2018) and "peacemaking criminology," as used by Pepinsky and Quinney (1991).

Yazzie (1993) calls peacemaking a "horizontal system of justice" because all participants are treated as equals. Its purpose is to preserve ongoing relationships and restore harmony among the involved parties. This is in sharp contrast to the European-based criminal justice system, based in European common law and justice procedures. This "Euro-based" justice system is an adversarial system where there must be a winner and a loser. It is a "vertical" system in which the judges "sit at the top over lawyers, jury members, parties, and all the participants in court proceedings. . . . [T]his vertical system relies on coercion to control and force people to do or not do something, according to the judge's decision" (Yazzie 1993, 411).

Navajo peacemaking was chosen as one of the case studies because it is perhaps the best-known and most-studied modern-day Indigenous form of restorative justice. As Zion and Yazzie (1997, 55–56) state, Navajo peacemaking is not alternative dispute resolution but "original dispute resolution," referring to its origins in the distant past. Nielsen (2005, 145) builds on this point describing how it differs from non-Indigenous restorative justice programs: the peacemaker is not a neutral mediator but may be a blood or clan relative; the process promotes the expression of feelings; consensus is sought, and the process does not end without it; spirituality is involved; the teaching and problem-solving role of the peacemaker goes beyond mediation; support group members are included, not just participants in the dispute; spiritual narratives are used as guides to problem-solving; and the peacemaker is not trained as a mediator but is knowledgeable about spirituality and culture.

The four case studies are analyzed in very general terms using concepts from Indigenous justice paradigms and Euro-based organizational theory to identify the transferable and nontransferable aspects of peacemaking. We realize that using a different spiritual group other than the modern Quaker group perhaps would add credibility in making the analysis more generalizable, but there is not a great deal of research available on other groups, and more importantly, present-day Quakers are involved in trying to further "right relations" with American Indians, a process that already includes peacemaking in some instances and has the potential for expanded peacemaking. To include slightly more diversity in our analysis, we focus on Modern Canadian Quakers combined with information on Modern American Quakers.

ANALYTICAL CONCEPTS

In order to carry out this analysis, we treated Indigenous communities (Old Lenape and Modern Navajo) and organized spiritual groups (Old and Modern Quakers) as organizations, despite the anachronistic application of this concept to the "Old" groups. A basic definition of organizations that allows us to do this is: "social structures created by individuals to support the collaborative pursuit of specified goals" (Scott 1981, 10). We recognize that in order to properly use social organizational theory to analyze these groups in any detail, it would take a lot more data than we have, and the results would end up being book-length. Another obstacle to a comprehensive analysis is the lack of historical data on the Lenape Indians from four hundred years ago. As a result, we are using only a few simple social organizational concepts to illustrate the potential or difficulty of transferability: organizational structures, processes, and values.

STRUCTURES

According to an organizational framework developed by Burrell and Morgan (1979, 168–81), all organizations have four structural subsystems: (1) the strategic control subsystem, comprising policy-makers and senior managers who monitor organizational environmental conditions, make key decisions about organizational goals and directions, balance the operations of the four subsystems, and ensure the legitimacy and survival of the organization; (2) the managerial subsystem, which internally integrates and controls the organization and expresses itself in the organization's authority structure and management style; (3) the human subsystem, which consists of organizational personnel; and (4) the operational subsystem, which converts inputs into outputs (that is, for example, converting clients in need into clients who have been rendered some service) using technology (in this case knowledge technology). In the operational subsystem is where we find the processes and values.

PROCESSES

Processes are the steps taken in accomplishing the goal of peacemaking. They are the "rituals" that Goldberg (1997) finds nontransferable. Four basic steps in accomplishing Indigenous justice are outlined by James Dumont (1993, 1996), a Canadian Métis scholar who, based on anthropological data, compared the justice values and practices of five different Indigenous cultures (including the early Navajo) with the practices of the Euro-based justice system. The Indigenous processes include teaching, warning and counseling, mediation and negotiation, and compensation—all essential elements of peacemaking. In table 1, we compare the Indigenous and the Euro-based justice system processes, as found in Dumont's paradigm, to the justice processes we found in our four case studies, looking for similarities and differences. The similarities that support peacemaking should be transferable to other groups. The similarities that overlap with those of our non-Indigenous groups, that is, old and modern Quaker, are of particular note.

TABLE 1 Justice Processes Found in Research, Compared with the General Indigenous and Euro-Based Justice Processes Paradigm by Dumont

	GENERAL INDIGENOUS JUSTICE PROCESSES PRE-CONTACT AND TODAY	GENERAL EURO-BASED JUSTICE PROCESSES	OLD LENAPE	OLD QUAKER	MODERN NAVAJO	MODERN QUAKER
CENTRALITY OF LAW ("VALUES" AS UNWRITTEN LAW)	Regular teaching of community values by elders and other respected community members	All under obligation to obey laws set by supervising state authority	Regular teachings of community values	Right of government to govern. Quaker principles override state law. Members must obey principles and detailed rules. Values taught by elders and overseers	All under obligation to obey laws set by supervising authorities	State law contestable when in conflict with Quaker principles. To become members, Friends must accept structure and principles but broader acceptance of value interpretations
JUSTICE PROCEDURES	Warning and counseling of offenders by leaders or council representing the community as a whole	Society reserves the right to protect itself from individuals who threaten to harm its members or property	Warning and counseling of members by leader	Warning and counseling of members by two or three "esteemed Friends"	Choice of Euro-based justice system or peacemaking	Discernment process initiated by Ministry and Council members to determine nature of problem. Process of clarification and negotiation

WHO CARRIES OUT JUSTICE?	Mediation and negotiation by elders, community members, clan leaders aimed at resolving disputes and reconciling offenders and victims	Retributive punishment, suffering in proportion to moral wrongdoing, set by legislation, judgment imposed	Mediation and negotiation by sachems aimed at resolving disputes and reconciling victims and offenders	Mediation by esteemed Friend(s) aimed at resolving disputes. If parties cannot agree at local level continues through regional levels to Yearly Meeting. Ultimate authority is all members in consensus at Yearly Meeting	Retributive imposed punishment set by legislation or naat'aanii-led peacemaking processes of prayer, talking it out, teaching and reconciliation	Mediation and negotiation continues through regional and national Ministry and Council Meetings aimed at reconciliation. Ultimate authority is with all members in consensus at Yearly Meeting
RESOLUTIONS	Compensation by offenders or clan to victims or victim's kin, even in cases like murder	Perpetrator is the object of sentencing retribution, incarceration, and rehabilitation, to be deterred and punished	Reparations though gift-giving and ceremony to victims or victim's family or clan, even in cases of murder	Restorative approach to restore peace in Meeting; aims at mutual understanding or fair and just settlement. Member who refuses to settle may lose membership or both parties involved may be advised to go to courts. No instances of reparation found but Quaker criminal law in Pennsylvania provided for reparation	Reparations through restitution, apology, community service; treatment plans for underlying problems	Mutual satisfaction and a return to peace in Meetings. Reparations rare. In cases of material goods or land, a negotiated settlement would be reached. Criminal acts are taken to the courts but the victim(s) and often also the offender are supported and encouraged by the local Ministry and Council

Adapted and expanded from Dumont (1996, 32).

VALUES

Values are part of the culture of any organization. Culture is relatively stable and is composed of assumptions and shared meanings that are the backdrop for action. Among other functions, cultures are the context in which structures and processes are formed (Hall 1999, 93).

As Goldberg (1997) rightfully points out, some cultural terms do not carry the same meaning for their Indigenous users and for outsiders. For example, we argue that while the Navajo term *hózhó,* (very) roughly translated as "harmony," means that Navajo peacemaking participants once again "walk in beauty," the general concept of harmony is a value and a goal in many cultures, though it doesn't have exactly the same meaning as in Navajo. As another example of values, Old Quakers wanted to avoid conflict and practice their faith in peace. In other words, if a justice value related to peacemaking exists within a cultural group, then it can be incorporated into a peacemaking process that fits that specific group. We compare the justice values for Indigenous and Euro-based justice found in Dumont's paradigm with the justice values of our four researched groups. If our groups' justice values are closer to Indigenous justice values, then they are more likely to be values that support peacemaking (see table 2). These comparisons of values and processes across the four cultures are by their nature very broad.

ANALYSIS

In addition to comparing our organizations to Euro-based and Indigenous paradigms as above, we also compare the structures, processes, and values across the four researched groups in tables 3 and 4, looking for similarities and differences among them. The authors did historical research on the Old Lenape and the pre-1750 Quakers at the Haverford Quaker Special Collections Library, including documentary analysis of Quaker historical records. This was supplemented with data from modern (20th and 21st century) writings of Canadian and American Friends on Quaker history and augmented by observational and interview data on the Navajo Nation peacemaker program collected from 1995–2003 by Nielsen as well as a review of the literature written about peacemaking especially by Navajo Nation scholars. Finally, data on the current Society of Friends comes from Heather's extensive reading of Quaker materials, including from Yearly Meeting websites for Canadian Friends and American Friends Service Committee as well as her longstanding membership in the Society of Friends. Data recorded by Heather are used here after consultation with philosophy professor Jeff Dudiak, whose studies have included extensive work on Quaker history.

TABLE 2 Justice Values Found in Research Compared with General Indigenous and European Justice Values from Dumont[a]

GENERAL JUSTICE INDIGENOUS VALUES	GENERAL EURO-BASED JUSTICE VALUES	OLD LENAPE[b]	OLD QUAKER	MODERN NAVAJO	MODERN QUAKER
Autonomy defined as individual responsibility and respect, knowledge for decision-making	Autonomy defined as assertiveness, competitiveness, adherence to rules, persistence	Self-control	Adherence to Testimonies expected. All of life sacred. Autonomy in decision-making. Individual spiritual practices underlie decisions and relationships. No leaders or priests but respect for discernment and unity of the whole	Recognition of self and others as sacred, no coercion	Individual spiritual practices and expanded Testimonies underlie decision-making relationships and material responsibility toward others. No leaders or priests. Respect for decisions made in unity of Meeting at any level.
Sharing defined as generosity and cooperation recognizing the interdependence of all life, harmony for collective good	Sharing defined as obligation, right for all to well-being and equal opportunity, maximizing individual success	Sharing and generosity to all, including strangers, harmony	Generosity and compassion, respect for others' values, goals must respect good of all	Cooperation	Generosity and compassion, respect for others' values, goals must respect good of all

TABLE 2 *continued*

GENERAL JUSTICE INDIGENOUS VALUES	GENERAL EURO-BASED JUSTICE VALUES	OLD LENAPE[b]	OLD QUAKER	MODERN NAVAJO	MODERN QUAKER
Wholeness defined as interconnectedness of all	Totality defined as the sum or the whole, calculations of connections to total	Interconnectedness of the universe	Community defined as the basis for discernment of a calling. Recognition that individual actions affect the whole community	Wholeness defined as interconnectedness of all	Community defined as the basis for discernment of a calling. Recognition that individual actions affect the whole community
Honor defined as respect for freedom and autonomy of beings, kinship with life	Consideration defined as courtesy and fair play, stewardship toward the less fortunate	Honor, see respect	Respect for others includes expectation of autonomy, caring, and equality of treatment, responsibility toward the whole	Respect for all living things and as found within clan system, respecting the integrity of oneself and others	Respect for others includes expectation of autonomy, caring and equality of treatment, responsibility toward the whole. Testimonies expanded to include Sustainability and Community. Esteemed or honored Friends are those who in themselves most express Truth
Kindness defined as a desire for harmony and amiability with all beings	Charity defined as exercising compassion because of acceptance of common humanity, motivation for personal development	Desire for harmony	Desire for harmony balanced with individual autonomy, belief in equality and compassion	Desire for harmony and well-being in interpersonal relationships	Desire for harmony balanced with individual autonomy, belief in equality and individual responsibility mixed with compassion. Harmony and community within Meetings highly valued

Bravery defined as the exercise of courage and bravery to accomplish security, peace, dignity, and freedom	Courage and valor defined as being in a noble cause or higher authority even if infringes on others' freedom	Bravery, peacefulness	Spiritual courage recorded as guide for others. Patience and discernment important. Inner Light's guidance sought communally and individually when faced with challenges	Having the courage to accomplish Peace	Spiritual courage in face of opposition to beliefs recorded as guide for others. Patience and discernment important. Continual seeking the Inner Light for personal and community guidance especially under pressure
Honesty defined as truthfulness and integrity in all relationships, recognizing inherent autonomy, dignity, and freedom of oneself and others	Honesty defined as truthfulness and respectability in accordance with laws	Truthfulness	Integrity a basic tenet. Laws may be disobeyed if they contribute to inequality or disrespect of individuals, groups, or community or threaten Peace	Truthfulness and Integrity in all relations, respect for elders	Integrity a basic tenet. Laws may be contested by entire community or disobeyed if they violate any of the Testimonies. Recognition of autonomy and potential for good in everyone
Respect defined as for one's own and others' freedom and autonomy, the inherent dignity of the person, and the maintenance of the collective	Respect defined as for personal and private property of oneself and others, the right to achieve personal gain	Respect for others	Respect for the autonomy, beliefs, and values of others. Respect for communally discerned decisions	Respect for all living things	Respect for the autonomy, beliefs, and values of others even when in conflict, and pressure to expect same respect, autonomy, and integrity of self. Respect for communally discerned decisions

[a] This table is adapted and expanded from Dumont (1993, 59–61; 1996, 24). The Indigenous and Euro-based values in the first two columns are taken from his work. Our conclusions are based on the values implied in the justice practices

[b] It should be noted that there is little data on Lenape values from four hundred years ago. Our conclusions are based on the values implied in the justice practices and other writings of Lenape contacts.

TABLE 3 Research Findings: Organizational Traits of the Four Groups

ORGANIZATIONAL CHARACTERISTICS	OLD LENAPE	OLD QUAKER	MODERN NAVAJO	MODERN QUAKER
Strategic Control	Sachem and council	Monthly, Quarterly, and Yearly Meetings (members of committees are "servants of the Meeting")	Navajo Nation Judicial Branch	Preparatory, Monthly, Quarterly, and Yearly Meetings each have Ministry and Council Committees. Clerks and recording clerks are "servants of the Meeting"
Managerial	Sachem and council	Yearly Meeting consists of volunteer members. Authority rests in decisions made by Friends attending Yearly Meetings or on committees.	Peacemaker coordinator and peacemakers	One or two paid staff have no structural authority. Work with volunteer committee members of specific committees, who report to overall authority such as Yearly Meeting
Human	Sachem	Ad hoc committees of esteemed Friends at each level up to Yearly Meeting. Meeting for Sufferings receives reports about Friends in need and acts to support with advice or assistance	Peacemakers	Ministry and Council (pastoral care) Committees at each level up to Yearly Meeting. American (AFSC) and Canadian (CFSC) Friends each have Service Committees reporting to Yearly Meeting and informing all members of activities. AFSC and CFSC have subcommittees working on peace, Indigenous support, and education services for Friends, such as conflict resolution

Operational Practices	Counseling, ceremony, speech-making, reparations	Warning, counseling, negotiation, canceling membership ("Disownment"). Advising legal redress	Ceremony, prayer, talking it out, teaching, reconciliation	Ministry and Council Committees meet when conflict arises at any level. Process shaped by nature of conflict or offence. "Wrestle with" recalcitrant Friends when conflict between individuals or within a Monthly Meeting. No disownment. Conflict more likely to be over issues than between individuals. Issues discussed at local Meetings until agreement reached and/or forwarded to Quarterly, Half Yearly, and Yearly Meetings, until Friends reach a united decision.
Operational Values	Autonomy, sharing, wholeness, honor, kindness, bravery, honesty, respect	That of God within everyone. Testimonies include Peace Equality, Integrity, and Simplicity. Value of peacemaking underlies all others	Autonomy, sharing, wholeness, honor, kindness, bravery, honesty, respect	That of God within everyone. Testimonies include Peace Equality, Integrity, Simplicity, Community, and Sustainability. Values of peacemaking and peacekeeping underlie all others because all others have that of God in them and must be treated as such

These organizational traits are only those related to peacemaking.

TABLE 4 Transferability of Organizational Traits Related to Peacemaking

ORGANIZATIONAL CHARACTERISTICS	LENAPE	OLD QUAKER	NAVAJO	MODERN QUAKER
Strategic Control	Transferable: flat structure **but:** not exact composition of immediate community leaders	Transferable: flat structure **but:** ultimate authority rests in unity at Yearly Meeting	Transferable: flat structure **but:** not exact composition of bureaucratic hierarchy	Transferable: flat structure **but:** ultimate authority Yearly Meeting. Smaller Meetings with authority on matters reaching beyond local affairs
Managerial	Transferable: local community members involved	Transferable: no hierarchical authority structures **but:** Monthly or Quarterly Meeting members in unity forward discussions to Yearly Meetings on matters of general concern	Transferable: local community members involved	Transferable: no hierarchical structures **but:** ultimate authority is unity at Yearly Meeting. Smaller Meetings also use discernment process and forward decisions or discussion/reports as appropriate with recommendations to Yearly Meetings on matters reaching beyond local affairs
Human	Transferable: respected community members	Transferable: ad hoc appointed members	Transferable: respected community members	Transferable: ad hoc appointed members

Operational Processes	Transferable: all processes **but:** content of ceremonies	Transferable: Appointing Committees to work with Friends in conflict or in need. Use of elders or "Weighty Friends" in conflict resolution **but:** Friends refusing recommendations might be "disowned" as reversible decision	Transferable: all processes **but:** content of ceremonies and prayers	Transferable: dependence on spiritual foundation. Processes shaped by nature of conflict, need, or "calling" **but:** Ministry and Council Committees at all levels meet; waiting on the Inner Light until unity
Operational Values	Transferable: similar interpretations of self-control, sharing, interconnectedness, honor/respect, harmony, peacefulness, truthfulness	Transferable: four basic principles—Equality, Simplicity, Peace, and Integrity **but:** Quaker principles part of revealed truths, understood through that of God; value accorded Friends who clearly live in the light	Transferable: similar interpretations of sacredness of self and others, cooperation, interconnectedness, honor/respect, harmony, peacefulness, truthfulness	Transferable: Six basic principles—Equality, Simplicity, Peace, Integrity, Community, and Sustainability **but:** Quaker principles part of revealed Truth understood through the Inner Light. Value accorded Friends who clearly live in the light

LENAPE PEACEMAKING PRE-1750

As the colonial era gained hold, Lenape land became home to not only the Lenape but also many other American Indian groups who were refugees from conflicts elsewhere along the Eastern Seaboard (Jennings 1984, 215). These groups, along with most of the Lenape, migrated to Ohio and points west as the settlers' encroachment continued. Our case study is based on the Lenape peacemaking structure, processes, and values at the beginning of this diaspora.

Structure. The <u>strategic control,</u> <u>managerial</u> and <u>human subsystems</u> for all early Lenape communities were the same. In each community, leadership (strategic control and managerial) was provided by the sachem who acted as a spokesman, and council of "old and wise men" who advised him on decisions to be made. They had mainly influence, not authority over the community (Weslager 1972, 33; Myers 1970, 36; Wallace 1961, 53; Hunter 1978, 21). The sachem ensured community order and justice so that, for example, members were avenged or restitution was made in disputes (Gimber 2000, 53). This made the sachem the <u>human subsystem</u> for providing peacemaking services. The <u>operational subsystem</u> was based in Lenape traditional processes and values.

Processes. The Lenape practiced peacemaking both internally and externally. Justice values and practices (as part of general socialization) were taught to children by the elder generation, and an individual's family mainly controlled his or her behavior (Wallace 1961, 62; Harrington 1913, 213–14). Not many descriptions of peacemaking processes exist, although extrapolations can be made from contemporary descriptions of ceremonies or events. Early writings indicate that internal reconciliation agreements involved meetings where the spiritual realm was invoked, opinions were stated, consensus was reached, restitution agreed upon, and gift-giving and feasts were used to seal internal and external reconciliation agreements (Grumet 2001, 24; Heckewelder 1876, 57–58; Weslager 1972, 58–59, 66; Dunn and Dunn 1982, 454; Merrell 1999, 167). Speechmaking, often very emotional, was a part of all ceremonies as was the participation of the spiritual realm (Heckewelder 1876, 57–58; Weslager 1972, 58–59, 66). Restitution for wrongdoing was common (Dunn and Dunn 1982, 454), although corporal punishments also occurred if they would lead to peace (Harrington 1913, 217). An example of a reparation ceremony, "Clearing the Road," taken from Merrell (1999, 50), is described earlier in the book.

The Lenape were also the peacemakers among the members of the Five and then Six Nations Confederacy. In order to carry out this role they were given the status of "women." Women were respected family and community leaders, participants in council meetings, and authorities within traditional Lenape and other Confederacy Nations (Weslager 1972, 62). Just as it was the role of the Lenape women to propose peace among community groups in conflict, it was the role of the Lenape Nation to propose peace among warring Nations. See also Wallace (1961, 59) and Brinton (1885, 109).

These descriptions suggest that peacemaking practices were facilitated by the sachem in the community and the Lenape among the Nations as follows: the problem was stated and discussed (including the expression of emotions), a resolution was negotiated, ceremonies and feasts were used, and gifts were given as restitution. The objective of the process was to restore harmony and peace within the community or between communities and Nations so that the communities or Nations could continue good relations and work effectively together. See table 1 for a comparison of Lenape justice processes with the other case studies.

Values. Peacefulness was an essential part of Lenape spirituality (Speck 1931, 21). The values of honor, harmony, peace, bravery, sharing, and respect for others were operationalized in the organizational processes. Other values included truthfulness (Wallace 1961, 56), interconnectedness of the universe (Wallace, 1961, 72), self-control (Wallace 1961, 78), courage, endurance (Wallace 1961, 78), and sharing with and generosity to all, including strangers (Weslager 1972, 51; Wallace 1961, 79; Heckewelder 1876, 78). That they almost exactly overlap with the values found in Dumont's Indigenous paradigm is no surprise (see table 2).

In sum, this means that at the time of contact with Europeans, the Old Lenape had a flat organizational structure that enabled immediate dispute resolution, had well-developed peacemaking practices that worked, and had values that supported peacemaking both internally and externally. They were the "acknowledged peacemakers" in Iroquois territory (Brinton 1885, 112).

QUAKER PEACEMAKING PRE-1750

Quakers differ from the Lenape and Navajo in that they have only existed for some 360 years, rather than for thousands of years (Brinton 2002, vii). Quaker structures and processes have been consciously developed in a relatively short period of time to express evolving beliefs, for example, their use of negotiation was taken originally from the British courts of the time as well as from the Upland Court that that had been in effective operation for many years when Quakers arrived in Pennsylvania (Soderlund 2015, 154).

Quaker systems supporting peace and restorative justice practices began in England and included not only their values but also their response to religious persecution (Smith 2006; Birkel 2004). Friends did not withdraw into secrecy as did other groups such as the Hutterites, but they did attempt to define and differentiate themselves from other Protestant groups including refuting the need for an organizational structure of priests and higher authorities and in attempts to persuade authorities that they posed no danger to the state. That differentiation included an early version of what later evolved into the Friends' Peace Testimony (Sykes 1958; Punshon 1984).

Dudiak (2020, n.p.) describes the early Quaker approach as one in which "the authority of the sword was only legitimate for the State to use in a broken world." This was not peacemaking as it is used today, but it was a reaction to the widespread acceptance of violence among non-Quaker citizens. In Penn's government, peace was the means by which Penn and other Quakers guarded against the violence of their times. Kelsey (1917, 61) gives a typical example of external use of peaceful means when he describes the attempts of Rhode Island Quakers to end King Philip's War in 1675 and 1676.

> John Easton, the Quaker's Deputy Governor, with four others went unarmed among the sullen savages of King Philip's camp, and proposed to the Indians that all differences between them and the whites be settled by arbitration. King Philip recited the grievances of the Indians, and the injustices of the whites, and doubted the willingness of the other New England colonies to settle the things in dispute fairly, as proposed by Easton and his companions. The Rhode Islanders pleaded all day for arbitration and although they and the Indians "sat veri friendly together" the peaceful mission was unsuccessful. (Kelsey 1917, 61)

What became Quaker peacemaking was rooted in developing Quaker spiritual values and practices.

Structures. The formal organization of Friends occurred during the persecutions that continued from about 1650 and ended in about 1689. The Glorious (i.e., Bloodless) Revolution saw Catholic James II go into exile and Protestants William III and Mary II (James II's daughter) become Britain's monarchs. The end of most Quaker abuse came with their Toleration Act (1689), enacted shortly after ascending the throne (Brock 1971; Bauman 1971).

In 1671, Quakers returned to the process of settling local structures. In 1672, they held the first Yearly Meeting (Punshon 1984, 90). This was the beginning of what might be termed their *strategic control subsystem*. Although control was in the hands of all members, decisions tended to be strongly influenced by a few dominant, weighty or "esteemed" Friends. At this time, structures were institutionalized by George Fox and Margaret Fell, responding to an urgent need for guidelines for new "seekers" joining the "Friends of Truth" with incomplete understanding of its beliefs and procedures. The structures also incorporated care and support of imprisoned and "travelling" Friends (Friends travelling in the Ministry) (Vipont 1977, 60; Punshon 1984, 60, 77).

As in England, structures in North America began with the local Meetings for Worship, making decisions based on group discernment, that is, decision-making (Sykes 1958; Birkel 2004). These were often held in Friends' homes and gradually developed to incorporate Monthly and Quarterly Meetings (groups of Meetings for Worship based on geographical location and meeting monthly and four times a year respectively). Yearly Meetings, such as those in Philadelphia and Burlington, grew out of Meetings for Worship (Punshon 1984) and responded to the much larger geographical areas that challenged the ability of Friends to meet often.

The strategic control subsystem therefore comprised the Yearly Meetings, located in London, England and in American cities and provinces such as Philadelphia, Burlington, New Jersey, Rhode Island, and other locations as settlement spread and more settler colonists joined the Friends. The Yearly Meeting, an organized body, made key decisions about organizational goals and directions, ensuring the legitimacy and survival of the organization. A central difference from most organization structures is that Yearly Meetings were and still are flat structures; they are a culmination of decision-making (discernment) in smaller groups that enable Friends to exercise control as a collective (Gimber 2000, 170).

The managerial subsystem was and is completely integrated within a system of Meetings based on frequency of Meeting and location. What has changed dramatically over time are the means of communication. When everything is done by either travelling to a Meeting or by letter, the decision-making process is very slow, sometimes taking years. In the early days of Friends, when organizational structures each had relatively small membership numbers, unresolved local issues were likely to go to Yearly Meeting (Jones 1966). As the Society's membership grew, Quarterly Meetings and then Half Yearly Meetings were added to the organizational structure. Decisions recorded in the minutes there would be passed on to Yearly Meeting, in contrast to the more common, top-down structures used in Western societies.

The human subsystem comprised Friends' community members, some of whom were chosen as esteemed or weighty Friends to settle internal disputes in committees. While they neither led nor controlled Meetings, their influence could be considerable (London Yearly Meeting 1737), and they would recommend a negotiation process that served as the operational subsystem of peacemaking. In all Meetings for Worship—Weekly, Monthly, etc.—elders were responsible for the spiritual life of the Meeting and would remind those who violated expectations, for example, of how ministry should proceed. Overseers took care of all nonspiritual concerns in the life of the Meeting. Jones (1966, 151) comments that, "The work of oversight was not confined to moral and spiritual matters. It touched the whole of life." In this sense peacemaking was an integral part of all Quaker practice. Conflict within Meetings at any level was addressed using a focus on maintaining or reestablishing peace or harmony within the community.

Outside the Quaker Meetings, Penn also incorporated the future principles of peacemaking in his government. Instead of the usually harsh physical punishments required by English law, Pennsylvania law focused on imprisonment and restitution of varying degrees, depending on the seriousness of the offense and if it was a repeat offense (Beckman 1976). Peacemakers, established in Chester and Sussex counties in 1683, used a system of arbitration similar to one from England (Colonial Society of Pennsylvania 1910, 25–28; Futhey and Cope 1881, 25; Loyd 1910, 48; Turner 1909, 97, 102, 116). As Quakers lost political power, Pennsylvania laws became more retributive (Barnes 1922, 7, 13), and "regular" arbitration replaced peacemaking (Loyd 1910, 15–16, 49). Until 1692, the colonial governor and Executive Council oversaw peacemakers, and thereby comprised both the strategic control and managerial subsystems (Beckman 1976, 27), with the human and operational subsystems being the appointed peacemakers and the peacemaking process.

Processes. Details are missing for early Friends' practices since, as Birkel (2004) points out, much of early Quaker social history is more oral than written. The *Books of Discipline* by the Philadelphia Yearly Meeting record the use of arbitration by Quakers in 1704 and include the venting of feelings and seeking agreement, just as the practices of the old Lenape did. If a dispute remained unresolved, the disputing Friends would eventually be advised to use the colonial system by, for example, going to a lawyer (London Yearly Meeting 1737). Outside of Quaker Meetings three members from each Pennsylvania government "precinct" or district with peacemakers settled disputes voluntarily submitted by community members (Colonial Society of Pennsylvania 1910, 34; Futhey and Cope 1881, 25; Loyd 1910, 48).

Values. Quakers' pacifist and egalitarian principles, and their focus on integrity and simplicity, led to peacemaking both in their own governance and in interactions with American Indians from early in their settlements. Wealth distribution was a concern; Pennsylvania's extreme inequality in the eighteenth century was antithetical to their values of justice and peace (Moulton 1971, 238). Friends believed in practicing equality, respecting "that of God in others," or speaking to that of God in others, a reference to their belief in equality and respect. They continued to avoid complexity as found in everything from explanations to organizations (Punshon 1984). Friends used these beliefs in talking with American Indians and non-Quaker settlers and in their conflicts with government officials.

The discussion of values shows considerable overlap with the Indigenous and Old Lenape values laid out in table 2 in that Old Quakers embraced values of honesty, kindness, sharing, humility, and strength (e.g., Punshon 1984, 127). As stated earlier, Friends' emphasis on the Peace Testimony was initially a testimony against war, more than a valuing of peace for itself. In this they differed from the Indigenous paradigm, where warfare and capital punishment might be accepted as necessary.

NAVAJO NATION PEACEMAKING TODAY

Members of the Navajo Nation have practiced mediation of disputes from time immemorial, and in 1982 this traditional practice was modified and added to the Navajo Nation court system as an alternative to formal court proceedings. Navajo peacemaking (*hózhóji naat'aah*) is not mediation, and it is not exactly alternative dispute resolution. It has been called "reparative justice" and "participatory justice" (Zion 1999). See Nielsen and Zion (2005) for more detailed descriptions of its history and operations.

Structure. The Peacemaking Program is one of five divisions of the Navajo Nation court system. The judicial branch of the Navajo Nation, with its headquarters in Window Rock, provides strategic control for the program. The peacemaker coordinator, also located in Window Rock, provides managerial oversight in that he or she provides training opportunities and information dissemination to the peacemakers. In terms of day-to-day operations, the peacemakers (*naat'aanii*) have no direct supervision. There are a varying number of peacemakers (the <u>human subsystem</u>) located in the 110 chapters (decentralized districts) of the Navajo Nation. Disputants request peacemaker assistance through court-employed peacemaker liaisons to help them arrive at a harmonious settlement of a dispute. The disputants are usually referred to peacemaking by the Navajo courts. The peacemakers are respected members of the community who are chosen by their communities because they have "demonstrated character, wisdom and the ability to make good plans for community action" (Austin 1993, 10). They usually have some relationship with the disputants so that they are not neutral mediators. Disputes may be based in land use, grazing rights, and domestic conflict, including child custody and family violence. Criminal offenses up to and including sexual assault and wrongful death have also been dealt with, although most cases are civil disputes. The majority of disputants are adult members of the Navajo Nation, although a juvenile project was successfully run on grant funding for three years (Meyer 2005). Diné Family Group Conferencing became a service of the program in 2011 (Navajo Nation n.d.-a). Life Value Engagements, a kind of talking circle, can help prepare participants for peacemaking (Navajo Nation n.d.-c), and peacemaking was introduced as a part of the Diné K–12 school curriculum soon after.

Processes. The process is guided by the naat'aanii who plays an active part ensuring that all participants speak, underlying issues are uncovered, a plan to resolve the issue is developed, consensus is reached, and the participants understand the issues as they relate to the spiritual world and the community. The purpose of the Peacemaking Program is to restore harmony to the participants and thereby to the community. According to James W. Zion (2005), one of the developers of the modern-day Peacemaking Program, peacemaking occurs in four steps: ceremony, talking it out, teaching, and reconciliation. The naat'aanii establishes the ceremonial context of peacemaking by using prayers that bring supernatural beings into the process (Bluehouse and Zion 1993). During the "talking it out" step, all participants express their feelings and opinions. Venting controlled by the naat'aanii also happens at this stage. Zion (2005, 92) describes this as "an interactive discussion of the problem and what the group feels about how it should be resolved." During the "teaching" step, the naat'aanii builds a shared perception of the issue and a resolution (Zion 2005). He or she uses spiritual teachings to define the problem. The teachings are most often derived from the Navajo creation and journey narratives, but, depending on the spiritual beliefs of the peacemaker and the participants, alternatively may be derived from Christian teachings or those of the Native American Church. The final "reconciliation" stage builds a consensus about a plan to reconcile the parties and establishes agreement for follow-up (Zion 2005). A plan is drawn up and filed with the court. The program has been undergoing institutionalization in the last decade or so, and according to the Navajo Nation Judicial Branch in their "Institutional History of *Hózhóji Naat'aah*" (n.d.-b, n.p.), "Over time, it has become clear that the independence of the peacemakers needs to be reinforced, the goal of peacemaking clarified, and the traditional components of *hózhóji naat'aah* as a distinct and separate method need to be restored for the traditional method's effective and proper use."

Values. In peacemaking there is little or no coercion, and there are no "sides." No one is labeled the offender or the victim, the plaintiff, or the defendant. As Yazzie (1993, 412) writes, "the ultimate goal of the peacemaker process is to restore the minds, physical being, spirits, and emotional well-being of all people involved." The process is based on values of interconnectedness and wholeness and builds on consensus and respect for all living things as embodied within the Navajo clan system known as *k'e* (solidarity). The discussion above refers directly to or implies Dumont's Indigenous values as laid out in table 2: the desire for harmony and well-being in interpersonal relationships, cooperation, the respect for elders, the recognition of self and others as sacred, respecting the integrity of oneself and others, and having the courage to accomplish peace, truthfulness, and integrity in all relations.

In sum, Navajo peacemaking has the most formal structure of the four groups, uses practices generally similar to the Old Lenape, and like the Old Quaker peacemakers, must operate within a dominant justice system. Its values overlap with those of Dumont's Indigenous paradigm, the Old Lenape, and to a great extent, the Old Quakers.

QUAKER PEACEMAKING TODAY

As with the early Quakers, present-day Quakers see no need for priests or other intermediaries, but rather, regard all of life as sacramental (Franklin 2006). No one time or activity is regarded as more sacred than others. The overarching responsibility of all members is to contribute to the "peaceable kingdom." In this sense they differ from American Indian cultures. Their beliefs have led them to use peacemaking in their own Meetings but also to work for social justice and peace beyond Quaker communities. They understand peace as fundamental to healthy "right" relations, strong communities, and all of the characteristics of human interaction found desirable in many cultures. Included in this under-standing is their belief that "peace is the presence of justice and that peace and justice are indivisible" (Franklin 2006, 45). Where the opposite—dictatorship, military control, and competitive fighting of some kind—exists there can be no peace. As Friends say, you cannot fight for peace since inherently that cre-ates conflict. Thus, their organizational structure and daily interactions strive to enhance peace.

Canadian Friends have one unified Yearly Meeting. Their united stand on the essential relation of peace and social justice leads them to vocally disagree with practices that use physical and/or emotional/intellectual violence. When finding it necessary to, as they say, "speak truth to power," they model that belief through their use of a nonviolent approach, whether in one-to-one meetings, correspondence, or through demonstrations, including silent witnessing (see www.quakerservice.ca for recent activities).

American Friends' organizations on the other hand, still reflect to a great extent the schisms of the nineteenth century. Structures and practices vary somewhat among, for example, liberal, orthodox, and conservative Friends, and values may be prioritized differently. There are now only two organizations that reflect and express major trends in American Quaker thought and practice, Friends United Meeting and Friends General Conference.

Canadian and American "liberal" Quakers follow much the same structures, processes, and values as in the past, although some definitions and expressions have enlarged and changed a little since Quakers first established themselves in America, specifically in Pennsylvania. This discussion of modern Quaker peacemaking will focus mainly on Canadian Friends but will also refer to some American Quaker characteristics.

Structures. In the USA, the structure of the Society of Friends ranges from the national to the local level. There is a strategic control system consisting largely of national organizations. These may be part of the managerial control system that operates both nationally and regionally, sometimes with a human subsys-tem that is in some cases, paid staff and others run by volunteer staff. Many are Yearly Meetings. These organizations exist to advise and inform Friends, and to support specific sections of the American population who are not necessarily Friends, such as Indigenous groups. The closest to an operational subsystem would be the work of Half Yearly, Quarterly, and Monthly Meetings, reaching out to support and inform Friends on national or local issues. Many have news-letters or journals online and sometimes also in print.

In Canada, managerial subsystems include some very small Meetings and many Monthly Meetings in larger population centers. There are Quarterly Meetings in the more populous areas of eastern Canada, but in western Canada, Friends look to Half Yearly Meetings for their next step in discernment. Discernment focuses on a mutually satisfactory resolution that expresses the spiritual will of the Meeting, not on winning acceptance for one's own viewpoint. Yearly Meeting is a national event that also holds memberships in and communicates with Friends General Conference and Friends United Meeting. It also sends a representative to meetings of Friends World Committee for Consultation. These connections can be central to the peacemaking process (Punshon 1984), and Yearly Meeting itself is the strategic control system for Canadian Quakers. Recording the process are clerks of each Meeting or committee and recording clerks (part of the human subsystem). These are volunteer positions. All decisions on any topic under discussion are based on the collective discernment of gathered Friends in a designated Meeting (Monthly, Quarterly, or Yearly) affected by that decision. Only in this sense has Yearly Meeting ever been the ultimate authority. Authority is not vested in any individual status or social position (see for example "Organization and Procedure" sections in Yearly Meeting websites, and for a concise account of historical developments, see Brinton [1950; 2002]). This organizational structure supports Quaker peacemaking and energizes peacemaking activities. All contributions carry equal value and are often all built into the final decision. As well, Quakers take their decision-making processes with them into other peace organizations with which they work (Brinton 2002).

The managerial subsystem of Yearly Meeting in Canada includes the Canadian Friends Service Committee (CFSC), technically a Yearly Meeting Committee, that has the necessary independence to continue its work outside of Yearly Meetings (CFSC n.d.). As funds allow, it may have full or part-time paid staff (human subsystem). CFSC includes the Quakers Fostering Justice (QFJ) Committee, the Indigenous Issues Committee, and the Peace Committee. While Quakers have no leaders, there sometimes are what one might term "functional leaders." These are Friends whose service in one arena has been so long and so noteworthy that press representatives, other Quakers, and workers in the field will turn to them for information and advice, but they are still not regarded or used as leaders. CFS committees tend to furnish many of these functional leaders such as the clerks of the Peace Committee, and the committee working with Indigenous Peoples, as well as the clerk of CFSC itself.

In summary, internal structures at the local level are mostly the same in Canada and the USA. In his booklet on Quaker practice, Brinton (1952) states the Meeting (most often the Monthly Meeting that meets weekly for worship) is the "basic unit" of the Religious Society of Friends. The strategic control subsystem is operated through the "will of the Meeting" and not through any management positions or individuals. The managerial subsystem can be seen in the many committees (more among American than Canadian Friends) that carry on the work of Friends in specific areas; the human subsystem consists mainly of volunteer Friends who are willing to serve on local, regional or Yearly Meeting committees with a few paid staff. Volunteers may have their travel expenses paid but they receive no personal recompense; the operational subsystem operates through local and regional Meetings whose members do the actual work involved.

Processes. Peacemaking is supported by Friends' organizational structures and methods of making decisions. Friends begin all Meetings as they do for Meeting for Worship. Business Meetings are known as "Meeting for Worship for Business" and begin with a period of silence. Silence follows between each speaker and each round of speaking. The clerk gradually gathers the essence of what is said into "a minute" in consultation with the recording clerk, who will document and read what they have. Friends may be satisfied at this point or more often will modify and edit the minute before silence indicates that there is general agreement. The focus is on discernment. Discipline, including restraint, is needed and encouraged by elders.

The use of silence is perhaps the closest Quakers come to a formal ritual although they have many informal rituals such as the shaking of hands to end a period of silence and refreshments after Meetings. Silence is in and of itself a ritual. It is the basis of every Meeting of a Quaker group; silence begins, occurs between spoken contributions, and ends Meetings of all kinds. Brinton (1950, 15) comments that the silent Meeting for Worship is "central and fundamental in Quaker practice. Out of it, all other religious and social exercise is derived."

Members continue to use an arbitration and mediation approach to the resolution of conflict in their own Meetings, although the formal structures laid out by early Quakers in their *Book(s) of Discipline* published by Yearly Meetings, are no longer included in the successor to the *Discipline* (in Canada titled *Faith and Practice*) published in local versions by different Yearly Meetings. Peacemaking remains an essential part of this process. Peacemaking is embedded in the relationships and practices of Meetings at all levels, i.e., the organizational and human subsystems are not clearly segregated, and the maintenance of harmonious relations is behind every action within local Meetings and regional or Yearly Meetings.

Quakers practice peacemaking in all types of community work, including acting as allies with Indigenous Peoples. In regard to both criminal offenses and to conflict within Meetings, both "elders" and weighty Friends and members of Ministry and Council (this may overlap) act in a similar role to the Navajo peacemakers with the exception that they are unlikely to have any kinship with disputants. Outside of Quaker structures, many Friends are involved in the justice system, where their emphasis on peacemaking leads to the promotion of restorative approaches to justice. Overrepresentation of Indigenous Peoples in prisons has often led Friends into working with Indigenous elders. Old and Modern Friends' involvement in restorative justice flows naturally from these beliefs. It is clearly based on their commitment to and value for spiritual equality and peaceful relations.

Values. The teaching of Quaker values is carried out by example, through ministry in Meeting for Worship, and in study groups ranging from studies of Quaker history to issue-based study groups such as environmental or peace concerns (Smith 2006). Many Meetings have their own library and encourage its use.

As with the Old Quakers, Modern Quaker core values are expressed in the foundational belief the "Inner Light," on which their Testimonies or principles, especially peacemaking, are built. Expressed differently over the years, the belief remains an underpinning of the Society. It means that not only are individuals responsible for living in the Light, but also that all people are treated with respect as spiritually equal, as having "that of God Within," while recognizing that in the larger society statuses based on wealth, occupational position, or other factors perpetuate discrimination. Friends' peacemaking incorporates a strong rebuttal of such statuses, regarding inequality as a major contributor to conflict. This thinking is sometimes referred to as part of right relations, which applies to human relations but also to relationships with the environment and with all of life. It refers to being in harmony, or creating balance in relationships, similar to Indigenous values, and also basic to restorative justice.

Respectful treatment acknowledges and respects the beliefs of others. It cannot be violent and must involve listening and negotiating to resolve conflict. The Inner Light commands respect but also peacemaking and peacekeeping, i.e., keeping all life-forms as safe from harm as possible.

In summary, liberal Modern Quakers have a completely flat structure at every level, as did the Old Quakers. Their processes for reaching agreement are basically the same as the Old Quakers and have some overlap with Old Lenape and Modern Navajo processes in that full and willing agreement by all is needed for the process to conclude. Peacemaking values among both Old Quakers and Modern Quakers have the same core Truth as their predecessors although it may be expressed differently at times. Basically, its focus is on reintegration. This overlaps with the values of the Old Lenape and Modern Navajo. Both these groups recognize that not all individuals are capable of such reintegration.

DISCUSSION AND CONCLUSIONS

As shown in our comparisons, the Old Lenape, Old Quakers, Modern Navajo, and Modern Quakers share similar organizational traits in several key areas: the structure comprising the managerial subsystem, the human subsystem, and the operational subsystem, consisting specifically of practices and values (as summarized in table 3). Each trait revealed areas of similarity that could be used to argue for the possible transferability of peacemaking (see table 4).

STRUCTURE

Four patterns of similarity were found that suggested transferability:

1. The local collective played an important part in the management of all the groups. Managerial subsystems among both Old and Modern Quakers were volunteer-driven and used smaller groups (committees) each of which might be focused on one issue including conflict resolution or peacemaking. The Old Lenape and Modern Navajo peacemaking were managed by the peacemakers themselves, although in the Lenape case, the peacemaker was also the community's spokesman.
2. Strategic control was widely shared among members of three of the groups (Old Lenape, Old Quaker, and Modern Quaker). Both the Old and Modern Quaker societies had very "flat" organizational structures in which, even where there were recognized and respected statuses, there was also equality of rights to participate in decision-making, with no inequality of representation or power. Supervision is not used. The Old Lenape sachem and

council shared decision-making with community members and provided supervision. The Modern Navajo were the most unusual in that the peacemakers have to operate within an imposed bureaucratic hierarchy; however, in comparison to Euro-based justice organizations, this is also a relatively flat structure. Therefore, a flat structure is likely a transferable structure for peacemaking but the exact form the flat structure took with our groups varied too much for those individual forms to be defined as transferable.

3. The human subsystem in all cases was made up of individuals respected in the community, with deep knowledge of spiritual teachings, and who were not neutral (that is unconcerned) participants. Among the Old and Modern Quakers, the human subsystem for peacemaking was volunteer operated. Among the Old Lenape, the sachem provided peacemaking services. Even though the Modern Navajo have the most hierarchical structure, the human subsystem operated at the local level.

4. It is mainly in the operational subsystem, that is, in the processes and values, that startling similarities occurred, and where the greatest argument for universality can be made.

PROCESSES

Here we found four patterns that suggested transferability:

1. In all four cases, respected and known members of the community acted to facilitate the peacemaking. It is really not surprising that Penn should use words analogous to Friendly practices when he described the Lenape decision process as having powerful kings (sachems) "and yet how they move by the breath of their people" (Myers 1970, 36; Wallace 1961, 53). Leadership was by influence, just as esteemed or weighty Friends led by example. Clerks and recording clerks in Friends Meetings, like the Lenape sachems and Navajo peacemakers, have limited authority and no special privileges.

2. While Old Quakers appointed Friends for each instance of conflict, there were, if only for a short period, Friends called "peacemakers." This contrasts somewhat with the community-recognized peacemakers of the Old Lenape and Modern Navajo. In the old Philadelphia court system, peacemakers had the formal role of mediating and negotiating and if necessary, arbitrating outcomes. After that role was phased out, Friends turned to local commit-

tees to resolve conflict. A difference is that while Old Quaker families might have been involved as victims or offenders, family or clan networks were not used as the basis for appointment to the negotiating process as in Modern Navajo peacemaking. Rather, the local Meeting stepped into this role. This practice continues in present-day Quaker Meetings. Another difference is that Old and Modern Quakers preferred simplicity over formal ritual and ceremony, unlike the Old Lenape and Modern Navajo. On the other hand, it could also be argued that while Quakers do have some formal rituals, such as the use of silence, and the building of a minute, they have many informal rituals such as tea and coffee after Meeting for Worship, which is where community building is strengthened.

3. The underlying peacemaking practices of Old and Modern Quakers were the same as those of the Old Lenape and Modern Navajo: counseling, talking out the issues, encouraging those interested to have their say, including expression of emotion, teaching using spiritual values, and establishing reconciliation. Reparations varied depending on the culture in three groups, Old Lenape, Old Quakers, and Modern Navajo. Unlike the Old Lenape and Modern Navajo peacemaking practices, Old Quakers and Modern Quakers did and do sometimes limit the length of a verbal contribution in Meeting for Worship or during a business Meeting. This is generally done gently and informally by an elder. Like the Old Lenape, Old and Modern Quakers have practiced and do practice peacemaking internally and externally.

VALUES

We found four patterns that suggested that these values were transferable:

1. The values of the Old Lenape and Modern Navajo fell firmly within Dumont's Indigenous paradigm, which is no surprise. What is surprising is the strong overlap between these values and the values of the Old and Modern Quakers. The exact content of the meaning of the values varied with each group because of their history and experiences, but the same values existed and had somewhat similar meanings.

2. Values of equality, respect, and social justice were taught by all four groups. Old Quakers held to four main principles, based on their belief that all humans had an Inner Light. Those four principles remain in Modern

Quaker values but with some enlarging of interpretation and addition of
two more principles, with peace being not only central but also the value for
which Quakers are generally known to the wider public. The values of the
Old Lenape and Modern Navajo focused more on the survival of the collective but also emphasized peacefulness (harmony), equality, and integrity.

3. In all four groups respect for others was embedded in a spiritual context.

4. The values most relevant to peacemaking shared by all four groups seemed
   to be peacefulness, respect, and the personal integrity to follow through. This
   similarity may be a strong clue as to why peacemaking developed independently among the Old Lenape, Old Quakers, and Modern Navajo. If, as
   Yazzie (1993, 412) argues, "The ultimate goal of the peacemaker process is
   to restore the minds, physical being, spirits, and emotional well-being of all
   people involved," one cannot escape the similarities between Old Lenape,
   Modern Navajo, and Old and Modern Quaker peacemaking as they continue
   to express these very principles in their spiritual and temporal lives.

Based on this analysis, transferability is possible for groups with flat,
community-based structures; shared decision-making at the local level; values shared by all participants (respect, peace, and integrity especially); and
respected community members who are willing to take on the role of peacemaker. If the group does not already have practices that could be modified to
become peacemaking, group members should be willing to adopt the practices
of counseling, talking it out among all interested parties, teaching based in spiritual values, and reconciliation.

What is nontransferable are the details, for example, the exact positions within
the strategic control subsystem, and some of the content of the practices, such as
the use of ceremony, prayer, and extended speaking among the Old Lenape, Modern Navajo, and Old Quaker versus more limited time by means of a desire that
speech be organized and clearly relevant among Modern Quakers (see table 4).
Three groups (Old Quakers, Modern Navajo, and Modern Quakers) had no control over the larger social structures within which they historically or now exist,
requiring them to insert their practices into an existing framework predicated on
hierarchy rather than a flat organization, and on punishment more than reintegration. Although they had to operate within two justice systems, individuals had the
choice of peacemaking. This means that each group adapted to the imposition of
an outside system but kept essential characteristics of their practices—and kept
more or less the same ones despite their difference in time and place.

Peacemaking has been in operation for millennia in Indigenous societies. Indigenous peacemaking now exists parallel to Euro-based justice systems in many countries such as Canada, the USA, and New Zealand, and seems to be well used, although it is not always the system of choice, for example, among the Navajo. Restorative justice practices in general are gaining in popularity, but their full potential has not yet been reached (Hass-Wisecup and Saxon 2018). Scholars in the field of restorative justice suggest that these programs have the potential to be substitutes for ineffective or issue-ridden parts of the Euro-based criminal justice system if the conditions are right, thereby enhancing the human rights of individuals involved. Our first conclusion, based on these four case studies, is that peacemaking has the potential to be used by any group—and not necessarily a culturally or spiritually based group—with the appropriate structure and values and that already has, or is willing to learn, the basic justice practices that can be modified to become peacemaking.

Second, because of the similarities in the structures, processes, and values among the four groups, it gives us hope that peacemaking may be a potential tool in achieving some degree of amelioration between Indigenous Peoples and settler colonist descendants. Retributive justice, that is, the regular criminal justice system in colonial societies, is not set up to achieve reconciliation. It is a system with winners and losers, as Yazzie (1993) describes it, that does little to prevent further disputes or promote the healing of the participants. Restorative justice in general has been successful at the institutional level in dealing with all kinds of harms, including violence. See for example, Hass-Wisecup and Saxon (2018) and Council of Europe (2018). Our research suggests that peacemaking operated at the local community level is most likely to be successful in achieving social justice and that the communities should have the shared characteristics described above. In countries where Indigenous Peoples have suffered the ravages of colonialism, peacemaking has and could occur on the national level as well, as attempted in Canada with the Truth and Reconciliation Commission, but it is at the community level that it perhaps could be most effectively operationalized. Quakers and Indigenous Peoples, based on past experiences, have the motivation, skills, and knowledge about how to do this and facilitate such meetings and discussions as they have often done in the past. In other words, peacemaking and Quakers could indeed contribute to the greater social justice for Indigenous Peoples that Indigenous Peoples have been working diligently toward.

7

A FEELING OF RIGHTNESS

Quaker/Indigenous Relations, Past, Present, and Future

I N THIS final chapter, we summarize the harms committed against Indigenous Peoples, particularly the Lenape during the early colonial era and more
recently, focusing on the intentions and actions of the Society of Friends.
The intention of this chapter is to provide evidence that Quakers made serious mistakes in colonial times, learned from these mistakes, and are now allies
of many American Indian Nations. The first section summarizes our analysis
of past Quaker response to colonial events, Indian responses to Quaker colonial actions, Quaker colonial thinking, Quaker rethinking about right relations
with Indigenous Peoples, and Quaker/Indigenous right relations encompassing
social justice. We then briefly look at the current relationships between Quakers
and Indigenous Peoples in Canada and the USA. We conclude that Indigenous
Peoples and Quakers could be effective allies in ameliorating some of the harms
caused by colonialism and in preventing future harms, if Indigenous Peoples so
determine.

AN OVERVIEW OF PAST QUAKER RESPONSES
TO COLONIALISM

This book discusses major events affecting Quaker and Indigenous relations over
a period of some four hundred years, focusing on specific events to illustrate our

thinking. We discuss events in Quaker-Indigenous relations from the founding of Pennsylvania to nineteenth-century Quakers supervising boarding schools under Ulysses Grant's administration, and in this chapter, we look at today.

The roots of Quaker alienation from Indigenous Peoples begin in Penn's relations with the British government and its antagonism to his Quakerism. Penn's plan for a Holy Experiment for Pennsylvania governance supported peaceful relations with the Lenape and a prosperous society for about seventy years, but it was unable to respond adequately to outside pressures, such as non-Quaker settler colonists' violence. Although it was a remarkably democratic form of government, albeit sufficiently under the domination of the proprietors and of the British monarchy that it has been called "feudal" by some writers (e.g., Jennings 1984), it never achieved a full-fledged "rule by the people for the people." Nor did it express true equality of citizens, including a recognition of Lenape sovereignty. Penn limited equality further by insisting official leaders must be Christian, even though he made clear that Pennsylvania offered religious tolerance.

The Quaker way is to trust the Inner Light in everyone (Worrall 1980, 5), but that did not always bring out the best in early settler colonists to Pennsylvania, many of whom were known for their greed, theft of lands, and violently negative attitudes and actions toward the Indigenous Peoples they encountered (Pencak and Richter 2004). This undermined Penn's relations with the Lenape, becoming a contributing factor in the failure of his Holy Experiment, and the first of many harms to Indigenous Peoples that followed Quaker settlement.

While Penn built respect for and peaceful relations with the Lenape in words and promises, he was unable to put them into practice effectively. Pennsylvania laws incorporated Indian rights to fair trade and justice in the courts, but violations of those rights were increasingly frequent as settler colonists perceived that they could do so without consequences. As well, they cheated Penn himself, increasing his financial problems through their nonpayment of quitrents. Many settlers on the borders of Pennsylvania did not even pay for the land they occupied (Soderlund 1983). It was apparently too easy to take advantage of Penn and his government. At the same time, Penn's refusal to establish a militia caused even more contention between settler colonists (including squatters) and government.

The consequences of all these acts, as well as his extravagant living costs, added considerably to his debts (Soderlund 1983) and contributed to his loss of control over settler colonists and to serious rifts in the government itself as well as in government relations with the Lenape. It also contributed to the hostility of a succession of British monarchs to whom the province owed allegiance. William Penn may have had the advantage of a good education, and of coming from a relatively high-status family with connections to the British court, but he had also adopted a religious perspective that was not just contrary to current monarchical thought, but which appeared to threaten the very stability of the British establishment. He was never trusted by them, culminating with a costly charge of treason (fortunately not upheld) by William III (Soderlund 2015, 161).

Also, partly as a consequence of his troubles, Penn spent only four years over two visits in Pennsylvania, returning to England in 1701. He died there in 1718 after a lengthy illness, during which his widow Hannah Penn took over as governor. It is interesting to note that Hannah's skills as governor received presidential recognition in 1984 (Women History n.d.). The years of her governing, from 1710 to 1726 when she died, were exceptionally peaceful and prosperous for Pennsylvania (Women History 2008), although William Penn's promise of regular contacts with the Lenape diminished and eventually disappeared, undermining friendship with them at a time when this prosperity was threatened by its basis in stolen or fraudulently obtained Lenape lands. The worst example of land theft came in 1737, contributing to the complete breakdown of Quaker-Lenape relations and to Lenape participation in the French and Indian War (Treese 1992). The role of the proprietors, especially John and Thomas Penn, in the infamous Walking Purchase, plus many other instances of settler colonist disrespect, theft, and overt violence led the Lenape to a point where, justifiably, they had had enough.

At this point the Quaker-controlled government could no longer evade the practical realities of its Peace Testimony, but the only examples they could turn to were colonies, such as Rhode Island, that had set up a militia at their founding. Rhode Island also incorporated a right of conscientious objection, allowing for refusals to serve in the militia, but by embedding that militia in the government, the issue of militia costs did not arise. The Pennsylvania government was torn apart by arguments over having, and paying for, a militia, which Penn had refused to establish. There were no alternatives in place since the government had no funds to set one up. The Council and the Assembly had to reach agreement on what to do, with no time, no means, and no guidelines to do so. The raids by the Lenape and other Indian tribes on Pennsylvania's boundaries exacerbated tensions between settler colonists, squatters, the Assembly, Council, and Governor Thomas Penn.

The Philadelphia Yearly Meeting reacted to the dilemma facing Friends who remained in the Assembly by urging that all Friends quit political activity, as it was now antithetical to the Peace Testimony (Worrall 1980, 81), leaving the decision as to what action to take to the remaining members of the Pennsylvania Assembly and Council. Friends individually were divided on how to express the Peace Testimony when faced with violence and war. In seventeenth-century England they had refused to fight for either side of government, but now they *were* the government. The alternative extremes available to them in response were exemplified by some Friends who accepted the need for violence in defense and by others who refused to support war and its needs in any way. Individuals responded to this situation in a variety of ways. Some quit politics altogether, some quit the government, and others stayed on, believing they could continue to influence decisions toward peace. As a collective Quakers now did not have the political support or power to practice peacemaking with Indigenous Peoples.

A few wealthy Friends thought they might have an answer but could not persuade the government to try it. They set up the Friendly Association for Reclaiming and Preserving Peace with the Indians by Pacific Measures, immediately encountering much resistance from the Pennsylvania government and military leaders (Harper 2016, 5). Their actions were an overt attempt to go beyond a refusal to "win" by any means available (Harper 2016). The Friendly Association fought hard to have Lenape negotiators fairly treated but failed in their attempts (Harper 2016). They also took into consideration the need to make amends—reconciliation as one step toward social justice through peacemaking. This was innovative for colonial thinking but might have appeared familiar, even expected, behavior by the Lenape. A relevant comment is that Pemberton, a founding member of the Friendly Association, "echoed William Penn's intention for the colony in the 1680s" (Harper 2016, 12).

Given the short-lived Peacemakers set up by Penn, and the continuing tendency to use negotiation by Quakers to resolve conflicts, it is reasonable to assume that had the Friendly Association been listened to by all Quakers in (and outside of) government, reconciliation could have become a positive means to address present and future conflicts and harms, including a return of right relations with the Lenape. Instead, it was another opportunity lost to future America.

At this point Penn's government would be scarcely recognizable to Penn himself. The seeds of its failure were present from the beginning in Penn's need for, and encouragement of, settler colonists including many non-pacifists, his inability to put effective legal controls in place, and Penn's failure to fully appreciate Lenape culture. Added to this, the attempts at control by the British Crown and the governing practices of his sons and their supporting Council members made a continuation of the Holy Experiment questionable. Without the skills of Hannah Penn, it quickly fell apart. Its eventual death can be attributed to the 1756 French and Indian War (Punshon 1984, 117–18). Pontiac's Rebellion was at least in part a consequence of failure by the British and their allies to honor the treaties that were made. The Paxton Boys' massacre of the Conestoga Indians was influenced in part by this Rebellion (Merrell 1999; Silver 2008; Kenny 2009; Brubaker 2010).

Blame was widely placed. Governor John Penn, and in fact the Penn family in Pennsylvania, were no longer Quakers, and few Quakers remained in government. The Paxton Boys and their supporters, particularly members of Presbyterian churches, blamed Quaker government and their pacifism. Presbyterian ministers preached sermons about the evils of Quaker values (Fisher 1919). For Quakers, both war and the Conestoga massacres once again challenged their Testimonies and responses to violent events, continuing the debate among Friends concerning the legitimacy of using violence for defense and the practicality of total pacifism.

They were challenged again in the American Revolutionary War of 1775, which saw an end to the Penn family oligarchy. During this event Quakers were further challenged by the sympathy many felt toward the Revolutionaries, their traditional loyalty to the British government, and their pacifism, resulting in a wide range of individualized responses. Quakers continued to hold ambiguous positions when responding to violence but discovered that their motives in assisting citizens hurt by the war brought them more positive attention by non-Quaker citizens and by government members. The work of supporting civilians during the war began to be part of Meeting for Sufferings, a committee set up in many Yearly Meetings to respond to the needs of Friends suffering for their Faith and later, any Friends in need. Individually initiated charitable acts gave way to Meeting-sponsored benevolence that was used to aid civilians of all faiths hurt in any way by the fighting. They took another step toward conformity.

Post-Revolutionary Pennsylvania found Quakers willing to be a part of a government focused on assimilation of Native Americans through education in order to literally keep them alive, or so Quakers paternalistically believed. The recognition of cultural genocide and its often-fatal consequences came much later.

In the American Revolutionary War, they were regarded as cowards and traitors, reviled by both sides in the fighting. Their aid to fellow citizens was appreciated, but their general refusal to fight undermined and still undermines respect for them, especially in cultures where masculinity is measured by military service (Batchelor 2019). Today, all types of violence (physical, emotional, psychological) are generally abhorred by Friends.

Some were exiled, their estates seized, and two were hanged for treason. Similarly, in the World Wars conscientious objection was allowed, but objectors often experienced abusive treatment. Some became involved in the manufacture of armaments (Sykes 1958), and some Friends felt they could not even do the alternative service offered and went to prison. During these wars Quakers mainly participated by way of the Friends' Ambulance Unit. This was seen by some Friends as a violation of the Peace Testimony and was despised by many non-Quakers for its insistence on the rescue of all wounded, regardless of whose side they were fighting on (Sykes 1958). As in the Revolutionary War, Quakers upset all parties involved.

Quakers continue to react to wars in several ways, including remaining convinced pacifists who refuse to support war in any way, those who withdraw into their own communities, those who focus on providing for the needs of civilians in the cities experiencing attacks, and those who participate in defensive measures of some kind.

Colonial actions by Quakers, rooted more in beliefs than in reality, illustrate the great harms that their growing acceptance of colonial goals and ideology caused, despite efforts to ameliorate harms caused by other settler colonists (Punshon 1984). While Quakers were blinded by their faith in the universality of their "Truth" in early colonial times, and it stayed that way for 250 years, it is no longer the case. During the twentieth century they became cognizant of the harms caused by settler colonialism and are now deeply involved in social justice initiatives to help to ameliorate them.

AN OVERVIEW OF PAST AMERICAN INDIAN RESPONSES TO QUAKER COLONIALISM

Before the Quakers arrived on the East Coast of North America, the Indians who inhabited the valley along the Lenapewihittuck River had already been living for decades in relative peace in separate but connected communities with

European traders such as the Swedes and Finns. They treated with these new neighbors for land usage, not land ownership, and if these European neighbors overstepped these agreements, such as occurred with the Dutch and English on a number of occasions, the Lenape acted against them, usually lethally. This peace was based on their mutual trade and communication networks, and intermarriage, but especially on the Europeans' respect for Lenape sovereignty. The Lenape found that the early Quakers fit into this peaceable community because of mutual interests in trade and peaceful living as expressed to them by Penn. They appreciated the respect they were shown by Penn and the Quakers and formed right relations with them as they had with their previous trader neighbors. Their numbers began to decrease though, as the diseases brought by their new neighbors had their effect. The Lenape became more diverse as they were joined by other tribal groups that had been driven off their land by settler-colonist violence in other colonies, but even so, their numbers were soon no match against the incoming Europeans.

The new settler colonists invited by Penn were different. They brought more diseases, violence, and criminal dealings. The Lenape's authority over the region disintegrated as their population decreased and as a result of the violence and chicanery of the new settler colonists. Penn's ineffectiveness in controlling the new settler colonists had serious and lethal consequences for the Indians. Some groups such as the Conestoga Indians tried to adapt to living under these new conditions and institutions but became innocent and dead victims of colonial politics.

The permutations of European governance were mostly mysterious to the Indians so that when the Quakers lost power in the Pennsylvania government, the Indians felt abandoned and betrayed, for example, as Penn's family forced them off their land. Even the activities of the Friendly Association were not enough to stave off their disappointment and the end of right relations between Indians and Quakers. The Indians saw that Pennsylvania had become no different than the other American colonies in their treatment of their Indian inhabitants.

Various other Indian groups, including the Lenape, gave up on peaceful coexistence. They were losing their lands, their treaties were not being honored, and on the western borders of Pennsylvania, squatters were murdering their community members and destroying their villages.

Many Lenape and their allies moved north and west to avoid conflict: some allied with the French in the French and Indian Wars against the English colonists, some fought on the side of the English colonists, and some tried to be peacemakers. This reflects what many Indian groups did during the Revolutionary War: some fought for the Americans, some for the British, and some moved away. Not all the Lenape migrated, however; some stayed by keeping a low profile, and these groups continued their traditional cultures and activities and are still found in and around Pennsylvania.

Good relations between American Indians and the Quakers diminished at this point with a few exceptions, such as the travelling Quaker teachers and the day schools run by Quakers on Indian land. Even these relations were fraught by cultural insensitivity on the part of the Quaker teachers. When Quakers began to function as Indian agents and run the boarding schools, their relationship was no longer one of mutual benefit but of disrespect and ignorance on the part of the Quakers. Even so, some Indian leaders, well-aware of the advantage of an education in American ways, sent their children to Quaker-run boarding schools (if they had a choice), since Quaker schools were known to be less physically abusive than those run by others, though still thoroughly assimilative. Once the Friends as an entity removed themselves from the boarding school system, the relations between the Quakers and Native Americans remained low-key until the mid-twentieth century. Quaker-Indian right relations had almost ceased to exist.

COLONIAL THINKING AND RIGHT RELATIONS

A "feeling of rightness" relates to spiritual consensus—to an agreement that all of life is sacred. Quakers Brown and Garver (2009, 211) describe the Moral Economy Project in which they are engaged as "a vision of right relationship with the commonwealth of life." The origins of the term are not clear but its meaning is fundamental to Quaker faith in the equality of all life. For Quakers there will be no social justice without peace, and no peace without social justice, a phrase attributed to Martin Luther King from a speech on December 14, 1967 (goodmenproject.com). For Quakers social justice now includes not just all human life but all life on our planet and involves active involvement in positive, well-functioning communities. It is a fundamental aspect of the Quaker spiritual belief in that of God in every living thing, and in this sense has some commonality with Indigenous views of the wholeness of all. It also underpins Quaker social justice work including restorative justice and peacemaking.

Most American Indian cultures have values and principles that focus on similar ideas about right relations that extend beyond the human sphere to encompass the interconnectedness of all life, including nonhuman and non-animate entities (Dumont 1996). For example, the Navajo word *hózhó*, which cannot be translated directly into English, has been described by the Honorable Raymond Austin (2009, 54) formerly of the Navajo Nation Supreme Court, as a state "where everything, tangible and intangible, is in its proper place and functioning well with everything else, such that the condition produced can be described as peace, harmony and balance (for lack of better English terms)." This "everything" includes "the interconnected, interrelated, and interdependent elements . . . in this structure, human beings compose one facet or one element" (Austin 2009, 54). The phrase "all my relations" (also said as "all our relations" depending on the situation) is part of Lakota culture and is described by Chief Arvol Looking Horse (n.d., n.p.) as follows:

> When we say Mitakuye Oyasin "All Our Relations" many people don't understand the meaning of those words. The phrase Mitakuye Oyasin has a bigger meaning than just our blood relatives. Yes, it's true; we are all one human race. But the word Mitakuye means relations and Oyasin means more than family, more than a Nation, more than all of humankind, everything that has a spirit. The Earth herself, Maka Unci, is our relation, and so is the sky, Grandfather Sky, and so is the Buffalo and so are each of the two-leggeds, the four-leggeds, those that swim, those that fly, the root nation and the crawling beings who share the world with us. Mitakuye Oyasin refers to the interconnectedness of all being and all things. We are all interconnected. We are all One.

The phrase is also used in the Anishinaabe (Ojibwa) languages and others, indicating a similar value of interconnectedness. Rupert Ross (2014, 63), a well-respected non-Indigenous scholar of Aboriginal justice, summarizes his understanding of traditional Aboriginal lifeways in Canada by writing, "traditional life centred on striving at all times to create 'right relations,' not only with people but also with everything else that surrounded you, not only in the present but also in the past and future, and not only within the physical realm but with the spiritual realm as well."

Quakers have developed and used this foundational stance of right relations at different times in their history and in different ways. In the twenty-first century it appears to have reached greater clarity and determination. During the years covered in this research, Quaker actions and beliefs shifted from the radical religious insurgency of the seventeenth century to an intensely conservative reformation period and following that to colonial ideology and religious discipline in the nineteenth century (Punshon 1984). Quaker nonconformity was continually confronted by events that challenged and shifted their beliefs toward greater social conformity, but at the same time, they developed creative responses to conflicts between social and perceived spiritual demands.

To refuse to fight in anyone's army and to declare peace in a society in which violence was endemic was either incredibly courageous or foolish, depending on one's point of view. Quakers tried to teach peace by example but failed to pay enough attention to the power of colonial thinking, and in the colonization of America, settler colonist greed. Insisting on their truths and practices in Indigenous communities was deeply insensitive and culturally violent. Quakers contributed to cultural genocide in their insistence on the superiority of European beliefs enacted in boarding schools and through their support of severalty. In this, yet again, an opportunity for mutual understanding and reconciliation was lost, and severe harms resulted.

Many Quakers failed to identify their colonialism in values such as a focus on hard work for its own sake, rigid gender roles, individualism, abstract education, and ownership of land. They failed to recognize their colonial mentality even though some weighty Friends (such as Woolman and Benezet) warned them about it. Polly O. (Daksi) Walker (2006, 27), a member of the Cherokee Nation and Quaker, states that Woolman, more than Penn, acknowledges "the possibility that Indians' spiritual beliefs may have had something in common with those of Quakers." Walker goes on to quote Woolman, speaking of his mission to the Indians in the summer of 1763:

> Having many years felt love in my heart toward the natives of this land who dwell far back in the wilderness, whose ancestors were the owners and possessors of the land where we dwell, and who for a very small consideration assigned their inheritance to us. . . . And in conversation and conduct, I believed some of them were measurably acquainted with that divine power which subjects the rough and the froward will of the creature. (P. Walker 2006, 27 from Moulton 1971, 122)

Woolman never used the term, but his words suggest right relations as the heart of his concern. P. Walker adds "Woolman recognized the dangers of colonial racism (even if he did not use this terminology) and the privileges it conferred on Whites" (P. Walker 2006, 27), but he was not listened to.

Right relations for both Quakers and Indigenous Peoples point to an ideal—a respectful, healthy, and ongoing relationship with both humans and with life as manifested in plants, animals, insects, terrain, climate, etc., an ideal that evolves as respect for life deepens. For First Nations activist Max FineDay (2020) reconciliation and right relations must include Indigenous relations to the land itself, therefore right relations cannot happen without the return or payment for stolen Indigenous lands—land return, among other things. Right relations, then, are an expression of social justice values as practiced by Quakers and as have been practiced by Indigenous Peoples since time immemorial.

QUAKER RIGHT RELATIONS AND SOCIAL JUSTICE

Ross (2019, 115) identified two key components of the Philadelphia Yearly Meeting Indian Committee's purpose and its consequences in 1795:

> First . . . Quakers were aware that what they called a "war of extermination," was being waged against Indigenous communities. . . . Second, in spite of their acute awareness of the persecution of the Indigenous communities and their sustained and vocal protest against it, these Quakers themselves were implicated in perpetuating patterns of misunderstanding and mistreatment of Indians . . . the Quakers working with them persisted in advocating for the "civilization" strategy even in the face of abundant evidence that the process was not advancing as they imagined it would.

Ross (2019, 123) notes that in recorded interactions between Quakers and Indians, "the Quakers were listening but missed important opportunities to hear Indian communication." This was also true of their agricultural policy, and Ross's second theme (related to Quaker work with the Seneca), of perpetuating misunderstandings and mistreatment. The third theme was their paternalism. When Quakers situated themselves as superior to their erstwhile Indian friends, they denied their own principle of equality, and however well-intentioned their actions may have been, they contributed to the destruction of Indian language, way of living, and spirituality.

Having initially begun by establishing right relations with the Lenape, Pennsylvania Quakers eventually lost right relations with the Lenape. Several important components, such as learning their language and working at understanding and respecting their culture, were missing even in the early relationships. Most Quakers did not listen with deep attention to the Lenape or later, to the Seneca and other Nations. Although some, such as Joseph Elkinton, learned the Seneca language, they appear to have been a minority. Consequently, seventeenth- and eighteenth-century Quakers generally did not fully understand and appreciate the cultures of the Indigenous Peoples they encountered. A probability is they were centered on their own messages and saw no need to incorporate those of others, since they already had the "Truth" (Dudiak 2015).

Violence is antithetical to the concept of right relations, and the use of force such as Quakers applied in the boarding schools challenges claims to Quaker peacemaking. At several moments in Pennsylvania's development, opportunities to incorporate a different perspective were missed, due to the Quaker need for social and political acceptance. For example, Rothenberg (1976, 148) writes: "the Seneca evidence time and again demonstrates flexibility and receptivity to new ideas, techniques and behavior which would belie the hypothesis that the Seneca were bound within the tight constraints of a previous culture model." Quakers seem not to have recognized that ability.

The evidence in each chapter supports the claim that settler colonialism and its inherent violence and social harms destroyed any potential that Penn's Holy Experiment had for shaping an America that integrated Native Americans and non–Native Americans in an equal and respectful relationship based in social justice. Colonialism is a great social harm that has been left unrepaired by the colonizing countries (M. Walker 2006, 12). As M. Walker (2006, 34–35) states, "There really is such a thing as adding moral insult to injury, whether willfully or not, and thus adding additional injuries, and there is also the fact that certain wrongs over time become larger ones when they involve continuing neglect or disrespect, or when wrongful harms themselves worsen for lack of response to them. Unremedied historic injustices toward groups or peoples [add and compound] injuries, as do continuing neglectful or bad treatment among individuals." She also writes that,

> Where wrongs persist unrepaired repeatedly, in an extended series of refusals
> or failures to repair, the lack of reparative effort on the part of those responsible
> for repair accrues layers of disregard, indifference, disrespect, contempt, belittle-
> ment, or intended or careless humiliation. In addition to the original injury and

the failure to repair, the added insult is the attitude of "That's their problem," or "That all happened so long ago," or "Get over it." Unrepaired wrongs on a large scale, which determine life experiences and life chances for generations, do not go away; even when they are silenced, they have a way of coming back. They tend to get worse as new generations not only inherit the continuing patterns of disadvantage and injustice that stem from grave wrongs in the past, but also experience outrage, mistrust, and despair at the continuing denial, indifference, or self-justification of those who have profited or continue to profit not only from the original wrong but also from its continuing effects. (M. Walker 2006, 205)

Colonialism in all its forms creates social harms (Nielsen and Robyn 2019). Colonial actions have reverberated for almost four hundred years until finally in North America attitudes have begun to change. For instance, victim-blaming has begun to wane in that Indigenous Peoples are being blamed less for what Dodge (2016, 272) describes as deserving the consequences because they engaged in some sort of risky behavior, such as defending their homes and lives against invasion and colonialism. P. Walker (2006, 30) writes, "we are responsible for addressing colonial racism in peaceful ways." Part of that is working to decrease the physical and structural violence and other harms that still exist against Indigenous People in colonized countries.

The need for apology, restitution, and rebuilding of right relations has been recognized as urgent in the USA and Canada. Peacemaking has begun among those willing to acknowledge the truth of colonialism, the depth and breadth of the damage that has resulted, and to accept responsibility for the benefits that had accrued to the descendants of settler colonists. We address a random handful of such events below as examples of potential changes that are and could be made to advance social justice.

CURRENT SITUATIONS IN CANADA AND THE USA: SOME OBSERVATIONS

Our research inevitably raised the question as to whether peacemaking and restorative justice between settler colonist descendants and Indigenous Peoples can be practiced in the USA and Canada today. Could we be any more successful than William Penn? Elaine Bishop at the 2018 Truth and Healing Conference held at Pendle Hill, Pennsylvania, pointed out that making an apology is fine, but does not carry much weight if it does not include specific plans for making amends. This could range from returning stolen lands to Indigenous trusteeship to immersing one's body and mind into as much of the Indigenous experience as is possible without being present at the time of the oppressive structures, such as residential schools. Returning Indigenous lands currently in private or corporate hands entails legal and personal challenges that are not easy to overcome. This could include financial costs but also personal costs, for example, the return of land that has been in one family for several generations but was never legally and fairly bought. The following sections outline some of the initiatives that Quakers have taken so far.

We wish to point out and acknowledge that Indigenous Peoples have made enormous strides in overcoming the impacts of colonialism with and without the aid of allies. Self-determination as recognized in American law means that American Indians and Alaskan Natives have inherent sovereignty and therefore the ability to make their own choices and take action within the parameters set by American federal Indian law and policy. In the USA, state and local movements have held Truth or Healing and Reconciliation gatherings; for example, the Wanabago (Haudenosaunee) People, "People of the Dawn," have an annual event for Truth and Reconciliation commemorating the "Two Row Wampum." This wampum belt depicts two separate canoes moving down the river in the same direction. This is friendship and comradeship between two groups of people each leading their lives according to their own beliefs and practices (*Dawnland* directed by Pender-Cudlip and Mazos 2018, shown at Pendle Hill Truth and Healing Conference, May 2018). In Canada, one major first step has been a national Truth and Reconciliation Commission (TRC) (TRC 2015).

As well, in Canada, bill C-15 enshrines the UN Declaration of Rights of Indigenous Peoples into national and provincial laws. It worked its way through the lower house with support from a range of organizations based on fears that an election would derail the effort as had happened before with the similar bill C-262. See Nielsen and Robyn (2019, 203–25) for a description of these extensive efforts, not only in Canada and the USA but also globally, as well as efforts settler colonists need to make.

THE UNITED STATES OF AMERICA

American Quaker-based educational institutions such as Pendle Hill, a conference center; Haverford College; and Bryn Mawr College (along with other organizations) have sponsored conferences focusing on relationships between Quakers and Native Americans. The two authors attended a 2016 Pennsylvania University conference presenting a wide range of papers, some of which were eventually published in a book, *Quakers and Native Americans*, edited by Ignacio Gallup-Diaz and Geoffrey Plank (2019). At a Pendle Hill, Pennsylvania, conference in 2018, two documentaries were shown about current American efforts toward reconciliation and healing in the USA. One was the film *Dawnland* (Pender-Cudlip and Mazo 2018; https://upstanderproject.org/dawnland) about the 2018 Maine Wabanaki-State Child Welfare TRC, and the ongoing program (http://www.mainewabanakireach.org/). The other was *Two Rivers* (Mitchell 1996), a story of a white American couple who moved from a multi-ethnic community to one in which there appeared to be only white people. They went looking for the missing "Others" and found a First Nations community. Over time they developed Native American / white in-home gatherings and community activities that eventually culminated in an annual powwow. It has been so successful that other communities are picking up on the idea (http://www.tworiversfilm.com/index.htm).

At the same conference, Dr. Denise Lajimodere (2018) presented on her own experiences as a researcher studying American Indian boarding schools and connecting with survivors. She shared both personal experiences with survivors in her own family and the stories of those she met through her research. Focusing on what healing would look like after apologies from all those religious organizations involved in the schools, Lajimodere argued for a national curriculum on residential schools for all levels of education, and the use of healing models with Native American counseling and holistic healing to support survivors and their families and to restore what was taken away, including language and spirituality. Broad-based decolonization and indigenization is needed, she said.

Three Lenape chiefs attended the conference: Chief Dennis Coker, Chief Dwayne Perry, and Chief Mark Gould, with the opening keynote address coming from Chief Coker of the Delaware Lenape, who spoke of the fight for state recognition and civil rights for his People (Coker 2018; see also Indian Country Today 2019).

A number of Quakers are working as allies with American Indian Nations, such as in Colorado, where the Boulder Friends Meeting has set up activities related to boarding school survivors and returning to a right relations with Indigenous Peoples (Boulder Friends n.d.). Quaker scholar and researcher Paula Palmer (Boulder Friends Meeting) and others are providing ministries under the Friends Peace Teams to "explore painful truths about the U.S. and Quaker history and create opportunities for individuals, Meetings, and communities to take steps toward right relationship" (Palmer 2020, 21) as well as writing articles for publications such as *Friends Journal*. One widely experienced exercise designed with their Indigenous partners is the "Blanket Exercise" that vividly models how land was stolen from Indigenous Peoples.

Friends' efforts to educate on the need for right relations are not just limited to the educational realm, however. There are also federal political groups such as the Friends Committee on National Legislation (FCNL) (https://www.fcnl .org) that has been providing advocacy for Native American concerns specifically since 1976. It has representatives across the United States and intervenes in legislation directly or indirectly through lobbying and the media when these are possible. FCNL has been active since 1943 when it was founded as a "religious lobby in the public interest" (FCNL n.d.-b) and has intervened in many aspects of federal legislation. Most recently it has supported the passage of American Indian health, education, cultural preservation, housing, and justice bills (FCNL n.d.-b), as well as calling for peace building support in the fiscal year budget for 2021 (March 2020). They describe their work this way: "FCNL's Native American Advocacy program has worked to restore and improve U.S. relations with Native Nations so that our country honors the promises made in hundreds of treaties with these groups." FCNL (n.d.-b) issues a regular "Native American Legislative update" (see, for example, https://www.fcnl.org/updates/native -american-legislative-update-2646). Its website lists "Seven Priorities for Native American Advocacy," which include Healing Past Wrongs (forced assimilation; reclaiming Native languages), Investing in Safety and Well-Being (Native youth, justice systems), and Self-Governance and Self-Determination (religious freedom; advancing self-determination; and preserving land and resources).

CANADA

Relations between settler colonists and the Indigenous Peoples of Canada may not have been as overtly and directly violent as those south of the border but followed a similar pattern of structural and cultural violence and deep disrespect, including the creation of reserves (reservations) governed by Indian agents legally empowered to control reserve residents. These policies included: the use of pass books when they left the reserve, the banning of spiritual practices such as the potlatch, and the establishment of residential schools under the 1876

Indian Act. The first large residential schools opened in western Canada in 1883. The last residential school closed in Saskatchewan in 1996. The schools were staffed by several churches—the Roman Catholics, Anglicans, Presbyterians, Methodists, and the United Church. Quakers took no active part in the schools but neither did they protest them, even though the abuses that occurred there were widely recognized and known to the federal government and members of the public (see Nielsen and Robyn 2019). It may not be possible at this time to establish how much Quakers knew about the abuses taking place either in Canada or in the USA.

Class action suits by survivors of the residential schools against the federal government and the churches that ran schools in Canada led to a compensation package in 2007 (CA\$1.9 billion), making this class action settlement one of the largest in Canadian history (Schwing 2021). The settlement also included a Truth and Reconciliation Commission (TRC) that began its work in 2010. Its findings, published in 2015, shook up relations between governments, churches, settler colonist descendants, and Indigenous Peoples (TRC 2015). It contained ninety-four calls to action that are also published in a separate booklet by the National Centre for Truth and Reconciliation (National Centre n.d.). This, often together with a booklet on the 2007 United Nations Declaration on the Rights of Indigenous Peoples (UNDRIP) (UN 2007), has reached schools and universities, religious and community groups, sparking discussions and acts of reconciliation.

Canadian Friends Service Committee (CFSC) recommends that Friends educate themselves about issues, such as the legacy and impacts of the residential schools (including reading the TRC Report Summary), and carry out actions such as contacting their local members of Parliament, urging them to ensure UNDRIP is integrated into Canadian laws, to raise Friends' awareness of the concerns of Aboriginal Peoples, to stimulate active participation in acts of reconciliation, and to focus on Indigenous rights, joining with Indigenous Peoples in common issues (CFSC n.d.-b). A recently resurgent concern in Canada is the "Sixties Scoop," referring to a time in the 1960s when social workers across Canada seized children from Indigenous parents, accusing them of being unfit to parent, and placed the children for adoption without parental consent. Children were separated from siblings and sent to homes within and outside Canada, where many were abused and once again divorced from their People and their culture. A similar initiative occurred in the USA. The repercussions of the Sixties Scoop are still being experienced by a generation of Indigenous individuals as they try to heal from the personal, family, and community trauma (see Nielsen and Robyn 2019).

In its summary of the TRC's final report titled "Honouring the Truth, Reconciling for the Future," the TRC (2015, 6–7) describes reconciliation as "establishing and maintaining a mutually respectful relationship between Aboriginal and non-Aboriginal peoples in this country. In order for that to happen, there has to be awareness of the past, acknowledgement of the harm that has been inflicted, atonement for the causes, and action to change behavior."

The churches involved have apologized, but few have taken any visible action. Prime Minister Stephen Harper apologized on behalf of the Canadian government in 2008. Bill C-262, later Bill C-15, was introduced by Romeo Saganish to address the United Nations Declaration on the Rights of Indigenous Peoples and its implications for Canadian laws. Bill C-262 died on the order book due to an election call. Bill C-15 contains C-262 with some additions. Bill C-15 was passed in both houses in May 2021. The Canadian government now has to replace any federal laws or sections of laws that do not accord with the Declaration. It is preceded by several important Supreme Court decisions that restate Indigenous rights.

Arthur Manuel (2015) states that recognizing Aboriginal title is a fundamental decolonizing action; however, he also points out the federal government continues to resist the idea that Aboriginal title incorporates the right to both land use permission *and denial*. For example, the Coastal Gaslink pipeline, which has been approved by the federal government, crosses the territory of the Wet'suwet'en, threatening their water supply, but their attempt to intervene in environmental hearings was denied. Worse, a court injunction against protestors blocking access roads *on Wet'suwet'en lands* was enforced by the Royal Canadian Mounted Police, which arrested protesters (Stueck et al. 2020; italics added). Many local Quakers were involved in these protests, and some were arrested. It should be noted that recently the Wet'suwet'en hereditary chiefs reached an agreement on their status with the federal government, but no resolution to the GasLink action has been reached as of May 2021 due to the pandemic. At the time of writing in 2021, work on the GasLink line is about one-third complete. Wet'suwet'en chief Na'moks told CBC news that the pandemic was disproportionately affecting First Nations in the north of British Columbia and temporarily shifting their attention away from this issue to caring for their elders (Trumpener 2021).

Quakers continue their work as allies of Aboriginal Peoples through the Quaker Indigenous Affairs Committee (QIAC), part of the Friends Service

Committee in Canada (Preston 2020). QIAC has its roots in a 1974 armed confrontation between the Anishinaabe and a Canadian government that failed to act when an upstream paper mill dumped gallons of organic mercury into the river system that served the Anishinaabe as household and drinking water and as a source of fish. This kind of action has not ended in Canada; in fact, the Justin Trudeau government was set to approve a huge oil sands development, until Teck Mines withdrew its application based on market projections in February 2020 (Rieger 2020).

Quaker Meetings across Canada are active in a range of justice issues, many of them related to Indigenous justice issues. For example, Matthew Legge, who at the time of this writing has been coordinating the Quaker Peace Committee since 2012, wrote the book *Are We Done Fighting? Building Understanding in a World of Hate and Division* (2019). The book is a "how to guide" to personal and group peacemaking work invaluable to activist Friends. An Education Committee, also part of CYM, also organizes online courses and supports educational projects by local Meetings and Friends. For many years Indigenous Rights program coordinator Jennifer Preston has worked at all levels from the United Nations to Yearly Meeting and with Monthly Meeting committees and individual Friends as allies of Indigenous groups (for example, see her "Submission to the Standing Committee on Indigenous and Northern Affairs House of Commons, Parliament of Canada; Study on Bill 262: The United Nations Declaration on the Rights of Indigenous Peoples," April 2018). In spite of the Truth and Reconciliation Commission Report, and former Prime Minister Harper's apology for the residential schools, the Canadian government continues to drag its feet on issues such as Indigenous land rights, housing and safe water, social services, and education on reserves. The shockingly high rate of violence, including murder, of Indigenous women and girls in Canada has finally made the news and continues to create headlines. It appears that more Canadians are aware that Indigenous Peoples' lives (physical, emotional, psychological) are at risk. As observed in many news reports, this includes situations that are on the edge of physical violence, and some have been verbally abusive on both sides. It is this kind of situation where peacemaking by Friends could become central.

Canadians have a reputation for being a peaceful people and have been involved in United Nations peacekeeping missions; yet many continue to hold dangerous stereotypes of Indigenous Peoples that can mar court decisions, such as in the Clayton Bushie shooting for which the shooter was acquitted by a local court and that also undermined respect for the RCMP (APTN 2018; Friesen

2018). Police also investigated online racist comments that followed the shooting, but today Canadians are aware that some police themselves use racist words and commit racist actions. As in the USA, too many Indigenous Peoples are involved as victims and offenders in the criminal justice system (Nielsen and Jarratt-Snider 2018; Malakieh 2020).

It is apparent that colonial governments in both Canada and the USA are still avoiding or denying their obligations to Indigenous Peoples, both fiduciary, as outlined in the treaties, and moral, in response to the great harms committed by settler colonists and their governments and continued today by their descendants. Members of the Society of Friends, in contrast, have taken up the challenge to assist with the amelioration of past and present harms and prevention of future harms. This is part of their social justice mandate. Friends have committed themselves to not only live peaceably with both equality and justice but to work towards increasing the expression of these values in the world (for example see section on peace in "Faith and Practice" by the Canadian Yearly Meeting, Religious Society of Friends 2011, 114).

CONCLUSION

According to M. Walker (2006, 15–16), restorative justice is the tool needed to repair relations. Peacemaking is a promising tool for achieving reconciliation between Indigenous Peoples and settler colonist descendants. Quakers have played the role of peacemaker in the past, both in early colonial times and in more recent history, as have many Indigenous Peoples, such as the Lenape. The potential is there for Quakers to take a more active role in future reconciliation attempts, working alongside Indigenous Peoples. Quakers have learned from their past arrogance and sense of superiority. They have seen the consequences of having good intentions that they could not carry out, as with protecting their Indian allies in early colonial times, or that they carried out all too well, as with the boarding schools. As Echohawk (2019, 313) writes, "Too much of the wrongs of the past were . . . conceived and advanced as the attempts of one side to help the other in the best way it knew how. Yet the actions taken in pursuit of those good intentions resulted in harm."

In the United States and Canada, Indigenous communities are still here. Their survivance is based in resilience and adaptability. They are not waiting for assistance from their colonizers; they are practicing de facto sovereignty, that is, they are working with creativity and innovation to resolve their own issues (see Nielsen and Jarratt-Snider 2018). As part of this, they are exercising their right to self-determination in terms of what assistance they ask for and accept, and from whom. It is their choice with whom they enter into right relations. Some American Indian Nations, as seen with the Lenape leaders who attended the Quaker conference in 2018, are willing to hear what Quakers have to offer.

The majority of Quakers feel that they owe Indigenous Peoples for the wrongs that have been committed against them. They are not indifferent to the injustice suffered by Indigenous Peoples at the hands of the settler colonists and that continue at the hand of their descendants. As M. Walker (2006, 202) writes:

> The problem of contempt for, or indifference or hostility to, those harmed also plagues cases of historical injustice. With historical injustices—long-running and still-running eras of unjust treatment—there is the question of what is owed now by contemporary societies to groups, peoples, or other societies who continue to suffer the life-diminishing effects of prior conquest, slavery, cultural destruction, and expropriation of land and resources. For the white settler societies of the United States, Canada, and Australia, for example, the continuing and often ravaging effects on indigenous people of forced removal from ancestral lands, genocidal and ethnocidal political and social policies, impoverishment in health, income, and education may be somewhat less denied or disputed than they used to be. Yet the telling of these histories often still prompts impatience or resentment in those who do not belong to the historically subjected and violated population.

M. Walker (2006, 37) also suggests that what is needed is sincerely attempted "moral repair," and states, "otherwise, those of us who have done wrong, or others of us who are witnesses, bystanders, or beneficiaries, but who refuse to address that wrong, will add to, compound, or deepen the damage done and augment the insults it carries." Quakers hold deep beliefs in social justice that overlap with Indigenous values. With their acknowledgement of past wrongs committed against Indigenous Peoples by members of their own faith and by settler colonialism in general, Quakers could continue to play important roles as allies of Indigenous Peoples, but such roles must be determined and defined by Indigenous Peoples.

Quakers are currently working politically and on individual-level right relations, but there is much more that can be done to undo the harms of the past and present. Quakers are taking communal responsibility for moral repair (M. Walker 2006, 6–7; see also Young 2013; Shin and Bounds 2017 and CFSC n.d.-b). As M. Walker (2006, 6–7) writes, "if moral repair means anything it means the attempt to address offense, harm, and anguish caused to those who suffer wrong. It is about 'setting things right,'" She specifically addresses the removal of Indigenous children, forced removal of Indigenous Peoples from their lands, and "the knowing suppression and destruction of cultures by colonizers" as injustices that need reparation (2006, 12) and writes that restorative justice is well-suited for repairing the "hard cases" of historical wrongs (2006, 207).

Quakers, non-Indigenous People, and scholars still have a great deal to learn—about social justice, about social harms, and about Indigenous Peoples and cultures. As part of their continuing efforts, Quakers might consider learning Indigenous languages or reading some of the increasing publications, both fictional and factual, now available. There are "150 ways" (Fraser and Komarnisky n.d.) to become involved in reconciliation, especially if by doing so, Quakers can pressure the governments of Canada, the USA, and the provinces and states to respond to Indigenous issues more respectfully and responsibly.

Indigenous Peoples have a great deal of knowledge that is theirs to share, if they determine they want to, and many do (Echohawk 2019). In her book about the "Never Broken Treaty" between Quakers and the Lenape, Chandler (2001) quotes Cheryll Coull who interviewed a Wsanec elder, Gabriol Bartleman, who said, "There is a word in our language—'kwagwatul'—which means 'talking together.' The time has come for this. The first Europeans came to live among us when my grandmother was a child. Now I am a great grand-father, and still, very little is known of our history and values" (Chandler 2001, 32).

This world, which is sorely afflicted by climate change, greed, disinformation, and violence, could benefit from the wisdom that many Indigenous communities have, with which they functioned successfully for tens of thousands of years. If Indigenous societies choose, Quakers could be allies in this. Together they could contribute to some of the social and political changes that are so desperately needed today. As Echohawk (2019, 317) writes, "A more accurate picture of our ancestral traditions and accomplishments would help to advance the understanding of how a life more conducive to continued existence on earth is possible." He states that more respectful ways of treating each other and of handling conflicts are essential, and that "tribal traditions can provide models for this way of relating." As well, the value of interconnectedness, whether it is called "right relations," as Quakers do, or hózhó or "All My Relations" or other similar terms used by Indigenous Peoples, is knowledge that can be adopted and adapted by non-Indigenous individuals, communities, and even nations, in an effort to overcome the many daunting and looming disasters that we have inflicted upon ourselves. We argue that sharing these practices could have important implications for future social and political developments in America.

GLOSSARY

The majority of the terms that follow are rooted in Quaker usages. This glossary contains common usages, not "official" definitions.

ALLOWED MEETINGS: See worship groups.

BENEVOLENCE / CORPORATE BENEVOLENCE: This term, also called philanthropy, has been applied by several writers who specifically relate the change from individual charity to carefully considered group charity after the Revolutionary War. It is the name for group charity by a Monthly, Quarterly, Half Yearly, or Yearly Meeting, which donates to or assists in some way a charity that reflects their principles, such as a nonprofit organization working with trauma victims.

BOOK OF DISCIPLINE: This was a set of guidelines for Friends to follow that became rigid during the Reformation that began in the early 1700s. Currently it takes the form of a set of quotations on a variety of topics taken from Friends' writings or statements overheard and recorded (known as "gleanings") and put together in a book known as *Faith and Practice*.

CHARTER OF PRIVILEGES: This is William Penn's title for his final Frame of Government, edited and changed to better meet the demands of his settlers.

CLERK OF MEETING: The clerk is responsible for facilitating Meetings for Worship for Business, including setting a time and date, making an agenda, and distributing any materials needed prior to the Meeting. The clerk works with the recording clerk to identify the sense of the Meeting on each issue. The position of clerk does not carry higher position or power.

CORPORATE BENEVOLENCE: See Benevolence.

DINÉ NATION CHAPTERS: These are the decentralized local government districts found on the Navajo (Diné) Nation.

DISCERNMENT: Discerning of the will of a Meeting is a sensitive and highly developed skill used by clerks and recording clerks to identify the core of Meeting discussion. It is presented to the Meeting and will often be edited and can be rejected entirely, although this is rare.

DISOWNMENT: Not used for many years, this was the ultimate discipline against a member not behaving according to Quaker ways. Disowned members could be reinstated if they wrote a letter of apology and mended their ways.

ELDERS (QUAKER): Elders are responsible for the spiritual life of the Meeting. This responsibility may also take the form of a Ministry and Council Committee in any level of Meeting.

ETHNOVIOLENCE: Violence and harassment based on race, ethnicity, religion, sexual orientation, and other diverse characteristics. These could be criminal actions but also include slurs, literature, symbols, and hostile, though legal, acts.

EXECUTIVE COUNCIL / COUNCIL: Appointed proprietors who represented the interests of the governor.

FRAME OF GOVERNMENT: William Penn called his design for the Pennsylvania government "A Frame of Government."

FREE SOCIETY OF TRADERS: Penn granted extensive trading privileges to the Free Society of Traders, whose objectives were to trade with the Indians and promote Philadelphia businesses.

FRIENDS GENERAL CONFERENCE (FGC): The website states that the FGC, serving the USA and Canada, has three main areas of endeavor. In brief, these are conferences and consultations, religious education, and hosting programs and initiatives "for and on behalf of our members." FGC also organizes the annual Meeting of liberal Friends in the USA and Canada.

HALF YEARLY MEETINGS: Friends' Meetings that occur every six months for a specific geographical area.

INNER LIGHT / THE LIGHT / INWARD LIGHT / LIGHT WITHIN / THAT OF GOD: These are terms used interchangeably to refer to the sense of inward spiritual guidance individually or in a group.

LEADING: A pressing sense of inner guidance to deliver a message or take up a specific action by an individual or group.

LEGISLATIVE ASSEMBLY / ASSEMBLY: The elected council in Penn's form of government that provided elected representation for settler colonists (small landowners or renters) as opposed to the appointed large landowners or proprietors who formed the Executive Council.

LORDS OF TRADE COUNCIL: This was part of the Privy Council of Charles II that was responsible for the colonies and trade.

MEETINGS: This is the term for any group of Friends gathering regularly for worship and/or worship and business, locally or regionally.

MEETINGS FOR WORSHIP: These are silent Meetings where members actively listen for spiritual guidance for the group.

MEETINGS FOR WORSHIP FOR BUSINESS: This is a Meeting for Worship during which business matters are discussed and resolved in a worshipful manner.

MEMORIAL: This is a Meeting for Worship during which a deceased Friend is remembered.

MINISTRY: These are spoken messages during a Meeting for Worship, for which there was no preparation and that come out of a strong feeling by the speaker of being led.

MINISTRY AND COUNCIL: A committee that may be set up by Monthly and Yearly Meetings to nurture the spiritual health of the Meeting including the quality of ministry during Meeting for Worship. The committee developed from "Ministry and Oversight," which originally focused on discipline among Friends as well as their Meeting's spiritual health.

MINUTE: This is the record made by a recording clerk of discernments by a Meeting for Worship for Business.

MONTHLY MEETING: Friends Meetings for Worship and for business held once a month for a specific geographical area, often a town, city, or metropolis.

NAAT'AANII: This is a Navajo/Diné peacemaker, a respected community member knowledgeable about Diné narratives.

OVERSEERS: These are Friends appointed by their Meeting (Monthly, Quarterly, Half Yearly, or Annual) to be responsible for the appropriate Quaker behavior of Meeting members. During the Reformation Years they were disciplinarians. Today, where they still exist, they are more likely to be responsible for pastoral care (see also elders).

PEACE TESTIMONY: This is the first of six Testimonies (see below). The Peace Testimony states that Quakers will not participate in violence, including war or other armed conflict. First published by Margaret Fell in 1660 (Quakers in the World n.d.), it gradually expanded to include not supporting any armed conflict and to active peacemaking work.

PEACEMAKING: This is a type of restorative justice process aimed at restoring harmony among the participants.

PREPARATIVE MEETINGS: See worship groups.

PRIVY COUNCIL: British royalty after the period of Cromwell's Commonwealth had a council of members, usually aristocrats of a similar background to the king or queen, who were his or her advisors.

PROGRAMMED MEETINGS: These are Meetings for Worship that are not held entirely in silence but draw on the more common format of hymns, prayers, and sermons, usually also with a period of silence included.

PROPRIETORS / PROPRIETORS COUNCIL: The council set up to represent the will of the proprietor, originally William Penn. It became that part of Penn's Frame of Government that represented proprietor interests and whose members were appointed by the governor. See Executive Council.

QUAKER PRINCIPLES: This is another name used to denote their Testimonies.

QUARTERLY MEETINGS: These are regionally based Meetings for Worship for Business, held four times a year and attended by Friends living in a specific geographical area.

QUITRENTS: These were fees charged by Pennsylvania proprietors (landowners) to those who bought lands from them. The fees were recompense for payments by proprietors, namely William Penn and his successors, to Indigenous Peoples who originally inhabited the lands. They could be seen as a form of taxes.

RECORDED MINISTERS: These are Quakers with a particular gift for speaking, usually on a specific topic, who may be recorded as such for the benefit of Meetings looking for speakers. In the past there were many more recorded ministers who felt called to visit Friends in their own or other countries. George Fox and John Woolman are two well-known Friends who traveled extensively.

RECORDED MINUTES: The written record of any minutes of the Meeting, whether Meeting for Worship for Business or other Meetings.

RECORDING CLERK: Recording clerks are analogous to secretaries but are *not* secretaries. They will listen and may note down the trends of what Meeting members are offering on a topic and when comments and ideas seem to be closing, work with the clerk to draw up a "minute" that expresses the will of the Meeting. Their work then is that of intense listening to discern God's will, as voiced by all present.

REPRESENTATIVE COMMITTEES: These are committees of the Yearly Meeting.

REPRESENTATIVE MEETING: This is a Canadian Committee that acts as a Yearly Meeting between annual events.

RESTORATIVE JUSTICE: This is a system of justice in which the offender takes responsibility to put things right, underlying issues are sought, and healing for the victim, offender, and the community are goals.

RIGHT RELATIONS: Applies to human relations but also to relationships with the environment and with all of life. It refers to being in harmony or creating balance in relationships. It is similar to many Indigenous values, and also basic to restorative justice.

SACHEMS: These are Lenape community leaders. They were termed "sachema" or "sachems" by the settler colonists and the term is now used in most scholarly work.

SETTLER COLONISTS: These are the invaders of Indigenous lands who come to stay. They will eliminate the Indigenous inhabitants if necessary to replace them.

SEVERALITY: This is private ownership of land by individual members, rather than by the Nation as a whole.

SILENCE: Silence is not a mere absence of noise for Friends. It is the occasion to listen for God's will, whether alone or together. Every Meeting begins with, and is conducted out of, silence.

TESTIMONIES: Friends currently have six basic principles or truths they try to live by: Peace, Simplicity, Integrity, Community, Equality, and Sustainability (SPICES).

TRAVELING FRIENDS: These are Quakers who feel called to travel "in the Truth," over varying distances, to witness or to encourage Friends, especially isolated Meetings or individuals. Similar to Recorded Ministers.

TRUTH: Friends use the term "Truth" as the revelation of God's will that is understood by Friends over time, i.e., it is revelatory, not absolute. Quakers' focus on following their own Inner Light, and in Meetings for Worship for Business seek the guidance of the Inner Light for the entire Meeting. Truth also is universal—every human being has that Light Within. Quakers are called to speak to that Light and draw it out, i.e they believe every human has a core of essential goodness within that can be fostered.

UNITY: A Quaker Meeting is "in unity" when Friends reach a decision with which all present are comfortable. This is not consensus but rather the gradual understanding and/or building of a spirit-led conclusion.

WEIGHTY FRIENDS: These are Friends esteemed for their wisdom and Quaker knowledge.

WITNESSING: This is to speak or act out of religious conviction, either intended to convey a belief or intended to contribute, e.g., to ending conflict, by drawing on one's Quaker faith.

WORSHIP GROUPS: These are similar to Allowed and Preparative Meetings, but definitions vary. In Canada, Worship Groups are usually small and localized Meetings for Worship that are often "under the care" of a larger Meeting or in some cases, under the care of Friends General Conference, which offers more resources for them. Generally, Allowed or Preparative Meetings, more common in the USA than Canada, also exist under the care of a Monthly Meeting. All three, if they grow in size and participation in larger bodies, can become Monthly Meetings.

WORSHIP SHARING GROUPS: Relatively new, these groups meet in the spirit and format of a Meeting for Worship to share personal insights, issues, concerns, or joys with each other.

YEARLY MEETING: This incorporates all Meetings in a given area. Canada has one national Yearly Meeting. In the United States there are a variety of different Yearly Meetings, both for different Quaker sects and by state or region.

REFERENCES

Adams, David Wallace. 1995. *Education for Extinction: American Indians and the Boarding School Experience 1875–1928*. Lawrence: University Press of Kansas.

Adler, Cyrus, and A. S. W. Rosenbach. 2011. "Pennsylvania." *Jewish Encyclopedia*. http://www.jewishencyclopedia.com/articles/12007-pennsylvania.

Alford, Susan. 1997. "Professionals Need Not Apply." *Corrections Today* 59 (7): 104–6.

Ali-Joseph, Alisse. 2018. "'Exercising Sovereignty: American Indian Collegiate Athletes." In *Crime and Social Justice in Indian Country*, edited by Marianne O. Nielsen and Karen Jarratt-Snider, 96–115. Tucson: University of Arizona Press.

Anaya, S. James. 1996. *Indigenous Peoples in International Law*. New York: Oxford University Press.

Anderson, Fred. 2000. *Crucible of War: The Seven Years' War and the Fate of Empire in British North America 1754–1766*. New York: Alfred A. Knopf.

Angell, Stephen W. 2003. "'Learn of the Heathen': Quakers and Indians in Southern New England, 1656–1676." *Quaker History: The Bulletin of the Friends Historical Association* 92 (1): 1–21. https://doi.org/10.1353/qkh.2003.0016.

Applegarth, Albert C. 1892. *Quakers in Pennsylvania*. Baltimore, Md.: Johns Hopkins University Press.

APTN National News. 2018. "Gerald Stanley Acquitted of All Charges in the Death of Colton Boushie." https://www.aptnnews.ca/national-news/gerald-stanley-acquitted-of-all-charges-in-the-death-of-colten-boushie/.

Archuleta, Margaret, Brenda J. Child, and K. T. Lomawaima, eds. 2000. *Away from Home: American Indian Boarding School Experiences, 1879–2000*. Phoenix, Ariz.: Heard Museum.

Austin, Raymond D. 1993. "Freedom, Responsibility and Duty: ADR and the Navajo Peacemaker Court." *The Judges Journal* 32 (2): 8–11.

Austin, Raymond D. 2009. *Navajo Courts and Navajo Common Law: A Tradition of Tribal Self-Governance.* Minneapolis: University of Minnesota Press.

Auth, Stephen F. 1989. *The Ten Years' War: Indian White Relations in Pennsylvania, 1755–1765.* New York: Garland.

Bacon, Margaret Hope. 1986 [1997]. *Mothers of Feminism: The Story of Quaker Women in America.* San Francisco: Harper & Row.

Bankhurst, Benjamin. 2009. "A Looking-Glass for Presbyterians: Recasting a Prejudice in Late Colonial Pennsylvania." *Pennsylvania Magazine of History and Biography* 133 (4): 317–48.

Barbour, Hugh, and Arthur O. Roberts, eds. 1973. *Early Quaker Writings 1650–1700.* Wallingford, Pa.: Pendle Hill Publications.

Barnes, Henry E. 1922. "Criminal Code of Pennsylvania." *Bulletin of the Friends Historical Society* 11 (1): 3–16.

Barton, Lois. 1990. *A Quaker Promise Kept: Philadelphia Friends' Work with the Allegany Senecas 1795–1960.* Eugene, Ore.: Spencer Butte Press.

Batchelor, Ray. 2019. "'Cast under Our Care': Elite Quaker Masculinity and Political Rhetoric about American Indians in the Age of Revolutions." In *Quakers and Native Americans,* edited by Ignacio Gallup-Diaz and Geoffrey Plank, 75–92. Boston, N.Y.: Brill.

Battey, Thomas C. 1875 [1968, 1972, 2012, 2017]. *The Life and Adventures of a Quaker among the Indians.* Boston: Lee and Shepard.

Battey, Thomas C. 1899. "Introduction." In *Our Red Brothers and the Peace Policy of President Ulysses S. Grant,* by Lawrie Tatum, vii–xix. Lincoln: University of Nebraska Press.

Bauman, Richard. 1971. *For the Reputation of Truth: Politics, Religion, and Conflict Among the Pennsylvania Quakers 1750–1800.* Baltimore, Md.: Johns Hopkins University Press.

Becker, Marshall, J. 1976. "The Okehocking: A Remnant Band of the Delaware Indians." *Pennsylvania Archaeologist* 43 (3): 24–61.

Becker, Marshall, J. 1980. "Lenape Archaeology: Archaeological and Ethnohistoric Considerations in Light of Recent Excavations." *Pennsylvania Archaeologist* 50 (4): 19–30.

Beckman, Gail M. 1976. *The Statutes of Pennsylvania in the Time of William Penn.* Vol. 1: *1680–1700.* New York: Vantage Press.

Berkhofer, Robert F. 1979. *The White Man's Indian: Images of the American Indian from Columbus to the Present.* New York: Vintage Books.

Berthrong, Donald J. 1976 [1992]. *The Cheyenne and Arapaho Ordeal: Reservation and Agency Life in the Indian Territory, 1875–1907.* Norman: University of Oklahoma Press.

Bierhorst, John. 1995. *Mythology of the Lenape.* Tucson: University of Arizona Press.

BillyPenn. 2020. "Meet Hannah Callowhill Penn, PA's First and Only Woman Leader." https://billypenn.com/2018/03/08/meet-hannah-callowhill-penn-pas-first-and-only-woman-leader/.

Birkel, Michael L. 2004. *Silence and Witness: The Quaker Tradition.* Maryknoll, N.Y.: Orbis Books.

Bishop, Elaine. 2018. "Apologies and Beyond." Presented at Truth and Healing: Quakers Seeking Right Relationship with Indigenous Peoples conference, May 3–6, Pendle Hill, Pa.

Blaut, J. M. 1993. *The Colonizer's Model of the World.* New York: Guilford Press.

Bluehouse, Philmer, and James W. Zion. 1993. "Hoozhooji Naat'aanii: The Navajo Justice and Harmony Ceremony." *Mediation Quarterly* 10 (4): 327–37.

Blumenfeld, Warren. 2018. "Reverend Dr. Martin Luther King Jr. and No Peace Without Justice." April 2, 2018. https://goodmenproject.com/featured-content/reverend-dr-martin-luther -king-jr-and-no-peace-without-justice/#:~:text=strong%3E%E2%80%9CThere%20can%20 be%20no,protesters%20on%20December%2014%2C%201967.

Boulder Friends Meeting. No date. "Boulder Friends Meeting." www.boulderfriendsmeeting.org.

Bowden, James. 1850. *The History of the Society of Friends in America*. London: Charles Gilpin.

Brinton, Daniel G. 1885. *The Lenape and their Legends*. Philadelphia: Brinton's Library of Aboriginal American Literature.

Brinton, Howard. 1950 [1993, 2006]. *Guide to Quaker Practice*. Pendle Hill Pamphlet no. 20. Wallingford, Pa.: Pendle Hill Publications.

Brinton, Howard. 2002. *Friends for 350 Years: Edited and Updated by Margaret Hope Bacon*. Wallingford, Pa.: Pendle Hill Publications.

Brock, Peter. 1971. *Pioneers of the Peaceable Kingdom: The Quaker Peace Testimony from the Colonial Era to the First World War*. Princeton, N.J.: Princeton University Press.

Bronner, Edwin B. 1953. "Philadelphia County Court of Quarter Sessions and Common Pleas, 1695." *Pennsylvania Magazine of History and Biography* 77 (4): 457–80.

Bronner, Edwin, B. 1968. "The Quakers and Non-Violence in Pennsylvania." *Pennsylvania History: A Journal of Mid-Atlantic Studies* 35 (1) 1–22.

Bronner, Edwin B. 1981. "A Time of Change: Philadelphia Yearly Meeting 1861–1914." In *Friends in the Delaware Valley: Philadelphia Yearly Meeting 1681–1981*, edited by John M. Moore, 103–37. Haverford, Pa.: Friends Historical Association.

Brown, Peter G., and Geoffrey Garver. 2009. *Right Relationship: Building a Whole Earth Economy*. San Francisco: Berrett-Koehler Publishers.

Brubaker, Jack. 2010. *Massacre of the Conestogas: On the Trail of the Paxton Boys in Lancaster County*. Charleston, S.C.: The History Press.

Burrell, Gibson, and Gareth Morgan. 1979. *Sociological Paradigms and Organizational Analysis*. London: Heinemann.

Camenzind, Krista. 2004. "Violence, Race, and the Paxton Boys." In *Friends and Enemies in Penn's Woods: Indians, Colonists, and the Racial Construction of Pennsylvania*, edited by William A. Pencak and Daniel K. Richter, 201–20. University Park: Pennsylvania State University Press.

Canadian Friends Service Committee (CFSC). No date-a. "Canadian Friends Service Committee: Quakers Working for Justice and Peace." Accessed April 13, 2020. www.quakerservice.ca.

Canadian Friends Service Committee (CFSC). No date-b. "Our Work: Indigenous Peoples Rights." Accessed April 6, 2021. https://quakerservice.ca/our-work/indigenous-peoples -rights/.

Canadian Yearly Meeting of the Religious Society of Friends. 2011. Faith and Practice. Ottawa, Ont.: Canadian Yearly Meeting.

Chandler, Sarah. 2001. "The Never Broken Treaty? Quaker Witness and Testimony on Aboriginal Title and Rights: What Canst Thou Say?" *Sunderland P. Gardner Lecture 2001*. Canadian Quaker Pamphlet Series 54. Argenta, B.C.: Argenta Friends Press.

Coates, Ken S. 2004. *A Global History of Indigenous Peoples: Struggle and Survival*. New York: Palgrave Macmillan.

Cocks, Joan. 2012. "The Violence of Structures and the Violence of Foundings." *New Political Science* 34 (2): 221–27.

Coker, Dennis, Chief, Lenape Indian Tribe of Delaware. 2018. "Words from the Lenape Chiefs." Presented at Truth and Healing: Quakers Seeking Right Relationship with Indigenous Peoples conference, May 3–6, Pendle Hill, Pa.

Colonial Society of Pennsylvania. 1910. *Record of the Courts of Chester County, Pennsylvania, 1681–1697.* Vol. 1. Philadelphia, Pa.: Patterson & White.

Comack, Elizabeth. 2018. "Corporate Colonialism and the 'Crimes of the Powerful' Committed Against the Indigenous Peoples of Canada." *Critical Criminology* 26: 455–71.

"Concessions and Agreements of the Proprietors, Freeholders and Inhabitants of the Province of West New Jersey in America." 1676 [1951]. Burlington, N.J.: Burlington Press.

Council of Europe. 2018. "Promoting More Human and Socially Effective Penal Sanctions. Recommendation CM/Rec (2018) 8 Concerning Restorative Justice in Criminal Matters." https://rm.coe.int/CoERMPublicCommonSearchServices/DisplayDCTMContent?documentId=09000016808e35f3.

Cullen, Frances. 2005. "The Twelve People Who Saved Rehabilitation: How the Science of Criminology Made a Difference." *Criminology* 43 (1): 1–42.

Cunneen, Chris. 1997. "Hysteria and Hate: The Vilification of Aboriginal and Torres Strait Islander People." In *Faces of Hate: Hate Crime in Australia*, edited by Chris Cunneen, Stephen Tomsen, and David Fraser, 137–61. Annandale, NSW: Federation Press.

Daiutolo, Robert, Jr. 1988. "The Role of Quakers in Indian Affairs During the French and Indian War." *Quaker History* 77 (1): 1–30. https://doi.org/10.1353/qkh.1988.0016.

Delaware Historical Society. 2019. "Delaware Facts or Interesting Things About the First State." http://dehistory.org/delaware-facts.

Dewees, Watson W. 1912. "Thomas Penn's Walking Purchase." *Bulletin of Friends Historical Society* 4 (2): 124–32.

Dodge, Mary. 2016. "White-Collar Crimes, Harm and Victimisation." In *A Companion to Crimes, Harm and Victimisation*, edited by Karen Corteen, Sharon Morley, Paul Taylor, and Jo Turner, 271–73. Bristol, UK: Policy Press.

Dorland, Arthur Garratt. 1968. *The Quakers in Canada: A History.* Toronto: Ryerson Press.

Dudiak, Jeffrey. 2020. "Quakers and Their Truth." Personal Communication.

Dudiak, Jeffrey, ed. 2015. *Befriending Truth: Quaker Perspectives.* Philadelphia, Pa.: Friends Association for Higher Education.

Dumont, James. 1993. "Justice and Aboriginal People." In *Aboriginal Peoples and the Justice System: Report of the National Round Table on Aboriginal Justice Issues*, edited by the Royal Commission on Aboriginal Peoples, 42–85. Ottawa, Ont.: Ministry of Supply and Services.

Dumont, James. 1996. "Justice and Native Peoples." In *Native Americans, Crime and Justice*, edited by Marianne O. Nielsen and Robert A. Silverman, 20–33. Boulder, Colo.: Westview.

Dunbar, John R., ed. 1957. *The Paxton Papers.* The Hague: Martinus Nijhoff.

Dunbar-Ortiz, Roxanne. 2014. *An Indigenous Peoples' History of the United States.* Boston: Beacon Press.

Dunn, Richard S., and Mary Maples Dunn, eds. 1982. *The Papers of William Penn.* Vol. 2: *1680–1684.* Philadelphia: University of Pennsylvania Press.

Duran, Eduardo, and Bonnie Duran. 1995. *Native American Postcolonial Psychology*. New York: SUNY Press.

Dutta, Kalpalata. 2020. "Violence Triangle of Johan Galtung in Context of Conflict Theory." Institute for Human Rights. March 31, 2020. https://www.aihrhre.org/understanding -violence-triangle-johan-galtung-conflict-theory/.

Echohawk, John. 2019. "A Shared Vision for Healing." In *Quakers and Native Americans*, edited by Ignacio Gallup-Diaz and Geoffrey Plank, 312–20. Leiden, Netherlands: Brill.

Elkinton [Elkington], Joseph. 1859 [1914, 1994]. *Quaker Mission Among the Indians of New York State*. Ithaca, N.Y.: Cornell University Library Digital Collections.

Ellwood, Lisa. 2018. "Nanticoke-Lenape of NJ Win Six-Year Battle to Restore State Recognition." *Indian Country Today, Newsmaven*. November 21, 2018. https://newsmaven.io/ indiancountrytoday/news/nanticoke-lenape-of-nj-win-six-year-battle-to-restore-state -recognition-8NBx9aIzLomzUiU2D7Pk8g/.

Engels, Jeremy. 2005. "'Equipped for Murder': The Paxton Boys and the 'Spirit of Killing all Indians' in Pennsylvania 1763–1764." *Rhetoric and Public Affairs* 8 (3), 355–381.

FineDay, Max. 2020. "Reconciliation Can't Happen Without Reclamation of Land." *Canadian Broadcasting Company Radio*. January 20, 2020.

Fisher, Sydney George. 1919. *The Quaker Colonies: A Chronicle of the Proprietors of the Delaware*. University of Toronto reprint catalog record MARCXML. http://www.archive.org/details/ quakercoloniesoofish.

Fixico, Donald L. 2013. *Indian Resilience and Rebuilding: Indigenous Nations in the Modern American West*. Tucson: University of Arizona Press.

"Frame of Government of Pennsylvania May 5th 1682." New Haven, Conn.: The Avalon Project, Yale Law School.

Franklin, Ursula M. 2006. *The Ursula Franklin Reader: Pacifism as a Map*. Toronto, Ont.: Between the Lines.

Fraser, Crystal, and Sara Komarnisky. No date. *150 Acts of Reconciliation for Canada's 150*. Accessed May 2, 2021. http://activehistory.ca/wp-content/uploads/2017/08/150acts.pdf.

Friends Committee on National Legislation (FCNL). No date-a. "Friends Committee on National Legislation." Accessed March 27, 2020. https://www.fcnl.org.

Friends Committee on National Legislation (FCNL). No Date-b. *FCNL's Native American Policy Program*. Pamphlet. Washington: Friends Committee on National Legislation.

Friends General Conference (FGC). No date. Homepage. Accessed May 16, 2020. https://www .fgcquaker.org/discover/.

Friends United Meeting (FUM). No date. Homepage. Accessed May 16, 2020. https://friends unitedmeeting.org.

Friends World Committee for Consultation (FWCC). No date. "World Office." Accessed March 17, 2021. https://www.fwcc.world.

Friesen, Joe. 2018. "The Night Colton Boushie Died: What Family and Police Files Say About His Last Day and What Came After." https://www.theglobeandmail.com/news/national/ colten-boushie/article32451940/.

Futhey, J. Smith, and Gilbert Cope. 1881. *History of Chester County, Pennsylvania with Genealogical and Biographical Sketches*. Philadelphia, Pa.: Louis H. Everts.

Gallup-Diaz, Ignacio, and Geoffrey Plank, eds. 2019. *Quakers and Native Americans*. Leiden, Netherlands: Brill.

Galtung, Johan. 1990. "Cultural Violence." *Journal of Peace Research* 27 (1): 291–305.

Gerona, Carla. 2004. "Imagining Peace in Quaker and Native American Dream Stories." In *Friends and Enemies in Penn's Woods: Indians, Colonists, and the Racial Construction of Pennsylvania*, edited by William A. Pencak and Daniel K. Richter, 41–62. University Park: Pennsylvania State University Press.

Giago, Tim. 2006. *Children Left Behind: The Dark Legacy of Indian Mission Boarding Schools*. Santa Fe, N.Mex.: Clear Light Publishing.

Gimber, Steven G. 2000. "Kinship and Covenants in the Wilderness: Indians, Quakers and Conversion to Christianity, 1675–1800." PhD diss., American University. ProQuest (9965829).

Globe and Mail. 2020. "Wet'suwet'en Chiefs, Blockades and Coastal GasLink: A Guide to the Dispute Over a B.C. Pipeline." https://www.theglobeandmail.com/canada/british-columbia/article-wetsuweten-coastal-gaslink-pipeline-rcmp-explainer/.

Goddard, Ives. 1974. "The Delaware Language, Past and Present." In *A Delaware Symposium*, edited by Herbert C. Kraft, 103–10. Harrisburg: Pennsylvania Historical and Museum Commission.

Goldberg, Carole E. 1997. "Overextended Borrowing: Tribal Peacemaking Applied to Non-Indian Disputes." *Washington Law Review*, no. 72, 1003–19.

Graber, Jennifer. 2014. "'If a War It May Be Called': The Peace Policy with American Indians." *Religion and American Culture: A Journal of Interpretation* 24 (1): 36–69.

Green, Howard L., ed. 1995. *Words that Make New Jersey History*. New Brunswick, N.J.: Rutgers University Press.

Grumet, Robert S., ed. 2001. *Voices from the Delaware Big House Ceremony*. Norman: University of Oklahoma Press.

Guenther, Karen. 2001. "A Crisis of Allegiance: Berks County, Pennsylvania Quakers and the War for Independence." *Quaker History* 90 (2): 15–34.

Hall, Richard H. 1999. *Organizations: Structures, Processes, and Outcomes*. 7th ed. Upper Saddle River, N.J.: Prentice-Hall.

Hamm, Thomas D. 2003. *The Quakers in America*. New York: Columbia University Press.

Hanna, Charles A. 1911 [1971]. *The Wilderness Trail or The Ventures and Adventures of the Pennsylvania Traders on the Allegheny Path*. New York: AMS Press.

Harper, Steven C. 2004. "Delawares and Pennsylvanians after the Walking Purchase." In *Friends and Enemies in Penn's Woods: Indians, Colonists and the Racial Construction of Pennsylvania*, edited by William A. Pencak and Daniel K. Richter, 167–79. University Park: Pennsylvania State University Press.

Harper, Steven C. 2016 "Friendly Association: The Alliance of Delawares and Quakers in the 1750s." Presented at Quakers, First Nations and American Indians conferences, November 10–12. Haverford College, Philadelphia, Pa.

Harrington, M. R. 1913. "A Preliminary Sketch of Lenape Culture." *American Antiquity*, no. 15, 208–35.

Harvey, Henry. 1855. "History of the Shawnee Indians, from the Year 1681 to 1854, Inclusive." Cincinnati, Ohio: Ephraim Morgan & Sons. Accessed June 3, 2012. www.archive.org/stream/shawneeomdoamsooharvrich.

Hass-Wisecup, Aida Y., and Caryn E. Saxon. 2018. *Restorative Justice: Integrating Theory, Research, and Practice*. Durham, N.C.: Carolina Academic Press.

Hayburn, Tim. 2005. "Words to Live By: Society of Friends, *Books of Discipline*, 1704–1747." Unpublished paper in Special Collections at Haverford College. Used with permission of author.

Heard Museum Guild. No date. "Princess Tsianina Red Feather." Accessed July 20, 2021. https://www.heardguild.org/princess-tsianina-red-feather/.

Heckewelder, Rev. John. 1876. *History, Manners, and Customs of the Indian Nations Who Once Inhabited Pennsylvania and the Neighbouring States*. Rev. ed. Philadelphia: Historical Society of Pennsylvania.

Hillyard, Paddy, and Steve Tombs. 2004. "Beyond Criminology?" In *Beyond Criminology: Taking Harm Seriously*, edited by Paddy Hillyard, Christina Pantazis, Steve Tombs, and Dave Gordon, 10–29. London: Pluto Press.

Hindle, Brooke. 1946. "The March of the Paxton Boys." *The William and Mary Quarterly: A Magazine of Early American History, Institutions, and Culture* 3 (4): 461–86.

Hirsch, Alison D. 2004. "Indian, Metis and Euro-American Women on Multiple Frontiers." In *Friends and Enemies in Penn's Woods: Indians, Colonists and the Racial Construction of Pennsylvania*, edited by William A. Pencak and Daniel K. Richter, 63–84. University Park: Pennsylvania State University Press.

Hixon, Robert. 1981. "Lawrie Tatum, Indian Agent; Quaker Values and Hard Choices." Pendle Hill Pamphlet no. 238. Wallingford, Pa.: Pendle Hill Publications.

Hunter, William A. 1978. "Documented Subdivisions of The Delaware Indians." *Bulletin of the Archaeological Society of New Jersey*, no. 35, 20–40.

Illick, Joseph E. 1971. "'Some of Our Best Indians Are Friends . . .': Quaker Attitudes and Actions Regarding the Western Indians During the Grant Administration." *Western Historical Quarterly* 2 (3): 283–94.

Indian Country Today. 2019. "Ramapough Lenape and Powhatan Renape Nations of New Jersey have State Recognition Reaffirmed." https://indiancountrytoday.com/news/ramapough -lenape-and-powhatan-renape-nations-of-new-jersey-have-state-recognition-reaffirmed -NUHKiCDZSU6qB0ZZyJp1fg.

Jackson, Maurice. 2009. *Let This Voice be Heard: Anthony Benezet, Father of Atlantic Abolition*. Philadelphia: University of Pennsylvania Press.

Jacobs, Margaret D. 2006. "Indian Boarding Schools in Comparative Perspective: The Removal of Indigenous Children in the United States and Australia, 1880–1940." In *Boarding School Blues: Revisiting American Indian Educational Experiences*, edited by Clifford E. Trafzer, Jean A. Keller, and Lorene Sisquoc, 202–31. Lincoln: University of Nebraska Press.

Jacobs, Margaret D. 2009. *White Mother to a Dark Race: Settler Colonialism, and the Removal of Indigenous Children in the American West and Australia 1880–1940*. Lincoln: University of Nebraska Press.

Jacobs, Wilbur R. 1969. "British-Colonial Attitudes and Policies Toward the Indian in the American Colonies." In *Attitudes of Colonial Powers Toward the American Indian*, edited by Howard Peckham and Charles Gibson, 81–106. Salt Lake City: University of Utah Press.

James, Sydney V. 1962. "The Impact of the American Revolution on Quakers' Ideas about Their Sect." *The William and Mary Quarterly* 19 (3): 360–82.

James, Sydney V. 1963. *A People Among Peoples: Quaker Benevolence in Eighteenth Century America*. Cambridge, Mass.: Harvard University Press.

Jennings, Francis. 1965. "Miquon's Passing: Indian-European Relations in Colonial Pennsylvania, 1674–1755." PhD diss., University of Pennsylvania. ProQuest (6604621).

Jennings, Francis. 1974. "The Delaware Indians in the Covenant Chain." In *A Delaware Symposium*, edited by Herbert C. Kraft, 89–102. Harrisburg: Pennsylvania Historical and Museum Commission.

Jennings, Francis. 1984. *The Ambiguous Iroquois Empire*. New York: W. W. Norton & Co.

Jones, Rufus, assisted by Isaac Sharpless and Amelia M. Gummere. 1962. *The Quakers in the American Colonies*. New York: Russell & Russell Inc.

Jones, Rufus, assisted by Isaac Sharpless and Amelia M. Gummere. 1966. *The Quakers in the American Colonies*. New York: W. W. Norton & Co.

Keil, Amanda. 2001. *The Peaceful People and the First Nations: A Brief History of Friends and Native Americans*. New York: American Friends Service Committee.

Kelsey, Rayner W. 1917. *Friends and the Indians, 1655–1917*. Philadelphia, Pa.: Associated Executive Committee of Friends on Indian Affairs.

Kenny, Kevin. 2009. *Peaceable Kingdom Lost: The Paxton Boys and the Destruction of William Penn's Holy Experiment*. Oxford, UK: Oxford University Press.

Keyser, Charles S. 1882. *Penn's Treaty with the Indians*. Philadelphia, Pa.: David McKay.

Kershner, Jon. 2020. "Personal Communication about John Woolman."

Kraft, Herbert C. 1974. "Indian Prehistory of New Jersey." In *A Delaware Symposium*, edited by Herbert C. Kraft, 1–56. Harrisburg: Pennsylvania Historical and Museum Commission.

Lajimodere, Denise. 2018. "The Past is Present: Intergenerational Trauma Suffered Today." Presentation at Truth and Healing: Quakers Seeking Right Relationship with Indigenous Peoples conference, May 3–6, Pendle Hill, Pa. Accessed May 19, 2020. Also available at https://www.youtube.com/watch?v=MnuoGIiO2QM as "Indian Boarding Schools and Historical Trauma."

Lednicer, Oliver. 1959. "Peacemaker Court in New York State." *New York University Intramural Law Review*, no. 14, 188–95.

Legge, Matthew. 2019. *Are We Done Fighting? Building Understanding in a World of Hate and Division*. Gabriola Island, B.C.: New Society Publishers.

Lenape Nation of Pennsylvania. 2018. "Lenape Nation of Pennsylvania." https://www.lenape-nation.org/.

Levy, Barry. 1988. *Quakers and the American Family: British Settlement in the Delaware Valley*. New York: Oxford University Press.

London Yearly Meeting. 1737. "Extracts of Advices and Minutes, 1675–1737." MC 976. Haverford, Pa.: Quakers and Special Collections, Haverford College.

London Yearly Meeting. 1960. *Book of Discipline*. Haverford, Pa.: Quakers and Special Collections, Haverford College.

Looking Horse, Chief Arvol. No Date. "White Buffalo Teachings (excerpts from)." https://www.thebridgekeepers.com/white-buffalo-teachings.html.

Loyd, William H. 1910. *The Early Courts of Pennsylvania*. Boston: Boston Book Co.

Making Peace and Sharing Power. 1997. *Proceedings of Making Peace and Sharing Power: A National Gathering of Aboriginal Peoples and Dispute Resolution.* Victoria, B.C.: University of Victoria Centre for Dispute Resolution.

Malakieh, Jamil. 2020. "Adult and Youth Correctional Statistics, 2018/2019." Statistics Canada. https://www150.statcan.gc.ca/n1/pub/85-002-x/2020001/article/00016-eng.htm.

Manuel, Arthur. 2015. *Unsettling Canada: A National Wake-up Call.* Toronto, Ont.: Between the Lines.

Marietta, Jack D. 1984. *The Reformation of American Quakerism, 1748–1783.* Philadelphia: University of Pennsylvania Press.

Marsh, Dawn G. 2014. *A Lenape Among the Quakers: The Life of Hannah Freeman.* Lincoln: University of Nebraska Press.

Martinson, Robert. 1974. "What Works? Questions and Answers about Prison Reform." *Public Interest,* no. 35, 22–54.

Matwick, Angela L., and Roberta L. Woodgate. 2016. "Social Justice: A Conceptual Analysis." *Public Health Nursing* 34 (2): 176–84.

McDaniel, Donna, and Vanessa Julye. 2009. *Fit for Freedom, Not for Friendship: Quakers, African Americans, and the Myth of Racial Justice.* Philadelphia, Pa.: Quaker Press of Friends General Conference.

McKellips, Karen K. 1992. "Educational Practices in Two Nineteenth Century American Indian Mission Schools." *Journal of American Indian Education* 32 (1): 12–20.

Mekeel, Arthur J. 1981. "The Founding Years 1681–1789." In *Friends in the Delaware Valley: Philadelphia Yearly Meeting 1681–1981,* edited by John M. Moore, 14–55. Haverford, Pa.: Friends Historical Association.

Merrell, James H. 1999. *Into the American Woods: Negotiators on the Pennsylvania Frontier.* New York: W. W. Norton & Co.

Meyer, Jon'a F. 2005. "Bił Háí'áázh ('I am His Brother'): Can Peacemaking Work with Juveniles." In *Navajo Nation Peacemaking: Living Traditional Justice,* edited by Marianne O. Nielsen and James W. Zion, 125–42. Tucson: University of Arizona Press.

Mihesuah, Devon A. 1993. *Cultivating the Rosebuds: The Education of Women at the Cherokee Female Seminary, 1851–1909.* Chicago: University of Illinois Press.

Milner, Clyde A., II. 1982. *With Good Intentions; Quaker Work among the Pawnees, Otos, and Omahas in the 1870s.* Lincoln: University of Nebraska Press.

Mitchell, Rodney, dir. 1996. *Two Rivers.* Eagle, ID: Greenleaf Street Production. DVD (Methone Valley Interpretive Center). http://www.tworiversfilm.com/index.htm.

Moore, John M., ed. 1981. *Friends in the Delaware Valley: Philadelphia Yearly Meeting 1681–1981.* Haverford, Pa.: Friends Historical Association.

Morse, Bradford W., ed. 1989. *Aboriginal Peoples and the Law.* Rev. 1st ed. Ottawa, Ont.: Carleton University Press.

Moulton, Phillips P., ed. 1971. *The Journal and Major Essays of John Woolman.* Richmond, Ind.: Friends United Press.

Mt. Pleasant, Alyssa. 2014. "Guiding Principles: Gus Wenta and the Debate over Formal Schooling at Buffalo Creek, 1800–1811." In *Hemispheric Perspectives on the History of Indigenous Edu-*

cation, edited by Brenda J. Child and Brian Klopotek, 114–32. Santa Fe, N.Mex.: School for Advanced Research Press (SAR).

Myers, Albert A., ed. 1970. *William Penn's Own Account of the Lenni Lenape or Delaware Indians*. Rev. ed. Somerset, N.J.: Middle Atlantic Press.

National Centre for Truth and Reconciliation. No date. *Truth and Reconciliation: Calls to Action*. Winnipeg: University of Manitoba.

National Park Service (NPS). 2020. "Zitkala-Ša (Red Bird / Gertrude Simmons Bonnin)." https://www.nps.gov/people/zitkala-sa.htm.

Native American Rights Fund (NARF). No date. "Indigenous Peacemaking Initiative." Accessed April 12, 2020. https://peacemaking.narf.org/.

Navajo Nation Judicial Branch. No date-a. "Áłchíní BáNdazhnit'á–Diné Family Group Conferencing." Accessed April 6, 2021. http://www.courts.navajo-nsn.gov/Peacemaking/Plan/fgc.html.

Navajo Nation Judicial Branch. No date-b. "The Peacemaking Program of the Navajo Nation: Institutional History of Hózhóji Naat'aah." Accessed April 6, 2021. http://www.courts.navajo-nsn.gov/indexpeacemaking.htm.

Navajo Nation Judicial Branch. No date-c. "The Peacemaking Program of the Navajo Nation: Nábináhaazláago Áłch'į' yáti'" Accessed April 6, 2021. http://www.courts.navajo-nsn.gov/indexpeacemaking.htm.

Nayar, Pramod K. 2015. *The Postcolonial Studies Dictionary*. Hoboken, N.J.: John Wiley & Sons.

New York Yearly Meeting, Religious Society of Friends. 1785. *Book of Discipline, New York Yearly Meeting, 1785 and Rules of Discipline of the Yearly Meeting Held in Rhode Island for New England*. New Bradford, Mass.: Abraham Shearman.

Nicholas, Mark A. 2006. "A Little School, A Reservation Divided: Quaker Education and Allegany Seneca Leadership in the Early American Republic." *American Indian Culture and Research Journal* 30 (3): 1–21.

Nickalls John L. 1952. *The Journal of George Fox*. Rev. ed. Cambridge, UK: Cambridge University Press.

Nielsen, Marianne O. 2005. "Navajo Nation Courts and Peacemaking: Restorative Justice Issues." In *Navajo Nation Peacemaking: Living Traditional Justice*, edited by Marianne O. Nielsen and James W. Zion, 143–55. Tucson: University of Arizona Press.

Nielsen, Marianne O., and Karen Jarratt-Snider, eds. 2018. *Crime and Social Justice in Indian Country*. Tucson: University of Arizona Press.

Nielsen, Marianne O., and Karen Jarratt-Snider, eds. 2020. *Traditional, National, and International Law and Indigenous Communities*. Tucson: University of Arizona Press.

Nielsen, Marianne O., and Linda M. Robyn. 2019. *Colonialism is Crime*. New Brunswick, N.J.: Rutgers University Press.

Nielsen, Marianne O., and James W. Zion., eds. 2005. *Navajo Nation Peacemaking: Living Traditional Justice*. Tucson: University of Arizona Press.

Nies, Judith. 1996. *Native American History*. New York: Ballantine Books.

Osterhammel, Jurgen. 1997. *Colonialism: A Theoretical Overview*. Princeton, N.J.: Markus Wiener Publishers.

Palmer, Paula. 2020. "The Land Remembers: Connecting with Native Peoples through the Land." *Friends Journal* (February): 21–25.

Passas, Nikos. 2016. "Legal Crimes—Lawful But Awful." In *A Companion to Crimes, Harm and Victimisation*, edited by Karen Corteen, Sharon Morley, Paul Taylor, and Jo Turner, 125–27. Bristol, UK: Policy Press.

Pemberton, Simon. 2004. "A Theory of Moral Indifference: Understanding the Production of Harm by Capitalist Society." In *Beyond Criminology: Taking Harm Seriously*, edited by Paddy Hillyard, Christina Pantazis, Steve Tombs, and Dave Gordon, 67–83. London: Pluto Press.

Pemberton, Simon. 2016. *Harmful Societies: Understanding Social Harm*. Bristol, UK: Policy Press.

Pencak, William A., and Daniel K. Richter. 2004. "Introduction." In *Friends and Enemies in Penn's Woods: Indians, Colonists, and the Racial Construction of Pennsylvania*, edited by William A. Pencak and Daniel K. Richter, ix–xxi. University Park: Pennsylvania State University Press.

Pender-Cudlip, Ben, and Adam Mazo, dirs. 2018. *Dawnland*. Upstander Project. https://upstanderproject.org/dawnland.

Penn, William. 1701. *Charter of Privileges Granted by William Penn Esq. to the Inhabitants of Pennsylvania and Territories*. October 28, 1701. https://avalon.law.yale.edu/18th_century/pa07.asp.

Pepinsky, Harold E., and Richard Quinney, eds. 1991. *Criminology as Peacemaking*. Bloomington: Indiana University Press.

Perry, Barbara. 2009. "'There's Just Places Ya' Don't Wanna Go': The Segregating Impact of Hate Crimes Against Native Americans." *Contemporary Justice Review* 12 (4): 401–18.

Petrosino, Carolyn. 1999. "Connecting the Past to the Future." *Journal of Contemporary Criminal Justice* 15 (1): 22–47.

Pointer, Richard W. 2007. *Encounters of the Spirit: Native Americans and European Colonial Religion*. Bloomington: Indiana University Press.

Pommersheim, Frank. 2009. *Broken Landscape: Indians, Indian Tribes, and the Constitution*. New York: Oxford University Press.

Presser, Lois. 2013. *Why We Harm*. New Brunswick, N.J.: Rutgers University Press.

Preston, Jennifer. 2018. "Submission to the Standing Committee on Indigenous and Northern Affairs House of Commons, Parliament of Canada; Study on Bill 262: The United Nations Declaration on the Rights of Indigenous Peoples." https://quakerservice.ca/wp-content/uploads/2018/04/INAC-Presentation-on-C-262-April-24-2018.pdf.

Preston, Jennifer. 2020. Quakers and Indigenous Rights Work for Canadian Friends Service Committee, Western Half Yearly Meeting of the Religious Society of Friends, May 16. Personal Communication.

Price, Richard T., and Cynthia Dunnigan. 1995. *Toward an Understanding of Aboriginal Peacemaking*. Victoria, B.C.: UVIC Institute for Dispute Resolution.

Ptolemy, Jayne Ellen. 2013. "'Our Native Soil': Philadelphian Quakers and Geographies of Race, 1780–1838." PhD diss., Yale University. ProQuest (3571920).

Punshon, John. 1984. *Portrait in Grey: A Short History of the Quakers*. London: Quaker Home Service.

Quakers in the World. No date. "Margaret Fell." Accessed April 6, 2021. https://www.quakers intheworld.org/quakers-in-action/14/Margaret-Fell.

Ream, Milton. 1981. "Philadelphia Friends and the Indians." In *Friends in the Delaware Valley: Philadelphia Yearly Meeting 1681–1981*, edited by John M. Moore, 200–14. Haverford, Pa.: Friends Historical Association.

Reyhner, Jon, and Jeanne Eder. 2004. *American Indian Education: A History*. Norman: University of Oklahoma Press.

Rieger, Sarah. 2020 (February 23). "Teck Withdraws Application for $20B Frontier Oilsands Mine." *CBC News*. https://www.cbc.ca/news/canada/calgary/teck-frontier-1.5473370.

Ross, Ellen M. 2019. "'The Great Spirit Hears All We Now Say': Philadelphia Quakers and the Seneca, 1798–1850." In *Quakers and Native Americans*, edited by Ignacio Gallup-Diaz and Geoffrey Plank, 115–35. Leiden, Netherlands: Brill.

Ross, Rupert. 2014. *Indigenous Healing: Exploring Traditional Paths*. Toronto, Ont.: Penguin.

Rothenberg, Diane. 1976. "Friends like These: An Ethnohistorical Analysis of the Interaction between Allegany Senecas and Quakers, 1798–1823." PhD diss., City University of New York. ProQuest Dissertations Publishing, 1976. 7611970.

Schutt, Amy C. 2007. *Peoples of the River Valleys: The Odyssey of the Delaware Indians*. Philadelphia: University of Pennsylvania Press.

Schwing, Emily. 2021 (June 30). "What the US Can Learn from Canada's Commission on Indigenous Residential Schools." *World*. https://www.pri.org/stories/2021-06-30/what-us-can-learn-canada-s-commission-indigenous-residential-schools.

Scott, Anne F. 1982. "Fishing in Troubled Waters." *Friends Journal* 1 (15): 8–11.

Scott, W. Richard. 1981 [1998]. *Organizations: Rational, Natural and Open Systems*. Englewood Cliffs, N.J.: Prentice Hall.

Seger, John H. 1934 [1957]. *Early Days Among the Cheyenne and Arapahoe Indians*, edited by Stanley Vestal. Norman: University of Oklahoma.

Sharpless, Isaac. 1898 [1902, 2002]. *A Quaker Experiment in Government VI: History of Quaker Government in Pennsylvania, 1682–1783*. Philadelphia: Ferris and Leach.

Sharpless, Isaac. 1906. "Presbyterian and Quaker in Colonial Pennsylvania." *Journal of the Presbyterian Historical Society (1901–1930)* 3 (5): 201–18.

Sharpless, Isaac. 1907. "A Pennsylvania Episode." *Bulletin of the Friends' Historical Society of Philadelphia* 1: 70–74.

Shin, Wonchul, and Elizabeth M. Bounds. 2017. "Treating Moral Harm as Social Harm: Toward a Restorative Ethics of Christian Responsibility." *Journal of the Society of Christian Ethics* 37 (2): 153–69.

Silver, Peter. 2008. *Our Savage Neighbors: How Indian War Transformed Early America*. New York: W. W. Norton & Co.

Smith, Lisa Ann. 2006. "Lives Lived in Spirit: Quaker Service for Peace and Social Justice in the Canadian Context." Unpublished master's thesis, Concordia University.

Smolenski, John. 2004. "The Death of Sawantaeny and the Problem of Justice on the Frontier." In *Friends and Enemies in Penn's Woods: Indians, Colonists and the Racial Construction of Pennsylvania*, edited by William A. Pencak and Daniel K. Richter, 104–28. University Park: Pennsylvania State University Press.

Soderlund, Jean R., ed. 1983. *William Penn and the Founding of Pennsylvania 1680–1684: A Documentary History*. Philadelphia: University of Pennsylvania Press.

Soderlund, Jean R. 2015. *Lenape Country: Delaware Valley Society Before William Penn*. Philadelphia: University of Pennsylvania Press.

Spady, James O. 2004. "Colonialism and the Discursive Antecedents of Penn's Treaty with the Indians." In *Friends and Enemies in Penn's Woods: Indians, Colonists, and the Racial Construction of Pennsylvania*, edited by William A. Pencak and Daniel K. Richter, 18–40. University Park: Pennsylvania State University Press.

Speck, Frank G. 1931. *A Study of the Delaware Indian Big House Ceremony*. Vol. 2. Harrisburg: Pennsylvania Historical Commission.

Stuart, Barry. 1997. *Building Community Justice Partnerships: Community Peacemaking Circles*. Ottawa, ON: Aboriginal Justice Directorate, Department of Justice of Canada.

Stueck, Wendy, Kristy Kirkup, and Justice Hunter. 2020. "Tentative Deal with Wet'suwet'en Nation Won't Stop Coastal GasLink Construction, B.C. Premier Horgan Says." https://www.theglobeandmail.com/canada/article-weekend-deal-with-wetsuweten-nation-wont-affect-pipeline/.

Swatzler, David. 2000. *A Friend among the Senecas: The Quaker Mission to Cornplanter's People*. Mechanicsburg, Pa.: Stackpole Books.

Sykes, John. 1958. *The Quakers: A New Look at Their Place in Society*. London: Allan Wingate.

Szasz, Margaret Connell. 1988. *Indian Education in the American Colonies 1607–1783*. Lincoln: University of Nebraska Press.

Tatum, Lawrie. 1899 [1970]. *Our Red Brothers and the Peace Policy of President Ulysses S. Grant*. Lincoln: University of Nebraska Press.

Thompson, Kari Elizabeth Rose. 2013. "Inconsistent Friends: Philadelphia Quakers and the Development of Native American Missions in the Long Eighteenth Century." PhD diss., University of Iowa. ProQuest 3566712.

Thurman, Melburn D. 1974. "Delaware Social Organization." In *A Delaware Symposium*, edited by Herbert C. Kraft, 111–34. Harrisburg: Pennsylvania Historical and Museum Commission.

Tiro, Karim M. 1997. "Words and Deeds: Natives, Europeans, and Writing in Eastern North America 1500–1850." Exhibition presented at the Rosenbach Museum and Library, Philadelphia, Pa., November 1997–March 1998.

Tiro, Karim M. 2006. "'We Wish to Do You Good': The Quaker Mission to the Oneida Nation, 1790–1840." *Journal of the Early Republic* 26 (3): 353–76.

Tombs, Steve. 2016. "Social Harm." In *A Companion to Crimes, Harm and Victimisation*, edited by Karen Corteen, Sharon Morley, Paul Taylor, and Jo Turner, 218–20. Bristol, UK: Policy Press.

Trafzer, Clifford E., Jean A. Keller, and Lorene Sisquoc, eds. 2006a. "Introduction: Origin and Development of the American Indian Boarding School System." In *Boarding School Blues: Revisiting American Indian Educational Experiences*, edited by Clifford E. Trafzer, Kean A. Keller, and Lorene Sisquoc, 1–34. Lincoln: University of Nebraska Press.

Trafzer, Clifford E., Jean A. Keller, and Lorene Sisquoc, eds. 2006b. "Preface." In *Boarding School Blues: Revisiting American Indian Educational Experiences*, edited by Clifford E. Trafzer, Kean A. Keller, and Lorene Sisquoc, xii. Lincoln: University of Nebraska Press.

Treese, Lorett. 1992 [2002]. *The Storm Gathering: The Penn Family and the American Revolution.* Mechanicsburg, Pa.: Stackpole Books.

Trennert, Robert A. 1983. "From Carlisle to Phoenix: The Rise and Fall of the Indian Outing System 1878–1930." *The Pacific Historical Review* 52 (3): 267–91.

Trigger, Bruce G. 1985. *Natives and Newcomers.* Kingston, Ont.: McGill-Queen's University Press.

Trumpener, Betsy. 2021. "A Year after Wet'suwet'en Blockades, Coastal GasLink Pipeline Pushes on Through Pandemic." *CBC News.* February 2005, 2021. https://www.cbc.ca/news/canada/british-columbia/coastal-gaslink-pipeline-bc-wet-suwet-en-pandemic-1.5898219.

Truth and Reconciliation Commission of Canada. 2015. *Honouring the Truth, Reconciling for the Future: Final Report of the Truth and Reconciliation Commission of Canada.* Vol. 1: *Summary.* Toronto, Ont.: James Lorimer.

Turner, C. H. B. 1909. *Some Records of Sussex County Delaware.* Philadelphia, Pa.: Allen, Lane and Scott.

Uhler, Sherman P. 1951. *Pennsylvania's Indian Relations to 1754.* New York: AMS Press.

United Nations (UN). 2007. "The Declaration on the Rights of Indigenous Peoples." https://undocs.org/A/RES/61/295.

United Nations Security Council (UN). 2004. "Resolution 1566" ("Concerning Threats to International Peace and Security Caused by Terrorism"). https://www.un.org/ruleoflaw/files/no454282.pdf.

United States Bureau of Indian Affairs, Department of the Interior. No date. "Frequently Asked Questions." Accessed February 13, 2021. https://www.bia.gov/frequently-asked-questions.

Van Ness, Daniel W. 1996. "Restorative Justice and International Human Rights." In *Restorative Justice: International Perspectives,* edited by Burt Galaway and Joe Hudson, 17–35. Monsey, N.Y.: Criminal Justice Press.

Van Ness, Daniel W., and Karen Heetderks Strong. 2006. *Restoring Justice: An Introduction to Restorative Justice.* 3rd ed. No location: LexisNexis.

Van Wormer, Katherine S., and Lorenn Walker, eds. 2013. *Restorative Justice Today: Practical Applications.* Los Angeles: Sage Publications.

Vipont, Elfrida. 1977. *The Story of Quakerism through Three Centuries.* 3rd ed. Richmond, Ind.: Friends United Press.

Walker, Margaret Urban. 2006. *Moral Repair: Reconstructing Social Relations After Wrongdoing.* New York: Cambridge University Press.

Walker, Polly O. (Daksi). 2006. "One Heart and a Wrong Spirit: The Religious Society of Friends and Colonial Racism." The James Backhouse Lecture. Kenmore, Queensland: The Religious Society of Friends in Australia.

Wallace, Paul A. W. 1961 [1971, 1981]. *Indians in Pennsylvania.* Harrisburg: Pennsylvania Historical and Museum Commission.

Weddle, Meredith Baldwin. 2001. *Walking in the Way of Peace: Quaker Pacifism in the Seventeenth Century.* New York: Oxford University Press.

Weslager, C. A. 1972 [2007]. *The Delaware Indians: A History.* New Brunswick, N.J.: Rutgers University Press.

White, Andrew P. 2003. "'Keeping Clear from the Gain of Oppression': 'Public Friends' and the De-mastering of Quaker Race Relations in Late Colonial America." PhD diss., Washington State University. ProQuest (3109901).

Wolfe, Patrick. 2006. "Settler-Colonialism and the Elimination of the Native." *Journal of Geno-cide Research* 8 (4): 387–409.

Woolford, Andrew. 2015. *This Benevolent Experiment: Indigenous Boarding Schools, Genocide, and Redress in Canada and the United States.* Lincoln: University of Nebraska.

Women History Blog. 2008. "History of American Women: Colonial Women | 18th–19th Cen-tury Women | Civil War Women: Hannah Penn." https://www.womenhistoryblog.com/2008/10/hannah-callowhill-penn.html.

World Health Organization. 2002. *World Report on Violence and Health: Summary.* https://www.who.int/violence_injury_prevention/violence/world_report/en/summary_en.pdf.

Worrall, Arthur J. 1980. *Quakers in the Colonial Northeast.* Hanover, N.H.: University Press of New England.

Wyatt, Tanya. 2014. "Invisible Pillaging: The Hidden Harm of Corporate Biopiracy." In *Invisible Crimes and Social Harms,* edited by Pamela Davies, Peter Francis, and Tanya Wyatt, 161–77.

Yazzie, Robert. 1993. "Navajo Justice Experience—Yesterday and Today." In *Aboriginal Peoples and the Justice System: National Roundtable on Indigenous Issues,* edited by Royal Commission on Aboriginal Peoples, 407–14. Ottawa, ON: Supply and Services.

Young, Iris Marion. 2013. *Responsibility for Justice.* New York: Oxford University Press.

Zehr, Howard. 2015. *The Little Book of Restorative Justice.* Rev. ed. New York: Good Books.

Zimmerman, Albright C. 1974. "European Trade Relations in the 17th and 18th Centuries." In *A Delaware Symposium,* edited by Herbert C. Kraft, 57–70. Harrisburg: Pennsylvania Histor-ical and Museum Commission.

Zion, James W. 1983. "The Navajo Nation Peacemaker Court: Deference to the Old and Accom-modation to the New." *American Indian Law Review* 11 (2): 89–109.

Zion, James W. 1999. "Monster Slayer and Born for Water: The Intersection of Restorative and Indigenous Justice." *Contemporary Justice Review* 2 (4): 359–82.

Zion, James W. 2005. "The Dynamics of Navajo Nation Peacemaking." In *Navajo Nation Peace-making: Living Traditional Justice,* edited by Marianne O. Nielsen and James W. Zion, 85–99. Tucson: University of Arizona Press.

Zion, James W., and Robert Yazzie. 1997. "Indigenous Law in North America in the Wake of Conquest." *Boston Law Review* 20: 55–84.

INDEX

Note: Page numbers in **bold** refers to tables.

ABOUT THE AUTHORS

Marianne O. Nielsen is a professor in the Department of Criminology and Criminal Justice at Northern Arizona University in Flagstaff, Arizona. She has worked for Indigenous organizations and has done research in Indigenous communities. She is the author with Linda M. Robyn of *Colonialism Is Crime* (Rutgers University Press, 2019) and is the co-editor with Robert Silverman of *Aboriginal Peoples and Canadian Criminal Justice* (Harcourt Brace, 1992), *Native Americans, Crime, and Justice* (Westview, 1996), and *Criminal Justice in Native America* (University of Arizona Press, 2009) and with James W. Zion of *Navajo Peacemaking: Living Traditional Justice* (University of Arizona Press, 2005). She is also co-editor with Karen Jarratt-Snider of the Indigenous Justice series from University of Arizona Press, which includes *Crime and Social Justice in Indian Country* (2018), *Traditional, National, and International Law and Indigenous Communities* (2020), and *Indigenous Environmental Justice* (2020), and two upcoming books in the series focused on Indigenous community health, resilience, and justice, and Indigenous women, two-spirited individuals, and justice.

Barbara M. Heather received her PhD from the University of Alberta in 1998. She has carried out research on Quaker politics, history, governance, and Native American relations since being awarded the Gest Fellowship with Marianne O. Nielsen at Haverford in 2005. Since 2001, she also has done research on same-sex schools and gender identities, work, and power among women in rural areas. Her areas of expertise are the sociology of gender and social inequality. She has taught and published in all of these areas. She has made presentations on our research at Quaker Meetings and conferences. She is a practicing Quaker and a retired professor from McEwan University in Edmonton, Alberta, Canada.